The authorship of the Pastoral Letters has been a matter of intense scholarly debate for almost two hundred years. The letters clearly purport to be written by the apostle Paul to Timothy and Titus, but perceived differences between the literary style, vocabulary, and theology of the Pastorals and those of the genuine Pauline letters suggest that this was not so. For many scholars, if Paul did not write the Pastorals, the author must be a disciple of Paul – a gifted pseudonymist– who composed these letters in Paul's name seeking to propagate Paul's thinking and to continue his effectiveness after his death.

Dr. Miller argues that the evidence demands a third solution, and suggests that no single author can be held responsible for much of this material. He presents a wide-ranging review of Jewish and early Christian literature, focusing on the compositional histories of these documents. This is the environment out of which the Pastorals emerged. Many biblical and extra-biblical documents are clearly compilations of materials, brought together by "editors" who sought to preserve material considered sacred by the communities of faith to which they belonged.

Miller's conclusion is that the Pastorals are composite documents based upon brief, but genuine, Pauline notes written to Timothy and Titus. The notes were preserved within the community's archives and later became that literary vehicle upon which other traditional material sacred to the community was loaded.

SOCIETY FOR NEW TESTAMENT STUDIES
MONOGRAPH SERIES
General editor: Richard Bauckham

93

THE PASTORAL LETTERS
AS COMPOSITE DOCUMENTS

The Pastoral Letters
as Composite Documents

JAMES D. MILLER

CAMBRIDGE
UNIVERSITY PRESS

PUBLISHED BY THE PRESS SYNDICATE OF THE UNIVERSITY OF
CAMBRIDGE
The Pitt Building, Trumpington Street, Cambridge CB2 1RP, United
Kingdom

CAMBRIDGE UNIVERSITY PRESS
The Edinburgh Building, Cambridge CB2 2RU, United Kingdom
40 West 20th Street, New York, NY 10011-4211, USA
10 Stamford Road, Oakleigh, Melbourne 3166, Australia

First published 1997

Printed in the United Kingdom at the University Press, Cambridge

Typeset in Times

A catalogue record for this book is available from the British Library

Library of Congress cataloguing in publication data

Miller, James D. (James David)
The Pastoral Letters as composite documents / James D. Miller.
    p.   cm. – (Society for New Testament Studies Monograph series: 93)
Includes bibliographical references and index.
ISBN 0 521 56048 9 (hardback)
1. Bible. N.T. Pastoral Epistles – Authorship.   2. Bible. N.T.
Pastoral Epistles – Criticism, interpretation, etc.   I. Title.
II. Series: Monograph series (Society for New Testament Studies); 93.
BS2735.2.M55   1997
227'.83066–dc20   96–29114 CIP

ISBN 0 521 56048 9 hardback

To Diane

my co-worker and teammate
whose spirit of adventure and industry
made this Edinburgh dream come true

To my parents, Edwin and Mary

"I am reminded of your sincere faith" (II Tim. 1:5).

CONTENTS

ACKNOWLEDGMENTS

I should like to express my grateful appreciation to all those who, by their guidance and encouragement, assisted me during the production of this book.

Special acknowledgment must be expressed to my advisor, Professor John O'Neill, for his generous gifts of time, encouragement, and keen observations; I am a richer man for having had him as a mentor in those three years; to Dr. Douglas Templeton, whose warmth and wit kept me sane on more than one occasion, for his provocative questions, kind support, and valuable suggestions; to the other members of the New Testament Faculty at New College, Edinburgh for their considerable assistance along the way. To each of them I express my thanks.

I am indebted to the New College library staff for their kindly and helpful work on numerous matters.

Acknowledgment must also be made of the way in which I was challenged and stimulated by my fellow graduate students; their friendship, questions, and criticisms have been received with appreciation.

My wife, Diane, contributed her considerable skills in the production of the final typescript; without her hard work, encouragement, and patience this work would not have been possible.

1

INTRODUCTION

The problem

The Pastorals claim to be personal letters from the apostle Paul to his two co-workers, Timothy and Titus, but the problem of the Pastorals, in a sentence, is that they do not seem to be what they claim to be.

They claim to be written by Paul, but in their diction, writing style, and theological emphases, they are hardly Pauline. Significant differences are acknowledged even by those who defend the Pauline authorship of these letters; C. F. D. Moule, for example, commenting on 1 Tim. 1:8, remarks:

> it is astonishing that anyone could seriously attribute to Paul at any stage of his life the definition there offered of where the goodness of the law lies.[1]

The Pastorals appear to be letters, but they only loosely follow the conventional epistolary format of the day;[2] I Timothy, for instance, omits the customary final greetings.[3] And the opening

[1] C. F. D. Moule, "The Problem of the Pastoral Epistles: A Reappraisal," *BJRL* 3 (1965), 431f. J. Jeremias (*Die Briefe an Timotheus und Titus* [Göttingen: Vandenhoeck & Ruprecht, 1953], p. 1) also concedes the peculiarity of the Pastorals: "The three Pastoral letters form materially and linguistically a special group within Paul's Letters."

[2] See the general discussion of first-century epistolary customs in G. J. Bahr, "Paul and Letter Writing in the First Century," *CBQ* 28 (1966), 465–477; W. G. Doty, "The Classification of Epistolary Literature," *CBQ* 31 (1969), 183–199; and R. W. Funk, *Language, Hermeneutics, and Word of God* (New York: Harper & Row, 1966), pp. 250–274.

[3] The lack of personal greetings is unusual in a personal letter and deserves close attention; J. L. White ("The New Testament Epistolary Literature in the Framework of Ancient Epistolography," in *Aufstieg und Niedergang der römischen Welt: Geschichte und Kultur Roms in Spiegel der neueren Forschung*, ed. H. Temporini and W. Hasse [Berlin: Walter de Gruyter, 1984], II. 25.2: 1753) observes

1

thanksgiving, which normally follows directly upon the salutation, does not appear at all in I Timothy or Titus.[4]

The letters claim to be written to two of Paul's closest co-workers, but the language is formal and distant, lacking the intimacy that one would expect among friends of long standing.[5] The admonitions directed to Timothy and Titus do not seem to accord with the status of these two men as veterans within the Pauline circle. After years of faithful service under Paul's supervision, it is strange that Timothy would need to be cautioned to "flee the evil desires of youth" (II 2:22). And it is equally odd that at this stage in his ministry Timothy would require a letter giving basic instructions on how one ought to behave in the household of God (I 3:15).[6] The general treatment of these two men is problematic throughout the Pastorals, given the special relationship that they had obviously enjoyed with Paul.[7]

The Pastorals purport to be occasional letters, but what actually occasioned them is not easily determined. I Timothy appears to be written in response to a threat from false teachers (1:3), but this concern soon gives way to matters that appear far less urgent and mundane by comparison (cf. 2:1ff., the exhortation to make prayers for all men, kings, etc.). The remarks at 3:15 suggest an altogether different motive behind the letter: to set right the conduct of the worshiping community. But the instructions given

that "the closing greetings are one of the marks of a real letter." Compare the final greetings in the letters of Philemon and III John.

4   I 1:12–17 differs considerably from the typical Pauline thanksgiving; it does not immediately follow the salutation, makes no reference to the addressee, and focuses upon Paul's own conversion. See the discussion in ch. 3 below. See also M. Wolter, *Die Pastoralbriefe als Paulustradition* (Göttingen: Vandenhoeck & Ruprecht, 1988), pp. 27ff.

5   Compare, for example, the formality of the salutation to Titus with that of Paul's letter to Philemon. J. Jeremias's suggestion (*Die Briefe*, pp. 3–4) that I Timothy and Titus are "official letters" does not adequately explain this oddity; Paul's letter to Philemon also has "official" character (the letter is addressed both to Philemon and to his "house-church"), but the language is far less formal than that of the Pastorals.

6   The elementary nature of the "church-order" instructions is surprising even if they are regarded as intended for "church leaders" in general; see, for example, the instructions on how to relate to various age groups within the congregation, I 5:1f.

7   The treatment of Timothy and Titus in the Pastorals caused A. Jülicher (*An Introduction to the New Testament*, ET by J. Ward [London: Smith, Elder, 1904], p. 186) to conclude that the Pauline authorship of these letters is "psychologically inconceivable." C. F. D. Moule ("The Problem of the Pastoral Epistles," p. 440) regards the treatment of Timothy in the Pastorals to be the greatest single difficulty facing those who seek to maintain the authenticity of these letters.

are hardly sufficient for such a task, and once again the letter trails off into other unrelated matters (cf. 4:1ff., concerns about the last days). The almost miscellaneous nature of the letter makes it difficult to determine what specific occasion (if any) gave rise to it. The epistolary motives behind II Timothy and Titus are equally difficult to specify.

Scholarship's response

The apparent discrepancies within the Pastorals are not easily explained on the assumption that these letters are authentic. Almost two centuries ago, F. D. E. Schleiermacher noted the literary oddities within I Timothy and concluded that the letter was nothing more than the patchwork of an imitator (a *zusammentragenden Nachahmer*).[8] Schleiermacher's assessment was soon followed by J. G. Eichhorn's rejection in 1812 of all three Pastorals.[9] Detailed studies by F. C. Baur (1835), H. J. Holtzmann (1880), M. Dibelius (1913), and P. N. Harrison (1921)[10] succeeded in convincing most scholars that the Pastorals are not authentic.[11]

Defenders of Pauline authorship[12] have consistently maintained that the literary peculiarities of these letters can be adequately accounted for by the special circumstances that surrounded their origin, among the most important of which are: (a) Paul's advancing age (which influenced his thinking), (b) Paul's long stay in the

---

8 F. D. E. Schleiermacher, "Ueber den sogennanten ersten Brief des Paulos an den Timotheos [*sic*]," reprinted in *Sämmtliche Werke* (32 vols., Berlin: G. Reimer, 1836), Vol. I, part 2, p. 317.

9 J. G. Eichhorn, *Einleitung in das Neue Testament* (Leipzig: Weidmannischen Buchhandlung, 1812), Vol. I, part 3, pp. 315–410.

10 F. C. Baur, *Die sogenannten Pastoralbriefe* (Tübingen: J. G. Gotta'schen, 1835); H. J. Holtzmann, *Die Pastoralbriefe kritisch und exegetisch behandelt* (Leipzig: Wilhelm Engelmann, 1880); M. Dibelius, *Die Briefe der Apostels Paulus an Timotheus I, II und Titus* (Tübingen: J. C. B. Mohr [Paul Siebeck], 1913); P. N. Harrison, *The Problem of the Pastoral Epistles* (London: Oxford University Press, 1921).

11 For a detailed review of critical studies on the Pastorals, see P. Trummer, *Die Paulustradition der Pastoralbriefe* (Frankfurt: P. Lang, 1978), pp. 19–56.

12 Among the most noted of these are: J. B. Lightfoot, "The Date of the Pastoral Epistles," in *Biblical Essays* (London: Macmillan, 1893), pp. 397–418; T. Zahn, *Einleitung in das Neue Testament* (Leipzig: A. Deichert [G. Böhme], 1897), Vol. I, pp. 398–389; A. Schlatter, *Die Kirche der Griechen im Urteil des Paulus* (Stuttgart: Calwer Vereinsbuchhandlung, 1936); Jeremias, *Die Briefe*; C. Spicq, *St. Paul: Les Epîtres Pastorales*, Etudes Bibliques (Paris: Gabalda, 1969); other advocates include: F. J. A. Hort, B. Weiss, E. K. Simpson, R. Parry, O. Roller, H. Schlier, M. Meinertz, W. Michaelis, B. Reicke, G. Holtz, J. N. D. Kelly, D. Guthrie, G. Fee.

West (which affected his use of language), (c) the new concerns addressed in the Pastorals (which required a different vocabulary), and (d) the employment of a new amanuensis (which altered the writing style).[13]

But such arguments have failed to convince most NT critics, who believe the discrepancies within the Pastorals to be much more serious and pervasive than the traditional approach allows.[14] The language, writing style, theology, literary character, and ecclesiastical concerns of these letters are all regarded as cumulative witnesses to the fact that the Pastorals are not Pauline, but stem from the hand of a pseudonymous author, who may (or may not) have had in his possession some genuine Pauline fragments.[15]

This position (in its various forms) has become so well entrenched that contemporary scholarship often takes the pseudonymous authorship of these documents for granted. J. T. Sanders, for example, in his work *Ethics in the New Testament*, reflects much current practice in his approach to these letters:

> That Colossians, Ephesians, II Thessalonians, 1 and 2 Timothy, Titus and I Peter are pseudonymous and imitate Paul's style and thought is not to be debated here but rather accepted as an assured result of critical historical scholarship.[16]

A similar starting point is taken by most contemporary students of

13 On the function and literary influence of an amanuensis, see especially O. Roller, *Das Formular der Paulinischen Briefe*, Beiträge zur Wissenschaft vom Alten und Neuen Testament 4.6 (Stuttgart: Kohlhammer, 1933), pp. 20ff.; Roller argues that Paul did not dictate the Pastorals but gave notes to an amanuensis who was responsible for the actual writing of these letters. W. G. Kümmel (*Introduction to the New Testament*, ET by H. C. Keel, revised ed. [London: SCM, 1975], pp. 251, 373–374) rejects this view, noting that the frequent breaks in the language of the Pauline letter suggest the practice of dictation.

14 E. F. Scott (*The Pastoral Epistles*, The Moffatt New Testament Commentary Series [London: Hodder & Stoughton, 1936], p. xxi), for example, thinks that "at almost every point [the pseudonymous author] has misunderstood Paul ... We cannot but feel that the mind at work in these Epistles is different, in its whole bent and outlook, from that of Paul."

15 The "fragments hypothesis" advocated as early as 1836 by K. A. Credner, and with great effect by P. N. Harrison (*The Problem*), is not really a mediating position in this debate since it also assumes that a pseudonymous author created a fictional letter (in which he placed genuine Pauline fragments). Cf. M. Dibelius and H. Conzelmann (*The Pastoral Epistles* [Philadelphia: Fortress Press, 1972], p. 5): "The secretary hypothesis and the fragment hypothesis are nothing but modifications of the declaration of inauthenticity."

16 J. T. Sanders, *Ethics in the New Testament* (Philadelphia: Fortress Press, 1975), p. 67n.

the Pastorals.[17] The acceptance of these letters as the product of a skilled pseudonymous author is increasingly being regarded as the *sine qua non* of Pastoral studies.

Continuing difficulties

But such a starting point is not easily defended. For although these letters contain anomalies that make it difficult to ascribe them to Paul, they present equally serious difficulties to the interpreter who presumes their pseudepigraphical character. Donelson surely overstates his case and undervalues the problems inherent in it when, in a chapter on the pseudepigraphical letter, he concludes that

> the Pastorals conform beautifully to the pseudepigraphical letter genre. They hold no surprises in either form or function.[18]

This sort of blanket endorsement of the Pastorals as pseudepigraphical suggests that the task of ascribing these letters to a pseudonymous author is virtually trouble-free. But that is not the case.

Considerable evidence suggests that early Christian circles did not knowingly endorse pseudepigraphical writings as authoritative.[19] Basic literary and historical questions were addressed by the

---

[17] So M. Wolter (*Die Pastoralbriefe*, p. 11), for example, begins his study by stating: "The wording of the title reveals that the following investigation flows out of the presumption that the Pastoral letters were not written by Paul, but stem from a later time in which the 'Apostolic' was only present as tradition." L. Donelson (*Pseudepigraphy and Ethical Argument in the Pastoral Epistles* [Tübingen: J. C. B. Mohr (Paul Siebeck), 1986], pp. 1–2) refers with approval to the "waning pressure to re-argue the question of authorship" and "the growing confidence that the author was not Paul."

[18] Donelson, *Pseudepigraphy*, p. 54.

[19] The view that the early church regarded pseudepigraphy as an innocent literary device (so F. C. Baur, *Paulus der Apostel Jesu Christi* (2 vols., Stuttgart: Becher & Müller, 1845), Vol. II, pp. 110–111) has been increasingly challenged. See, for example, J. S. Candlish, "On the Moral Character of Pseudonymous Books," *The Expositor*, 4.4 (1891), 91–107, 272–279; F. Torm, "Die Psychologie der Pseudonymität im Hinblick auf die Literatur des Urchristentums," in *Pseudepigraphie in der heidnischen und jüdisch-christlichen Antike*, Studien der Luther-Akademie 2 (Gütersloh: C. Bertelsmann, 1932); more recently: M. Rist, "Pseudepigraphy and the Early Christians," in *Studies in New Testament and Early Christian Literature: Essays in Honor of Allen P. Wikren*, ed. D. E. Aune (Leiden: E. J. Brill, 1972), pp. 75–91. Rist calls pseudepigraphy "an ancient, though not honorable, literary device" (p. 75); likewise, D. Meade, *Pseudonymity and Canon*, Wissenschaftliche Untersuchungen zum Neuen Testament 39 (Tübingen: J. C. B. Mohr [Paul Siebeck], 1986), p. 198. On the history of the debate, see D. Guthrie, "The Development of the Idea of Canonical Pseudepigraphy in New Testament

early church; Tertullian informs us, for example, that the authenticity of the book of Enoch was disputed by some who found it difficult to believe that the book (if written by Enoch) could have survived the great flood.[20] Origen had doubts about the authenticity of Hebrews on the grounds of its peculiar literary style:

> the verbal style of the epistle "to the Hebrews" is not rude, like the language of the apostle [Paul] ... The thoughts are those of the apostle, but the diction and phraseology are those of some one who remembered the apostolic teachings, and wrote down at his leisure what had been said by this teacher.[21]

The Petrine authorship of II Peter was disputed, according to Jerome, by some who took account of the differences in style between this letter and I Peter.[22]

That pseudepigraphical writings were not knowingly accepted by the early church is also indicated by Tertullian's report of the censure and removal of the presbyter in Asia who was convicted of composing the Acts of Paul.[23] Tertullian plainly rejects this document on theological grounds,[24] but his report also indicates a certain disdain for documents that "falsely bear the name of Paul." The number of pseudepigrapha that failed to achieve recognition because of their dubious literary or theological character underscores the church's sensitivity on this point.[25]

There is no convincing evidence to prove that pseudonymous authors aimed at versimilitude; but we do know, as J.S. Candlish

Criticism," in *Vox Evangelica*, ed. R. Martin (London: Epworth Press, 1962). Reprinted in *SPCK Theological Collections 4: Some Recent Studies by Kurt Aland, Donald Guthrie* [et al.] (London: SPCK, 1965).

[20] Tertullian responds to this early form of historical criticism by suggesting that Noah probably heard the teaching of Enoch from Methuselah and passed it on to posterity. See Tertullian, *De cultu fem.* 1.3, as cited by B.M. Metzger, "Literary Forgeries and Canonical Pseudepigrapha," *JBL* 91 (1972), 15.

[21] Cited by Eusebius, *Ecclesiastical History* 6.25.11–14 (Loeb edition).

[22] Jerome, *Lives of Illustrious Men* 1, as cited by Rist, "Pseudepigraphy," p. 87.

[23] The account appears in Tertullian's *De baptismo* 17. See the introductory article by W. Schneemelcher, "Acts of Paul," in *New Testament Apocrypha*, ed. W. Schneemelcher, ET by R. Mcl. Wilson (London: Lutterworth Press, 1965), Vol. II, p. 232.

[24] Tertullian opposed those who, pointing to Thecla as an example, maintained the right of women to teach and to baptize (*De baptismo* 17).

[25] The Muratori Canon refers to the rejection of the epistles to the Laodiceans and the Alexandrians, "forged in Paul's name for the sect of Marcion, and several others, which cannot be received in the catholic Church; for it will not do to mix gall with honey" (lines 63–67).

has noted, that no known pseudepigraphical writing was ever accepted as authoritative by the early church.[26] And if (as seems likely) pseudepigraphy was regarded as a "dishonorable device"[27] within the early Christian community, it is reasonable to suppose that an author writing pseudapostolic letters would employ every device to ensure that his composition appeared authentic. He would naturally be concerned to provide a convincing *Sitz im Leben* for the letters, and would be cautious about deviating too widely from the epistolary style of the one in whose name he wrote.

Judged by such criteria, however, the Pastorals do not read easily as pseudonymous documents. They pose serious difficulties, in fact, to the interpreter who decides to treat them as pseudepigraphical writings.[28]

To promote the appearance of genuineness, a pseudonymous author might be expected to build upon well-known traditions.[29] To a certain extent the Pastorals do reflect earlier Pauline traditions; for example, Paul's persecutions in Antioch, Iconium, and Lystra are described in II Tim. 3:11, and specific reference to a number of his known companions is made (see II Tim. 4:11ff.). But it is nonetheless remarkable that the Pastorals consistently refer to persons and events otherwise unknown within the NT; the names of sixteen persons appear in these letters who are mentioned nowhere else in the NT.[30] Nor is there any hint within early Christian literature that Timothy ever served as the leader of the community in Ephesus, or that Titus ever worked in Crete. As a fictional sphere of ministry, Spain would seem the more sensible

---

[26] Candlish, "On the Moral Character of Pseudonymous Books," p. 103.

[27] So Donelson, *Pseudepigraphy*, p. 16: "We are forced to admit that in Christian circles pseudonymity was considered a dishonorable device and, if discovered, the document was rejected and the author, if known, was excoriated."

[28] See, especially, the objections made by F. Torm in "Die Psychologie der Pseudonymität." Torm finds the theory of pseudonymity psychologically inconceivable: "It seems to me, that this interpretation of the letters which presents them as having an ethical purpose and as a cleverly devised account of an imagined drama in three acts, introduces us to an author whose personality is psychologically inconceivable. Such a peculiar person never lived" (p. 52). Torm's objections have weight and have not received adequate attention.

[29] The pseudepigraphical epistle to the Laodiceans, for example, builds upon the reference in Col. 4:16 to a letter from Laodicea.

[30] They are: Hymenaeus (I 1:20; II 2:17); Alexander (I 1:20; II 4:14); Lois and Eunice (II 1:5); Phygelus and Hermogenes (II 1:15); Onesiphorus (II 1:16; 4:19); Philetus (II 2:17); Crescens, Carpus, Eubulus, Pudens, Linus, Claudia (II 4:10, 13, 21); Artemus and Zenas (Titus 3:12ff.).

and compelling choice of a pseudonymous author, especially since Paul mentions it as his intended field of work (Rom. 15:24).[31]

And Demas, a man acknowledged and praised elsewhere in the Pauline corpus (Philemon 24; cf. Col. 4:14), is portrayed by the author of the Pastorals as "a forsaker who has abandoned the apostle and the Christian ministry for the love of this present age" (II 4:10).[32] Such disparaging remarks about a known disciple could raise questions that would not be in the interests of a pseudonymous author. The unfavorable picture of Timothy as young and inexperienced, needing to learn the basic principles of Christian service, seems equally difficult to ascribe to a pseudonymous author.[33]

The problem becomes even more pronounced if, as most commentators believe, the author of the Pastorals possessed an in-depth knowledge of Paul's other letters[34] (and the book of Acts?).[35] With the models of ten Pauline letters before him, and the concern to make his pseudepigraphic writings appear authentic, it is hard to understand why a pseudonymous author would not take more care in conforming the epistolary format of the Pastorals to that of the other Paulines. Why not include a conventional "thanksgiving" in I Timothy and Titus? Why omit the customary greetings at the end of I Timothy? Why deviate from the customary Pauline letter form by addressing the letters to individuals rather than to commu-

---

[31] It is possible, of course, that a pseudonymous author could have been relying upon traditions in which it was known that Paul did not visit Spain.

[32] It is not impossible that the Demas referred to here is a different one from that of Philemon 24 and Col. 4:14, but later tradition (see Epiphanius, *Haer.* 51) regards him both as Paul's colleague and an apostate from the Christian faith.

[33] See, for example, II 2:3, 7, 14, 22. T. Zahn (*Introduction to the New Testament*, ET by J. Trout et al. [3 vols., Edinburgh: T. & T. Clark, 1909], Vol. II, pp. 88f.) thinks it "inconceivable" that a pseudonymous author would paint such a portrait of Timothy.

[34] P. N. Harrison (*The Problem*, p. 8), for example, argues that "the real author of the Pastorals was a devout, sincere, and earnest Paulinist ... He knew and had studied deeply every one of our ten Paulines." Roland Schwarz (*Bürgerliches Christentum im Neuen Testament?*, Österreichische Biblische Studien 4 [Klosterneuburg: Österreichisches Katholisches Bibelwerk, 1983], p. 26) builds his study on this assumption: "The author of this writing [the Pastorals] is more than likely a direct disciple of Paul." See also the extensive tabulations of Pauline-like phrases in the Pastorals: Harrison, *The Problem*, pp. 167–175; A. E. Barnett, *Paul Becomes a Literary Influence* (Chicago: University Press, 1941), pp. 251–277; Schlatter, *Die Kirche der Griechen*, p. 15.

[35] So A. T. Hanson, *The Pastoral Epistles*, The New Century Bible Commentary (Grand Rapids, MI: Eerdmans, 1982), p. 13. Likewise, C. K. Barrett, *The Pastoral Epistles* (Oxford: Clarendon Press, 1963), p. 18. Barrett thinks it probable that II 3:11 shows a knowledge of Acts.

nities?[36] Conforming the Pastorals to the style of the other Paulines would contribute, one would think, to the verisimilitude needed in a pseudonymous undertaking of this kind.

But the peculiarity of the Pastorals extends beyond their external forms. The internal organization of the letters has no parallel within the Pauline corpus;[37] community rules, domestic codes, and non-parenetic materials appear in odd juxtaposition.[38] Unlike most other Pauline letters, the Pastorals have no specific parenetic section; instead, blocks of parenetic materials are scattered throughout the letters.[39] Such differences, as W. Stenger has observed, "lead to a highly significant difference between the Pastoral Epistles, the genuine letters of Paul and the Deuteropaulines."[40] The Pastorals do not read like other pseudepigraphic letters; A. T. Hanson finds their lack of any central or developing theme a distinctive feature that has no parallel within pseudepigraphic circles; he regards them as *sui generis*.[41]

On the assumption that the Pastorals are the product of a pseudonymous author, it is also difficult to explain their stark variations of pseudepigraphic "dress." II Timothy is full of personalia and information specific to Paul, but I Timothy and Titus contain relatively little that serves to set the occasions of the letter or to add a personal touch. Consequently, II Timothy seems far more convincing as a personal letter. But if the Pastorals are all written by the same pseudonymous author, why the striking differences in pseudepigraphic style? Why do I Timothy and Titus

---

[36] The personal nature of the Pastorals seems to have made their acceptance as authoritative community documents more difficult. The Muratori Canon hints at this when it describes the Pastorals as "[written] out of goodwill and love, *and yet* held sacred to the glory of the catholic Church for the ordering of ecclesiastical discipline" (lines 60–63, my italic).

[37] See the analysis of the Pauline letter form by W. Doty, *Contemporary New Testament Interpretation* (Englewood Cliffs, NJ: Prentice-Hall, 1972), p. 144. By comparing the internal organization of Paul's letters ("sequence analysis") Doty thinks a "more or less standard pattern" of a Pauline letter can be observed. Even if the specifics of Doty's "sequence analysis" are not accepted, it is hard to deny that the internal organization of the Pastorals is quite different from that of the other Paulines.

[38] H. von Campenhausen ("Polykarp von Smyrna und die Pastoralbriefe," in *Aus der Frühzeit des Christentums* [Tübingen: J. C. B. Mohr (Paul Siebeck), 1963], pp. 229–231) notes the unusual ordering of these materials in the Pastorals.

[39] R. Karris ("The Function and *Sitz im Leben* of the Paraenetic Elements in the Pastoral Letters," Ph.D. dissertation, Harvard, 1971, p. x) estimates that up to 75 percent of the Pastorals can be classified as parenesis.

[40] W. Stenger, "Timotheus and Titus als literarische Gestalten," *Kairos* 16 (1974), 262–263.

[41] Hanson, *The Pastoral Epistles*, p. 27.

lack the pseudepigraphic features that make II Timothy so compelling? Attempts to explain these differences in "dress" have been less than satisfactory; B. S. Easton argues that the success of II Timothy and Titus (which, in his opinion, were published first) lessened the need for a convincing display of pseudepigraphic personalia in I Timothy.[42] But Easton can produce no evidence to support such a view. Equally unconvincing is A. T. Hanson's suggestion that "by the time the author came to write Titus he was beginning to run out of material."[43]

Summary

From these preliminary observations, it is clear that in their present form the Pastorals are not easily attributed to the hand of any single author, be it Paul or a pseudo-Paul.

The arguments against the Pauline authorship of these letters do not need to be rehearsed here; they are well known and will be discussed at various points within this study. Suffice it to say that on literary, stylistic, historical, and linguistic grounds, the acceptance of the Pauline authorship of the Pastorals seems most untenable. This position gains support, I think, from the primary role that advocates of authenticity make the amanuensis play in the writing of these letters.[44] Although the use of another secretary could account for some differences in the Pastorals' literary style *vis-à-vis* the other Pauline letters, it cannot adequately explain the basic changes in the thought and outlook that characterize so much of the material within these letters. To attribute such differences to an amanuensis is to make him for all practical purposes the author of the documents.

But if the Pastorals are not easily ascribed to Paul, neither do they lend themselves readily to the view that they are pseudepigraphic writings, composed by a sophisticated and skilled pseudonymous author. This is an aspect of the problem that has been too frequently overlooked by NT critics. It has been largely assumed

---

[42] B. S. Easton, *The Pastoral Epistles* (London: SCM, 1948), p. 19. "Finally in 1 Timothy the method was so well known that the pseudonymity is a bare convention; it is only in 1.3 (copied from Titus 1.5) that any attempt is made to put the situation back into the past."

[43] Hanson, *The Pastoral Epistles*, p. 47.

[44] See Jeremias, *Die Briefe*, p. 8; J. N. D. Kelly, *A Commentary on the Pastoral Epistles* (London: Adam & Charles Black, 1963), pp. 25–26; Spicq, *Les Epîtres Pastorales*, p. 199; J. H. Bernard, *The Pastoral Epistles* (Grand Rapids, MI: Baker, 1980 [1899]), pp. XII, XXIV.

that there is only one alternative to the theory of Pauline authorship, namely, that the Pastorals were written by a pseudo-Paul. But
as we shall see, many of the same literary features that weigh
against the Pauline authorship of these letters speak with equal
force against theories that make them out to be crafted products of
an imitator.

Perhaps the most telling of these is the peculiar lack of sustained
argument and development of thought that characterizes these
letters (see below); the juxtaposition of unrelated materials without
logical connection raises fundamental questions about the composition of these letters that, in my thinking, are not resolvable on any
theory of authorship, be it Paul or a pseudo-Paul. The differences
in Pauline epistolary style and the stark variations among the three
letters in their supposed use of pseudepigraphic devices (personal
notices, greetings, etc.) raise further difficulties that must be more
carefully examined.

But if I am right in suspecting that the Pastorals were written
neither by Paul nor by a clever pseudonymous author, then the
problem of their origin remains, and poses even more complicated
hermeneutical questions to the interpreter. The complexity of the
issue, though frequently minimized by advocates on both sides of
the authenticity debate, has long been recognized; over one
hundred years ago, W. M. L. de Wette concluded his study of the
Pastorals with the rather despairing refrain (repeated three times)
that in their present form the letters are "neither historically nor
exegetically comprehensible."[45] A. von Harnack, likewise, noting
the seriousness of the textual difficulties, suggested that the origin
of the Pastorals is both an unresolved and an unresolvable puzzle.[46]
These assessments are sobering reminders of the massive historical
and exegetical questions that confront any interpreter of these
letters, and caution us against accepting facile solutions to the
problems encountered here.

So that we can understand the extent of the problems that
surround the Pastorals, the text of these letters must be allowed to
speak, as it were, on its own behalf. The letters are characterized by

[45] W. M. L. de Wette, *Lehrbuch der historisch-kritischen Einleitung in die kanonischen Bücher des Neuen Testaments* (Berlin: G. Reimer, 1860 [1826]), pp. 328,
332, 335.
[46] A. von Harnack, *Die Briefsammlung des Apostels Paulus und die anderen
vorkonstantinischen Briefsammlungen* (Leipzig: J. C. Hinrichs, 1926), p. 14: "The
puzzle that is hovering over these letters [the Pastorals] has never really been
solved and is, with our historical resources, also unsolvable."

certain literary features that can tell us much about their origin. It is to these features that we now turn.[47]

Examining the text

The diversity of literary forms

One of the Pastorals' most striking features is their remarkable array of diverse (and apparently "fixed") literary forms. The fact that many of these formal materials have no apparent connection to their immediate context is puzzling and raises questions as to their origin and composition. Perhaps even more important for understanding these letters is the fact that many of these fixed elements appear within other Jewish and early Christian documents.

Even a casual survey of the Pastorals reveals the formal character of much contained therein.[48] Among other elements to be noted later in this study, the Pastorals include:

> liturgical/creedal/hymnic formulas
> guidelines for selecting leaders
> household rules
> virtue/vice lists
> polemical sayings
> proverbial citations
> apocalyptic warnings
> admonitions
> midrashic expositions
> doxologies.

The arrangement of the materials

The presence of such literary diversity within personal letters is peculiar. But it is the loose arrangement of these materials that,

---

[47] The following pages contain a preliminary report of my findings. The central portion of the book (chapters 3–5) is designed to substantiate in detail the general observations presented here.

[48] M. Dibelius was instrumental in bringing the form-critical approach to bear on the study of the Pastorals: see his *Die Briefe des Apostels Paulus*, pp. 136–139. More recently, see A. T. Hanson's brief study of the Pastorals' "Technique of composition" in his commentary (*The Pastoral Epistles*, pp. 42–47). Hanson finds nine distinct types of material that have been incorporated into the Pastorals.

more than anything else, presents the exegete of the Pastorals with major hermeneutical problems.

Throughout the Pastorals topics are addressed and left off, only to reappear later for no apparent reason; the instruction about community leaders in I Tim. 3:1ff., for example, is picked up again in 5:17; the admonition regarding riches in I Tim. 6:9ff. resumes unexpectedly two paragraphs later in 6:17. Paragraphs, and even sentences, are frequently strung together without any logical link, sometimes appearing like a disorganized collage; it is not easy to fit the concern of I Tim. 5:1f. ("do not rebuke an elder") into its surrounding context; the unit just appears, without warning, and without apparent motive. The same is true of the puzzling admonition at I. Tim. 5:23 ("no longer drink only water").

The direction of thought in these letters is frequently broken by unexpected shifts in subject matter: see, for instance, the "plainly erratic boulders"[49] that appear at II 1:15–18 and 3:10–12. The letters lack any clear development of thought, sustained argument, or even unifying theme, and consequently defy any attempt at an orderly outline. This lack of order and cohesiveness is not confined to a small parenetic section of the letters (where one might expect it) but permeates the documents as a whole.

The content

Another notable feature of the Pastorals is their unusually high concentration of parenetic materials;[50] Robert Karris has estimated that up to 75 percent of the Pastorals can be categorized as parenesis.[51] The letters are permeated with clusters of proverbial sayings, ethical admonitions, and moral injunctions that in many respects show no specifically Christian features.[52]

Personal remarks appear sporadically throughout I and II Timothy, but seldom in a way that ties them closely to their

---

49 So J. Moffatt, *An Introduction to the Literature of the New Testament*, revised 3rd ed. (Edinburgh: T. & T. Clark, 1920), p. 403. Moffatt's *Introduction* contains a valuable survey of the literary problems inherent in the study of the Pastorals (pp. 395–420).
50 V. P. Furnish (*Paul's Exhortations in the Context of his Letters and Thought*, Microcard Theological Studies 36 [Washington: The Microcard Foundation for the American Theological Library Association, 1960], p. 40) defines parenesis as "essentially a collection of wise sayings and advice, authenticated by long use, and intended as ready reference for all sorts of moral directives."
51 Karris, "The Function," p. x.
52 See, for example, the discussion on pp. 78–82 (I 4:6–10); pp. 115–116 (II 2:22–26); pp. 126–128 (Titus 2:6–9) below.

immediate context.[53] The letter to Titus is devoid of any personal material except for the opening to the letter (1:1–5) and the conclusion (3:12–15). The polemical passages are remarkable both for their intensity and their ambiguity. Reprobate members, denounced with a scathing vehemence, are the target of vilification throughout the letters. Yet the polemic itself seems fragmented and disjointed, presenting no clear picture of who these opponents are. They have been variously identified as (1) Jewish Christians;[54] (2) Gnostics;[55] and (3) Marcionites,[56] but the evidence permits no certainty. In fact, it is not even clear whether one or several heresies are targeted in these polemical passages.[57]

Fixed expressions and traditional materials

The appearance of numerous fixed expressions and formulaic sayings is another striking feature of the Pastorals. While the most obvious of these is the "faithful word" formula, πιστὸς ὁ λόγος,[58] other fixed phrases include,

οἴδαμεν δὲ ὅτι (1:8);
εἰδὼς τοῦτο ὅτι (I 1:9; II 3:1);
ταῦτα ὑποτιθέμενος (... παράγγελλε, ... δίδασκε ...
μελέτα ... ὑπομίμνῃσκε ... λάλει ... παρακάλει ...
φεῦγε; cf. I 4:6, 4:11, 6:11, II 2:14; Tit. 2:15);
σὺ δέ (I 6:11; II 2:1, 3:10, 3:14, 4:5; Tit. 2:1);
ταῦτα φεῦγε, δίωκε δέ (I 6:11; II 2:22);

---

53   See, for example, I 1:20; 3:14–15; II 2:10–11.
54   So, for example, Lightfoot, "The Date," pp. 411–418. Lightfoot calls the heresy a form of "Judaic Gnosticism" or, more precisely, "Essene Judaism" (p. 416). See also F. J. A. Hort, *Judaistic Christianity* (Cambridge: Macmillan, 1894), pp. 135ff.; Spicq, *Les Epîtres Pastorales*, pp. lii–lxxii.
55   So, for example, Easton, *The Pastoral Epistles*, pp. 1–7.
56   The theory that the Pastorals were written in response to the Marcionite heresy was advocated by the Tübingen school, and especially by F. C. Baur, *Paulus der Apostel Jesu Christi*, Vol. II, pp. 492–499). A modern defender of this view is F. Gealy (*The First and Second Epistles to Timothy and the Epistle to Titus*, The Interpreter's Bible, Vol. XI (New York: Abingdon Press, 1955), pp. 358–360.
57   R. Karris, "The Background and Significance of the Polemic of the Pastoral Epistles," *JBL* 92 (1973), 549–564.
58   This formula occurs five times throughout the Pastorals: see I 1:15; 3:1a; 4:9; II 2:11; Titus 3:8. On the critical questions see G. W. Knight, *The Faithful Sayings in the Pastoral Letters* (Grand Rapids, MI: Baker, 1979 [1968]), pp. 4–30. See also the study by W. Nauck, "Die Herkunft des Verfassers der Pastoralbriefe," Th.D thesis, Göttingen, 1950, pp. 45–52.

διαμαρτύρομαι ἐνώπιον τοῦ θεοῦ (I 5:21; II 2:14, 4:1).

The repetition of these and other fixed expressions in the Pastorals is puzzling, and raises questions regarding their literary function within the letters. Sometimes they appear to serve as mere connecting tools, linking sentences and paragraphs together.[59] But frequently they occur at the beginning or the end of passages that read like set, probably preformed, pieces; in these cases, the fixed expressions act as "markers," signaling the inclusion of traditional pieces within the text. The "faithful word" formula in the Pastorals, for instance, seems to be functioning in this way.[60] The clearest example occurs at II Tim. 2:11, where the formula is immediately followed by a rhythmical (perhaps hymnic?) fragment of five lines, including two balanced couplets. The phrase πιστὸς ὁ λόγος sometimes appears at the beginning (I 1:15; II 2:11, and I 4:9?) and sometimes at the end (Titus 3:8 and perhaps I 3:1a) of such traditional material.

To take another example, the term ὁμολογουμένως occurs only in the NT at I Tim. 3:16, where its precise meaning is difficult to determine.[61] It occurs, however, three times in IV Maccabees (6:31; 7:16; 16:1), each time introducing the set expression: "devout reason is sovereign over the emotions." In I 3:16, it seems to be functioning in a similar way, introducing a fixed credal (hymnic?) fragment that, with its three rhythmically equal couplets, has long been suspected of having a pre-Pauline origin.

That the Pastorals contain some preformed materials has been widely recognized, by those who affirm as well as those who deny their Pauline authorship. A. Seeberg, for instance, argued in 1903 that the Pastorals contain several fixed catechetical-like units, including a creedal statement (II 2:8), an apocalytpic expression (II 4:1), and a hymn (I 3:16).[62] Since then an increasing number of scholars have recognized the traditional character of these letters. J. Jeremias suggests that they "cite a large number of established

59 So Hanson, *The Pastoral Epistles*, pp. 46–47.
60 The recognition that this formula marks the presence of preformed traditions goes back to at least 1852; see W. Conybeare and J. Howson, *The Life and Epistles of Paul* (London: Longman, Green, 1852), p. 752n.
61 Alfred Seeberg, in *Der Katechismus der Urchristenheit*, Theologische Bücherei 26 (Munich: Kaiser, 1966 [1903]), pp. 112–113, discusses the problem involved in translating this term. The options he suggests are: "correspondingly great," "great," "admittedly great."
62 Ibid., pp. 70ff., 96ff.

sayings and formulae" and gives as examples I Tim. 1:15, 2:5, 3:16, 6:13; II Tim. 2:8.[63]

But the extent to which these letters may incorporate preformed traditions has not, to my knowledge, ever been thoroughly examined. E. E. Ellis, who upholds the Pauline authorship of these letters, has recently written a remarkable article in which he argues that traditional materials make up at least 41 percent of I Timothy, 16 percent of II Timothy, and 46 percent of Titus.[64]

Although I cannot follow Ellis in his conclusions regarding the authenticity of the Pastorals, his insights into the formal characteristics of much of the material within the Pastorals corroborate, in significant ways, my own analysis of this material.

The problem of literary origin

The problem of the Pastorals is compounded by the fact that these letters show points of contact with all sorts of literature, both Jewish and pagan. This accounts for the remarkably diverse conclusions that have been drawn regarding the origins of the documents. W. Nauck, for example, observing the similarities between the Pastorals and certain Jewish literature, concludes that the author of the Pastorals must have been a converted Jew, rabbinically trained, and conversant from childhood with hellenistic thinking and lifestyle.[65] S. G. Wilson compares various linguistic features within the Pastorals to those of Luke/Acts and finds sufficient evidence to argue for the Lucan authorship of the Pastorals.[66]

On the grounds of the similarities between the Pastorals and

---

[63] Jeremias, *Die Briefe*, p. 5.
[64] E. E. Ellis, "Traditions in the Pastoral Epistles," in *Early Jewish and Christian Exegesis: Studies in Memory of William Hugh Brownlee*, ed. Craig Evans and W. Stinespring (Atlanta: Scholars Press, 1987), pp. 237–253. Ellis acknowledges that his work is only introductory, and suggests that "a more intensive study could ... identify a number of other passages that consists of or rest upon preformed material" (p. 248).
[65] Nauck, "Die Herkunft"; see especially his conclusions, pp. 103ff.
[66] S. G. Wilson, *Luke and the Pastoral Epistles* (London: SPCK, 1979); see, however, I. H. Marshall's critical review of Wilson's arguments in *JSNT* 10 (1981), 69–74. Marshall notes that the linguistic differences between the Pastorals and Luke–Acts are as striking as any similarities that might be shared between the two groups of writings (p. 72). Other advocates of Wilson's basic position include: J. D. Quinn, "The Last Volume of Luke," in *Perspectives on Luke–Acts*, ed. C. H. Talbert (Danville, VA: Association of Baptist Professors of Religion, 1978), pp. 62–65; Moule, "The Problem of the Pastoral Epistles," 403–452; A. Strobel, "Schreiben des Lukas? Zum sprachlichen Problem der Pastoralbriefe," *NTS* 15 (1969), 191–210.

Polycarp's letter to the Philippians, Hans von Campenhausen suggests that Polycarp might be responsible for the production of these letters.[67]

L. Donelson evaluates the Pastorals in light of various Greco-Roman writings, and concludes that the author was probably a Greek convert, skilled in Greco-Roman rhetoric, who wrote within literary circles much closer to Athens than Jerusalem.[68] B. Fiore compares the Pastorals to the pseudonymous Socratic letters, and concludes that the two letter collections must have originated within similar groups and situations, and that the author of the Pastorals himself probably came from a Cynic background.[69]

The sheer diversity of such opinion reflects the complexity of the problems posed by these letters, and cautions us against drawing hasty conclusions on the basis of literary parallels. As important as comparative analysis is (and it will play a vital role in this book), it is nonetheless a discipline that must always build upon, and not preempt, a close study of the text. This caution is especially important for the study of the Pastorals since these texts are characterized by compositional oddities and peculiar literary features.

Conclusions

A close reading of the Pastorals suggests that these documents are not simple letters from Paul to Timothy and Titus. They contain all sorts of diverse literary materials such as household rules, creedal fragments, proverbial sayings, and liturgical pieces. The arrangement of these materials is without apparent order; they seem to be linked together only in the loosest sense; topics are picked up and abruptly left off, only to be returned to later; sudden shifts in subject matter abound. The letters are marked by numerous fixed expressions which often seem to function as "markers" of cited or preformed traditional materials.

Such literary oddities contribute to the massive hermeneutical problem posed by the Pastorals, and require some explanation if these letters are to make sense. A controlling assumption of the

---

[67] Von Campenhausen, "Polykarp von Smyrna," pp. 197–252.

[68] The extent to which Donelson holds to this view is evident from the almost complete neglect throughout his dissertation of extra-canonical Jewish literature. Only IV Maccabees receives any attention.

[69] B. Fiore, *The Function of Personal Example in the Socratic and Pastoral Epistles* (Rome: Biblical Institute Press, 1986), p. 136.

present study is that the problem of the Pastorals revolves not so much around questions of authorship as of composition. That is to say, the primary question to be asked of these documents is not "Who wrote them?" but rather "Why do the letters read the way they do?"

This monograph seeks above all else to answer that basic question. Many NT scholars have addressed the literary problems inherent in these letters. Their insights provide the foundation upon which much of this work is laid.

Yet, it is nonetheless true that the compositional history of these documents has received relatively little consideration. It is hoped that by focusing attention upon the oddities within the texts of the Pastorals, and upon the techniques which brought these materials together, this study can contribute to a more adequate reading of these letters.

At the heart of this book is the belief that the Pastorals do not have a simple literary past; in their present form they are misread if understood as the product of one mind, be it that of Paul or a pseudo-Paul. The letters appear, rather, to be much more the work of a compiler than of an author. The texts of the Pastorals, it will be argued, bear all the marks of composite documents and, as such, must be read with an appreciation for their complex compositional history. To read the Pastorals in this way seems to accord best with both the internal evidence of the texts themselves, and with what we know of the surrounding literary environment.

2

RELIGIOUS WRITINGS AS COLLECTIONS

The compositional question

If I am right in thinking that the literary peculiarities of the Pastorals make it difficult to ascribe them either to Paul or to a pseudo-Paul, then the key to understanding these texts turns not so much upon the question of their authorship as upon the history of their redaction. To pose the problem in this way is, of course, to enter a controversial arena within contemporary NT scholarship. Little agreement exists on the extent to which the NT epistles have been editorially reworked;[1] the debate, in fact, reaches back to the very beginnings of modern NT historical-critical work when J. S. Semler proposed that II Corinthians was composed of distinct Pauline fragments.[2]

Controversy over redaction

More recently, however, a widespread skepticism has taken root within NT scholarship against the view that the Pauline corpus has suffered from redactional alterations.[3] Johannes Weiss lamented

---

[1] See W. Kümmel, *Introduction to the New Testament*, ET by H. C. Kee, rev. ed. (London: SCM, 1975), p. 251. The diversity of opinion is revealed throughout Kümmel's treatment of the integrity of individual NT letters.

[2] Semler's commentary on II Corinthians touched off a debate on the textual integrity of the Pauline corpus that continues to this day. See Gottfried Hornig, *Die Anfänge der historisch-kritischen Theologie: Johann Salomo Semlers Schriftverständis und seine Stellung zu Luther* (Göttingen: Vandenhoeck & Ruprecht, 1961).

[3] See, for example, the views of H. Gamble, "The Redaction of the Pauline Letters and the Formation of the Pauline Corpus," *JBL* 94 (1975), 403–418; W. Michaelis, "Teilungshypothesen bei Paulusbriefen," *TZ* 14 (1958), 321–326; K. Aland, "Glosse, Interpolation, Redaktion und Komposition in der Sicht der neutestamentlichen Textkritik," in *Studien zur Überlieferung des Neuen Testa-*

this development as long ago as 1910 when, in his commentary on I Corinthians, he wrote:

> Since all hypotheses that assume that the epistle requires to be cut up into pieces are received with the greatest suspicion in the prevailing climate of opinion today – Jülicher calls them "fantastic" – it may be that the following exegetical notes will remain without effect for the time being and perhaps first be discussed in some later age.[4]

During the last fifty years scholarly opinion on the integrity of NT texts has if anything set harder in the direction that Weiss had feared. The textual unity of the NT letters, in particular, is frequently taken for granted by contemporary NT scholars.[5]

This is nowhere more apparent than in the study of the Pastorals. The literary integrity of these writings is seldom questioned by current scholars; most critics begin their work on the presumption that these letters were written by an individual author, at a specific time and place.

Such a starting point is not limited to those who think the Pastorals are genuine Pauline writings; scholars who regard the letters as essentially pseudonymous conduct their research on similar assumptions. The work of P. N. Harrison is a case in point; to his credit, Harrison recognizes the need to inquire into the literary origins of the Pastorals:

> We speak of the "author" in the singular. But whether these writings are all by the same author, whether they are each of them to be regarded as a unity or composite, and as the work of one mind or of more than one, may not be taken for granted, but is precisely one of the questions we have to investigate.[6]

---

ments und seines Textes, Arbeiten zur neutestamentlichen Textforschung (Berlin: de Gruyter, 1967), see pp. 48ff.

4 J. Weiss, *Die Erste Korintherbrief* (Göttingen: Vandenhoeck & Ruprecht, 1910), p. xl.

5 To mention only one example: David Aune never addresses the question of the integrity of the NT writings in his otherwise valuable book, *The New Testament and its Literary Environment* (Philadelphia: Westminster Press, 1987). Except for II Corinthians, which he thinks may be a composite document consisting of between two and six separate compositions (pp. 208ff.), Aune seems to assume the literary integrity of all other NT documents.

6 P. N. Harrison, *The Problem of the Pastoral Epistles* (London: Oxford University Press, 1921), p. 2.

But while affirming the legitimacy of such questions, Harrison never really investigates the possibility that the Pastorals may be something other than unified literary compositions. And although he argues that two of the letters (II Timothy and Titus) contain some genuine Pauline notes,[7] thus implying that the Pastorals are in some sense the product of a redactor, he never examines the extent to which this redactional activity may have influenced the rest of the contents. His subsequent interpretation, consequently, remains governed by the assumption that the Pastorals are the work not so much of a redactor as of a creative author, writing "to meet the requirements of his own day."[8]

A. T. Hanson, likewise, tends to interpret the Pastorals as the composition of a single mind, even though he recognizes that the letters "are made up of a miscellaneous collection of material."[9] The question of whether the title "author" or that of "editor" is more suitable to the one (or ones?) who compiled this material is one that Hanson, unfortunately, never considers.

These two critics typify the approach to the Pastorals followed by most current scholars; similarities among the three letters (in content and subject matter, literary style and vocabulary, shared grammatical peculiarities, etc.) are interpreted as evidence of common authorship.[10] But the fact that two or more documents show close similarities in content, subject matter, vocabulary, etc. does not necessarily imply that they were written by the same author. Other equally plausible possibilities exist; it may mean, for example, as in the case of the Synoptic gospels, that various editors have been at work, drawing from the same storehouse of traditional materials. It may be that the Pastorals are the product of one author, but, if so, this must be carefully demonstrated and not simply presumed on the basis of general literary parallels.[11]

---

[7] Harrison revised his earlier findings (of five genuine notes) in later studies that appear in his book *Paulines and Pastorals* (London: Villiers, 1964), pp. 106–128. He divided the three notes as follows: (1) Titus 3:12–15; (2) II Tim. 4:9–15; (3) II Tim. 1:16–18, 3:10–11, 4:1, 2a, 5b–8, 16–19, 21b, 22a.

[8] Ibid., p. 14.

[9] A. T. Hanson, *The Pastoral Epistles*, The New Century Bible Commentary (Grand Rapids, MI: Eerdmans, 1982), p. 42.

[10] So Harrison, *The Problem*, p. 17. For similar judgments coming from different corners of the authenticity debate, see also Scott, *The Pastoral Epistles*, p. xxiv; Kelly, *The Pastoral Epistles*, p. 28; N. Brox, *Die Pastoralbriefe*, Regensburger Neues Testament VII.2 (Regensburg: F. Pustet, 1969).

[11] It is possible, as A. T. Hanson, E. E. Ellis and others argue, that the Pastorals are the product of a single author who made heavy use of traditional materials; the problem with this hypothesis, however, is that we would expect an author to link

The problem is intensified by the fact that stylistic differences are also to be found among (and within!) the Pastorals. W. Lock, for example, finds II Timothy "more intricate in structure and often less clear in expression" than I Timothy or Titus.[12] Such differences suggest that the stylistic witnesses within the Pastorals may not all be telling the same story. Nevertheless, students of the Pastorals have frequently accepted the verbal and stylistic similarities within these letters as proof of their common authorship and literary unity.

Such a starting point effectively eliminates the need to engage in any serious discussion of the compositional integrity of these documents. For if the Pastorals were originally written by one author in essentially the same form as we now possess them, then questions regarding their compositional history lose much, if not all, of their significance. As a result, the integrity of these letters has come to be regarded as a "given" upon which subsequent inter-pretation can be built.[13]

Literary integrity

But does the surviving literary evidence allow us to presume that we possess the Pastoral letters essentially in their original form? Or is there sufficient reason to suspect that these documents may have been editorially reworked in the course of their transcription?

In the concentrated study of the NT it is all too easy to treat these texts as though they were historically *sui generis*, somehow protected from the editorial vicissitudes that were so much a part of the literary world into which they were born. But the Pastorals were not transmitted within a literary vacuum. Like all other NT texts they were written and subsequently copied within literate

his miscellaneous materials together more smoothly, without the sort of abrupt transitions and logical discontinuities that Hanson admits characterizes these letters. The whole question of common authorship and continuity of thought within the Pastorals is treated more fully in appendix A below.

[12] W. Lock, *The Pastoral Epistles* (Edinburgh: T. & T. Clark, 1924), p. xxvii. Lock, however, thinks that the differences may have been caused by "a difference of mood." J. Moffatt (*Introduction*, p. 401) observes that I Timothy "is more discursive and miscellaneous than II Tim."

[13] So, for example, M. Wolter, *Die Pastoralbriefe*, p. 17: "The particular character-istic of the Pastoral letters (as Pseudepigrapha) as opposed to the other pseudepi-graphic letters of the New Testament lies in the fact that, we are now not just dealing with one but three fictitious letters *from one single author*" (my italic).

religious circles that were responsible for the production, the preservation, and the transmission of an enormous mass of religious documents.

There is no reason to think that early Christian scribes treated the transmission of the Pastorals any differently from the way they treated other sacred and esteemed writings; for this reason, an examination of the editorial activity within these other writings can contribute much to our understanding of the likely scribal influences that were brought to bear upon the Pastorals themselves.

Examining the literary environment

The aim of this chapter, then, is to provide a sketch of the wider literary context within which the Pastorals themselves were written and copied. Special attention in this survey is devoted to the literary integrity and the transcriptional histories of this literature. It will become clear from our investigation that the religious literature of Judaism and early Christianity shares basic compositional features, the most important of which are presented below, and which form the outline for the remainder of this chapter:

I   Substantial MS evidence suggests that most of the sacred literature of Judaism is composite, and has undergone extensive redaction during the course of transmission.

II Texts were subjected to many forms of editorial reworking, the most notable of which are listed below:
A   Previously independent texts were sometimes "stitched" together, often without any indication that originally separate texts had been so joined.
B   Large blocks of preformed materials (including prayers, hymns, psalms, apocalyptic admonitions, etc.) were often incorporated into existing texts.
C   Brief proverbial sayings and short traditional pieces were frequently added by scribes to existing texts.

III Similar editorial activity is apparent in the surviving MSS of "non-canonical" early Christian documents.

IV The NT writings possess equally complex compositional histories.

The composite nature of sacred Jewish literature

It has become a canon of OT scholarship that the Hebrew scriptures underwent a long process of redactional development and growth; in every division of the OT (the Pentateuch, the Hexateuch, the historical writings, the prophetic books, the wisdom materials, apocalyptic writings, the psalms) editorial revision has occurred; traditional materials of diverse origins have been gathered and added to earlier writings. No one disputes that this vast library of Hebrew literature has been profoundly influenced by the work of compilers and redactors.[14] Frequently this editorial work has resulted in alterations both in the form and in the content of the original writings.

The LXX, likewise, testifies in a striking way to this continuing process of textual growth and development; proverbial sayings, psalms, traditional stories, community "letters," etc. appear in the LXX that have no counterpart in the Hebrew Bible (see below). "New" materials have been added to "existing" texts, often with no indication that the original has been altered. Compiling, interpolating, appending, and prefixing – all of these editorial techniques are clearly visible within the LXX, and were frequently and freely employed. Only by appreciating the redactional histories of these texts can a proper interpretation of their significance and meaning be attained.

The great body of "intertestamental" Jewish literature is also replete with composite writings of various kinds. Few documents within this circle of literature present uncomplicated textual histories; on the contrary, the pervasive work of scribal editors and redactors is clearly apparent throughout these writings. No literary genre was exempt from this activity; letters, poems, apocalypses, community manuals, wisdom writings, and the like all show signs of having been subject to extensive editorial treatment.

An overview of the literature, showing various features of scribal redaction

The following literary survey builds upon the widely accepted

---

[14] See, for example, M. Noth, *A History of Pentateuchal Traditions* (Englewood Cliffs, NJ: Prentice-Hall, 1972). Noth emphasizes that the Hebrew scriptures must be read as a growing complex of living traditions. See pp. 1, 3, 5, 54, *et passim*.

findings of many scholars. The results, however, underscore a fact too often neglected by students of the NT: Jewish and early Christian communities regarded their sacred texts, not as copyrighted volumes, but as collections of living traditions; consequently, their scribes were not reluctant to weave previously independent materials together during transmission, believing that by this activity they were ensuring the preservation and wider circulation of the traditions that they had been charged to maintain.

Previously independent documents have been "stitched" together

It was not unusual for scribes to connect formerly independent documents together, often without giving any indication of the originally independent status of the texts so compiled.

The prophetic books of the OT provide clear examples of this. The book of Isaiah is a composite document consisting of various collections of prophetic oracles whose origins cannot be assigned to any one author and whose dates span several centuries (Isaiah 1–39; 40–55; 56–66). The Hebrew text of Jeremiah, likewise, comprises a miscellany of traditional materials including various collections of prophetic oracles, the memoirs of Baruch (chs. 26–35; 36–45), and a historical appendix (ch. 52). As H. Cunliffe-Jones has correctly remarked:

> The nearest analogy to the ordering of the material [in Jeremiah] is that of a library, in which the original collection had its own classification, but to which other collections of various sizes have been added, without their either conforming to the original classification or being given a new overall classification.[15]

The LXX contains a number of traditional stories that have been "stitched" together during the course of translation (or transmission?). Two previously independent stories (Susannah, and Bel and the Dragon) have been added, for example, to the Daniel material. These materials comprise some 174 verses which have no counterpart in the Hebrew Bible. According to G. Vermes and M. Goodman such additions

---

[15] H. Cunliffe-Jones, *Jeremiah* (London: SCM, 1960), p. 15.

appear to consist in an amalgam of different stories only loosely linked together, largely irrelevant to the story in Daniel, and probably complete before their insertion into the book.[16]

Depending upon which MS one reads, the story of Susannah appears "stitched" to different contexts, none of which seems particularly suitable. In some MSS the story appears as a sort of preface to the book of Daniel (for example, in "Theodotion," the old Latin, the Coptic, the Ethiopic, and the Arabic versions); in others it appears as the last chapter of the book (as in the LXX, the Vulgate, the Syro-Hexaplar).

The account of Bel and the Dragon shows a similar contextual fluidity: in "Theodotion" it follows immediately upon Daniel 12, while in the LXX it appears after the story of Susannah. Its originally independent character is also attested by the fact that Daniel is introduced formally and fully to his readers in the Bel narrative (cf. verses 2ff. LXX), even though in its present context such information only duplicates what is said of Daniel elsewhere in the larger Daniel corpus.

Two complete letters addressed to Jews in Egypt have been connected at some stage of transmission to the beginning of II Maccabees (cf. 1:1–9; 1:10–2:18).

The book of I Enoch (Ethiopic) shows a similar redactional history. Evidence from Qumran indicates that the diverse materials presently contained within I Enoch were originally separate texts written at different times by different authors. In its present form the text comprises at least six distinct segments:

1   The book of the Watchers (1–36)
2   The book of Similitudes (37–71)
3   The book of Astronomical Writings (72–82)
4   The book of Dream Visions (83–90)
5   The book of Admonitions (the epistle of Enoch, 91–105)
6   Appendix from the book of Noah (106–107)

From MSS discovered at Qumran, it is clear that book 3 of I Enoch (the book of Astronomical Writings) existed independently in scrolls that contained no other section of the corpus.[17]

[16] E. Schürer, *The History of the Jewish People in the Age of Jesus Christ*, rev. and ed. G. Vermes, F. Millar, and M. Goodman (3 vols., Edinburgh: T. & T. Clark, 1987), Vol. III, part 2, p. 723.

[17] See J.T. Milik and M. Black, *The Books of Enoch: Aramaic Fragments of Qumran Cave 4* (London: SCM, 1976), p. 8.

The same can be said of the excerpt from the book of Noah that appears as an appendix at the end of Enoch (chs. 105–106); this addition is not included in the Qumran MSS of Enoch, but has been preserved separately in another Hebrew document found in cave I (IQ19).[18] Other evidence from Qumran indicates that books 2 and 3 of Enoch were not written on the same manuscripts as books 1 and 5; this could mean that some, if not all, of these sections originally circulated independently and were only later compiled into a large collection of Enochic traditions.[19]

The Syriac Apocalypse of Baruch (II Baruch) is likewise a fusion of preformed materials. In this case, a previously independent "letter" attributed to Baruch (chs. 78–86) appears to have been appended to the larger apocalypse.[20]

The fusion of the Epistle of Jeremiah to I Baruch occurred much later in the textual history of Baruch, but shows how the process of compiling continued long into the Christian era. The epistle appears in the LXX as a separate book placed between Lamentations and Ezekiel.[21] But in some later Greek MSS it is appended without a break to the end of Baruch. And after the time of Jerome most texts show the epistle as ch. 6 of Baruch.

Complex literary histories also lay behind many of the Qumran writings. The Rule of the Community (IQS), for example, is clearly a composite work made up of various community source materials.[22] There is good MS evidence to suggest that the Rule was expanded during various stages of its transmission. Two originally

---

[18] On the evidence, see J. T. Milik, *Ten Years of Discovery in the Wilderness of Judea*, ET by J. Strugnell (London: SCM, 1959), pp 33f.

[19] See J. T. Milik, "Problèmes de la littérature hénochique à la lumière des fragments araméens de Qumran," *HTR* 64 (1971), 333–378.

[20] G. B. Sayler (*Have the Promises Failed? A Literary Analysis of 2 Baruch* [Chico, CA: Scholars Press, 1982], p. 5) analyzes the disparate materials collected in II Baruch and notes that "Jewish authors of the Greco-Roman period frequently integrated a variety of sources and traditions into an individual document, with no attempt to harmonize different or even conflicting viewpoints." See also the still valuable treatment of the book by R. H. Charles (*The Apocalypse of Baruch* [London: Adam & Charles Black, 1896], p. 23): "[Baruch] is a composite work put together about the close of the century, from at least five or six independent writings."

[21] The epistle, as an independent text, has also been found at Qumran. For MS evidence see M. Baillet, *Discoveries in the Judaean Desert*, Vol. III (Oxford: Clarendon Press, 1955), p. 143.

[22] See the discussion in Schürer, *The History of the Jewish People*, Vol. III, part 1, p. 384. "The Community Rule belongs to a type of literature for which it is inappropriate to speak of a single author."

separate documents, the Messianic Rule (IQSa) and the Blessings (IQSb), appear to have been added to the end of IQS at a later time.[23]

The same sort of literary development is apparent in the Damascus Document. On the basis of breaks in the text, content, and vocabulary, A. M. Denis has identified two documents of diverse origin that have been incorporated within the present Damascus Document.[24] J. Murphy-O'Connor has argued a very similar thesis, suggesting that cols. 2.14–6.1 were originally a missionary document.[25]

Although the Mishnah is a much later document than those mentioned above, it seems appropriate to include it at the end of this brief survey since it illustrates the continuing scribal tendency to gather together disparate materials into one document. Not only is the Mishnah a compilation of various sources, but each of the separate tractates it contains is composite too. Pirqe 'Aboth, for example, is a collection of sayings attributed to sixty or so rabbinic sages.[26] The earliest collection probably ended at 'Aboth 4:22. Chapter 5 contains a collection of numerical sayings (5:1–15) and other wise words which are not attributed to any rabbi or sage (except 5:20–23). Chapter 6 contains liturgical materials which were probably not originally a part of the 'Aboth.[27]

---

[23] So D. Barthélemy, *Discoveries in the Judaean Desert*, Vol. I (Oxford: Clarendon Press, 1956), pp. 107–108.

[24] A. M. Denis, "Les Thèmes de connaissance dans le Document de Damas," *Studia Hellenistica* 15 (1967), 139–146. See also his study entitled "Evolution de structures dans la secte de Qumran," in *Aux origines de l'église*, Recherches bibliques VII (Bruges: Desclée de Brouwer, 1964), pp. 23–49. Denis argues that the older text comprises cols. 1.1–4, 6a, while the more recent includes cols. 4.6b–6.11.

[25] J. Murphy-O'Connor, "An Essene Missionary Document? CD II, 14–VI, 1," *Revue Biblique* 77 (1970), 201. "Originally conceived as an instrument of conversion, CDII, 14–VI, 1 was later adapted to serve a different function by the addition of historical (I, 1–II, 1) and theological (II, 2–13) introductions. Moreover, within the missionary document in its present state various interpolations and glosses are to be detected."

[26] W. D. Davies ("Reflexions on Traditions: The Aboth Revisited," *Christian History and Interpretation: Studies Presented to John Knox*, ed. W. Farmer, C. F. D. Moule, and R. Niebuhr [Cambridge: University Press, 1967], pp. 127–159) likens the 'Aboth to "a miniature book of Proverbs."

[27] See H. Danby, *The Mishnah* (Oxford: University Press, 1933), p. 458, n. 12. Danby regards ch. 6 as "a very late gloss to the five chapters of Aboth."

Blocks of preformed materials

Compilation within Jewish documents did not only involve the stitching together of previously independent documents. The insertion of preformed blocks of traditional materials into existing texts is also well attested throughout Jewish literature.

A previously independent prayer (the Prayer of Azariah) and a poem (the Song of the Three Young Men) have been joined to each other (and to 3:23–24) by some brief narrative prose that functions to link them to the "received" religious text. The early use of these materials in a liturgical setting is likely since both the prayer and the hymn are found as separate odes (8 and 9) in the appendix to the Psalms within the text of codex Alexandrinus.

The LXX text of Esther adds a variety of preformed materials that do not appear in the Hebrew Bible, including: two prayers (of Mordecai and Esther, 13:8–14:19), biographical notes of Esther before the king (15:1–16), two royal decrees (of Artaxerxes, 13:1–7; 16:1–24), an interpretation of a dream, a conclusion, and a colophon (10:1–11:1).[28] It is unlikely that the translator of Esther composed any of these additions himself; if he did, it is hard to understand why he allowed various inconsistencies and contradictions to remain between the additions and the main text (cf. 11:3 and 12:1 against 2:21).[29]

Various blocks of traditional elements have been incorporated into I Baruch, including a prayer (1:15–3:8) and two poems (3:9–4:4; 4:5–5:9), each of which is probably the work of a different author.[30] At some point the various materials were bound together under the common theme of the Exile and the Return.

A sixteen-verse psalm of thanksgiving has been added to the text of Sirach (following 51:12) in the codex Vaticanus; the recurring refrain "for his mercy endures forever" is reminiscent of that which recurs in Psalm 136.

The text of the Sibylline Oracles has been subject to frequent editorial interpolations sometimes involving large blocks of mate-

---

[28] These additions (about 107 verses in all) were grouped together and placed at the end of Esther by Jerome. They appear in the KJV of the Apocrypha as Esther 10:4–16:24.

[29] There is also reason to think that these additions were not all inserted into the text at the same time. See Schürer, *The History of the Jewish People*, Vol. III, part 2, pp. 719f.

[30] See C. A. Moore, *Daniel, Esther, and Jeremiah: The Additions* (Garden City, NY: Doubleday, 1977), pp. 256, 275.

rial.[31] The group of Ψ MSS, for example, includes a long passage (Sib. Or. 2.56–148) that also appears in Pseudo-Phocylides (verses 5–79).[32]

Codex Vaticanus incorporates an extensive parenetic section into the book of Tobit (4:7–18) that does not appear in the text of codex Sinaiticus. It is very unlikely that a scribe would intentionally omit such a passage; but it is equally hard to imagine how he could have overlooked such a lengthy text by mistake. It seems very probable that the traditional parenetic material was added to the text by a later scribe.

The writings of Qumran also reflect this scribal tendency to add blocks of traditional materials to existing texts. At some stage in the development of the Community Rule, a number of disparate elements were gathered together, including: an initiation liturgy (1:16–2:19), a processional order (2:19–25), a teaching of the "Two Ways" (3:13–4:26), and a hymn (10:9–11:22).

In one copy of the War Scroll, 4Q491 (= 4Qm^a), a hymn (of the archangel Michael?) appears that is not found in 1QM (cf. 4Q491, II.8–18).[33]

In the incomplete Psalm Scroll at Qumran (11QPs^a) six "non-canonical" psalms have been added to the "canonical" collection.[34]

Short traditional pieces have been inserted into "existing" documents

It is well known that scribes often added short interpolations or glosses to existing texts. These additions were frequently motivated by the scribe's desire to complete an OT quotation, to explain an obscure phrase, or to fill out a well-known formula.

But an equally striking editorial feature of this literature is the

---

[31] Later Christian interpolations are obvious: see, for example, the teaching about the incarnation and career of Christ in 1.324–401; in 2.238–251 an editor has added sayings about the coming of Christ in glory with his angels; see also 2.311ff. (on the intercession of the virgin) and 2.264 (a reference to presbyters and deacons).

[32] See A. Kurfess, "Das Mahngedicht des sogenannten Phokylides im zweiten Buch der Oracula Sibyllina," *ZNW* 38 (1939), 171–181. See also the comments in P. W. van der Horst, *The Sentences of Pseudo-Phocylides* (Leiden: E. J. Brill, 1978), pp. 84–85. It is worthy of note that the interpolation omits Ps. Phoc. verses 70–75.

[33] So Milik, *Ten Years of Discovery*, p. 39: "the work was variously expanded, especially in the hymnic sections."

[34] See the remarks by G. Vermes, *The Dead Sea Scrolls in English*, rev. 3rd ed. (Harmondsworth: Penguin, 1987), pp. 208–214.

frequent and sometimes sudden intrusion into the text of short sayings, often of a proverbial, liturgical, or hymnic character.

The LXX offers numerous examples of how the sacred text could and did grow by the addition of small preformed traditional units. The LXX version of the Song of Moses, for example, adds a refrain not found in the MT:

> Let the sons of God
>   worship him,
> Rejoice, O nations,
>   with his people,
> and let all the angels of God
>   magnify him.[35]

The addition of small traditional sayings to existing texts is especially evident in the MS evidence that survives of the book of Sirach. Nearly 150 lines are added to Sirach in the MS group represented by Greek codices 55, 70, 106, 248, 253, and 254. The differences apparently reflect the early appearance of several Hebrew recensions, the later editions being enlarged to incorporate additional materials.[36]

The earliest witnesses to the text of Sirach 11, for example, omit 11:15–16:

> 15 Wisdom, understanding, and knowledge of the law come from the Lord; affection and the ways of good works come from him.
>
> 16 Error and darkness were created with sinners; evil will grow old with those who take pride in malice.

These two interpolations, and many others that appear within the text of Sirach, must be attributed to scribal activity during the course of transmission.[37]

Similar additions appear in the surviving MS witnesses of Pseudo-Phocylides.[38] Frequently, the scribal methods behind such interpolations can still be observed; verse 36, for example, is a

[35] See Deut. 32:43 (LXX).

[36] See W. O. E. Oesterley, *The Wisdom of Jesus the Son of Sirach or Ecclesiasticus* (Cambridge: University Press, 1912), p. xciii.

[37] Sirach is filled with these obvious scribal additions; see, for example, Sir. 1:5, 7, 21; 3:19, 25; 10:21; 13:14; 16:15–16.

[38] For example, verses 36, 116–117, 129, 144–146. See the commentary by van der Horst, *The Sentences of Pseudo-Phocylides*.

spurious sentence that seems to have been added and linked to verse 35 by means of word association:[39]

35 ἀγροῦ γειτονέοντος ἀπόσχεο,
    μὴ δ' ἄρ' ὑπερβῇς.

36 πάντων μέτρον ἄριστον,
    ὑπερβασίαι δ' ἀλεγειναί.

It seems likely that ὑπερβῇς in verse 35 suggested to a scribe another proverbial saying (containing ὑπερβασίαι) which he then added to the text.

Other additions to Pseudo-Phocylides reveal similar scribal techniques. Verses 116–117, for example, which appear in only one MS (V), seem to have been inserted into their present context out of thematic considerations:

116 Nobody knows what will be after tomorrow
     or after an hour.

117 The death of mortals cannot be foreseen,
     and the future is uncertain.

The following verses (118–121) also treat various aspects of life's instability.

Verse 144 (only in MS V) has apparently been added to the text to illustrate an aspect of the previous saying:

143 Nip the evil in the bud and heal the wound.

144 By a tiny spark a vast wood is set on fire.

We also see evidence in the Qumran MSS that very brief units, sometimes consisting of only a few words, were added by various editors of these documents. Referring to the apparent collaboration of scribes on the transcription of IQH, M. Martin observes:

> In IQH we concluded [cf. Vol. I, p. 62] that Scribe A finished his section, that Scribe B took up for *some four lines* and handed over then to Scribe C, and finally that, when Scribe C had finished his part and revised his own work and that of Scribe A, scribe B returned to the work and went over the work of both Scribes A and C. There is

---

[39] The verse is omitted by three important MSS: L, P, V.

here enough evidence to warrant our speaking of a mutual
collaboration and revision [my italic].[40]

Martin goes on to argue that the Qumran MS evidence suggests
that scribes deliberately left lacunae in the MSS for later insertions
which would be added by other scribes. Compilation, in his view,
was a community project that sometimes involved MS additions
(by various hands) of very small bits, as the document circulated
throughout the scriptorium.

Non-canonical early Christian documents show similar marks of scribal editing and redaction

The composite character of much Jewish literature is mirrored
throughout ancient Christian writings. Few of these documents can
be read as the product of a single author. Surviving MS evidence
indicates that early Christian compilers were at work, collecting
and combining traditional materials.

The Didache, for example, is a composite document that shows a
complex literary history.[41] Diverse blocks of preformed independent traditional materials can be discerned within this teaching
manual.[42] A version of the "Two Ways" (1:1–6:2), for example, has
at some stage been incorporated into the larger work.[43] Also
embedded within this document is a collection of three prayers
(8:2–10:8, including the Lord's prayer), and several clusters of
community instructions (on conduct toward church leaders, 11:3–
12; on hospitality, 12:1–5, etc.).

The Epistle of Barnabas, likewise, exhibits certain marks of
redaction; in Barn. 18:1, an editorial remark clearly reveals a
literary seam: "Now let us pass on to another lesson (γνῶσιν) and
teaching (διδαχήν)." This remark is followed immediately by a
version of the "Two Ways" (18:1–21:9) very similar to the one that

---

[40] M. Martin, *The Scribal Character of the Dead Sea Scrolls* (Louvain: University Publications, 1958), Vol. I, p. 388.

[41] R. A. Kraft (*The Apostolic Fathers*, ed. R. Grant [6 vols., New York: Thomas Nelson, 1965], Vol. III, *Barnabas and the Didache*, pp. 1–2, 64) regards the Didache as "evolved literature" and suggests that it is "as much the product of its sources as it is the work of any individual."

[42] See J. P. Audet, *La Didachè: instructions des apôtres*, Etudes bibliques (Paris: Gabalda, 1958), pp. 104–121 (on the composition of the text), and pp. 121–186 (on the sources).

[43] See the parallels to this material in the Qumran Community Rule (IQS 3:18) and Barn. 18:1–21:9.

appears in the Didache. Significantly, an ancient Latin version (L) of Barnabas only includes chs. 1–17, omitting altogether the "Two Ways" material; such MS evidence supports the theory that the epistle once circulated in a much shortened form.

The different recensions of the Ignatian corpus provide considerable textual evidence for this process of editorial revision and expansion.[44] Two facts emerge from the textual history of this corpus: (1) in the course of transmission, collections of letters could be enlarged by the "loading" of spurious letters onto the collection, and (2) genuine letters were sometimes subjected to massive scribal interpolation.[45] The Ignatian recensions provide a unique opportunity to view something of the textual development and editorial processes of early Christian texts.

There is reason to doubt the literary integrity of Polycarp's letter to the Philippians. Commentators have suspected that this letter (as transmitted) is not a unity but consists, rather, of two formerly distinct documents. The suspicion arises primarily from internal grounds; in 9:1–2 Polycarp seems to regard Ignatius as already dead, but later in the same letter (13:2) he requests news about him as though Ignatius were still alive.[46]

The Shepherd of Hermas, likewise, appears to be a composite document that was enlarged during the course of transmission. Scholars have identified at least three separate stages of growth in which later writings were appended to earlier materials.[47] The

---

[44] Each extant Ignatian recension contains a different number of letters: the shorter Syriac recension (edited by W. Cureton in 1844) includes only three: Ign. Poly., Ign. Eph., and Ign. Rom. The "middle" recension (edited by Bishop Ussher in 1644) contains twelve: the three Syriac letters plus Ign. Smyr., Ign. Mag., Ign. Phil., Ign. Tral., Mary of Cassobola to Ign., Ign. to Mary of Cassobola, Ign. Tars., Ign. Antioch., Ign. Hero., Ign. Rom. The long recension (edited by R. Grosseteste in 1250) has seventeen letters: the twelve letters of the middle recension (with many alterations) plus an account of the martyrdom of Ignatius and four letters of correspondence between Ignatius, St. John and St. Mary.

[45] See the detailed discussion in J. B. Lightfoot, *The Apostolic Fathers*, Vol. I, part 2, *St. Ignatius and St. Polycarp* (London: Macmillan, 1889), pp. 233–279; Lightfoot argued that the interpolator made extensive use of traditional materials taken from the Apostolic Constitutions. Compare T. Zahn, *Ignatius von Antiochen* (Gotha: Friedrich Andreas Perthes, 1873), pp. 75–166.

[46] So P. N. Harrison, *Polycarp's Two Epistles to the Philippians* (Cambridge: University Press, 1936), pp. 15–19. In ch. 3, Harrison examines other early Christian writings that appear to be composite. His examples include II Corinthians, Philippians, II Timothy, and Romans 16. *Pace* J. B. Lightfoot, *The Apostolic Fathers* (London: Macmillan, 1893), pp. 166–167.

[47] See the discussions on the literary character of this document by M. Dibelius, *Der Hirt des Hermas* (Tübingen: J. C. B. Mohr [Paul Siebeck], 1923), pp. 419–421.

Mandates and the Similitudes of the Shepherd appear to be based on older Jewish traditional materials. Mandates 2–10, 12, examine a series of virtues and vices, and the whole section is similar in many ways to the teaching of the "Two Ways" (compare Didache 1–6, Barnabas 18–20). The Similitudes, likewise, contain a collection of parables that most likely have a pre-Christian Jewish origin.[48]

Considerable MS evidence suggests that the apocryphal Acts of Paul has been editorially enlarged through the addition of various traditions about the apostle.[49] The correspondence between Paul and Corinth, for example, is in three parts:

1   a letter written to Paul from Corinth;
2   a narrative recounting the delivery of the letter to Paul in prison; and
3   a letter written by Paul to Corinth (III Corinthians).

The Latin text of this material is attested by five MSS, of which all but one (Z) omit part 2 (the narrative). Codex Z (which includes part 2) omits part 3. And codex P omits parts 1 and 2. A third-century Greek MS discovered among the Bodmer papyri (X) also omits part 2.

These omissions are significant, for they indicate the likelihood that parts 1 and 3 at one time circulated independently, and were only later added to the Acts of Paul. The narrative, then, may serve in its present context as an editorial link between the two originally separate "letters."

The epistle to Diognetus is plainly a composite document consisting of two previously independent texts, the first of which ends with chapter 10. Chapters 11–12 have no connection with the preceding ones, and it is generally recognized that they originally belonged to a different document. As J. B. Lightfoot has observed,

> The two remaining chapters belong to some different work which has been accidentally attached to it, just as in most of the extant MSS the latter part of the Epistle

---

[48] See, for example, Similitudes 8, the parable of the willow tree (8.3.2–3, extolling the general validity of the Jewish law?) and its secondary Christian application (8.3.4–11).

[49] See A. F. J. Klijn, "The Apocryphal Correspondence between Paul and the Corinthians," *Vigiliae Christianae* 17 (1963), 2–23; W. Schneemelcher's introduction to the Acts of Paul in *New Testament Apocrypha*, ed. E. Hennecke (London: Lutterworth Press, 1965), Vol. II, pp. 322ff.

of Polycarp is attached to the former part of the Epistle of Barnabas, so as to form in appearance one work. Probably in this case also an archetypal MS had lost some leaves.[50]

Conclusions

No matter where one looks in the literary landscape of which the Pastoral letters are a part, the textual evidence reveals unmistakable signs of frequent and substantial editing. Many of these texts are clearly amalgamations of previously independent materials. Traditional materials have been gathered together and woven into sacred collections.

It is clear from the above overview that the vast majority of these Jewish and early Christian writings are misinterpreted if they are read as the product of one hand; no single author was responsible for them. The surviving MS evidence shows the remarkable extent to which scribes collected and compiled disparate materials; the textual histories of every genre of literature (including historical narratives, prophetic and wisdom literature, apocalyptic writings, epistolary collections) show the marks of this scribal activity.

The editorial reworking of NT texts

Form criticism, together with its daughters, redaction criticism and narrative criticism, has demonstrated that the editors of the gospels both handed on sayings and traditions about Jesus and consciously and unconsciously shaped their traditional material to serve their own theological ends and the needs of the communities that they were serving. Redaction criticism and narrative criticism have emphasized that the gospels we have are distinctive products of authors or "schools." Yet these critics rightly assume theories about the literary interdependence of the Synoptic gospels. They have never lost sight of the fact that the gospel writers were passing on traditions that had come to their communities in either oral or written form.

When the church's oral traditions were first written down is a matter of speculation. Paul's references to the traditions he had received (cf. I Cor. 11:23; 15:3) seem to allow the possibility that

---

[50]   Lightfoot, *The Apostolic Fathers* (1893), p. 488.

written traditions circulated among the early Christian communities at a very early stage indeed.[51]

If so, it is likely that Christian scribes were at work from the beginning, "stitching" together small pieces of traditional materials that came into their care. As Bultmann and others have argued, these traditional materials probably circulated at first as isolated sayings or short stories which were slowly gathered into small and then larger collections; the editorial methods used to combine these materials often featured catch-word links that, not infrequently, tied sayings together that did not have any real integral relationship with one another. The Gospel of Thomas may represent an early collection of previously isolated Jesus sayings. As M. Fieger has argued:

> The Coptic Gospel of Thomas shows a "loose unity" (Haechen). Again and again there is to be seen a certain coherence in the grouping of this Logion with that: the individual sayings are bound together by catch-word connection, similarity of form, or relation to the same or a similar theme ... However a meaningfully unified editorial structure is not to be demonstrated for the Gospel of Thomas.[52]

The evangelists (and later editors) continued this process of compilation. To call the evangelists "compilers," however, does not mean that the gospels are simply a rag-bag of traditions woven together without any sense of structure or desire for coherence. There are clear signs of intentionality behind the formation of the gospels, particularly evident in their distinctive traits. Nor was the idea of the shaping of tradition new to the evangelists. They were continuing an editorial process which began as soon as Jesus' sayings were recalled and used in preaching and teaching, and as soon as stories were told of his deeds. In short, the evangelists, for all that they were authors, were also servants of their collected traditions. Whatever else they did, one of their aims was to preserve their community's sacred traditions.

So, in addition to isolated sayings, the evangelists seem to have

---

[51] E. E. Ellis, "New Directions in Form Criticism," in *Jesus Christus in Historie und Theologie [Festschrift in honor of H. Conzelmann]* (Tübingen: J. C. B. Mohr, 1975), pp. 299–315, notes the tendency among modern form-critics to emphasize the formative role that *written* transmission played within early Christianity.

[52] M. Fieger, *Das Thomasevangelium: Einleitung Kommentar und Systematik*, Neutestamentliche Abhandlungen, NF 22 (Münster: Aschendorff, 1991), pp. 5–6.

had in their possession preformed collections of materials which they then incorporated into their own collections of traditions.[53] The five "conflict-stories" of Mark 2:1–3:6 probably illustrate such a preformed collection. As M. Albertz has argued, these stories show a loosely joined unity and structure, but it is very unlikely that the evangelist wrote the section himself; the material has all the marks of a preformed literary unit and probably existed as a collection when it came into the hands of the gospel compiler. V. Tayor (following Albertz) notes:

> What Mark does is to take over this complex, either from a document or from oral tradition; in a conservative spirit he weaves it into his Gospel (cf. ii. 1 and 13), even though it does not entirely suit his plan.[54]

The "sermons" on the mount (Matt. 5:1–7:27) and the plain (Luke 6:17–49) may represent other early collections of prayers, beatitudes, parables, etc. that antedate both Matthew and Luke. H. D. Betz has proposed that the "sermon" appearing in Matt. 5–7 is a pre-Matthean source compiled around AD 55 by a redactor of Jesus' sayings.[55] Betz's arguments on the origin of this material are not all equally convincing, but his suggestion that the evangelist had access to an independent written collection of Jesus' sayings and incorporated it into his gospel seems very possible.

The "Little Apocalypse" of Mark 13 is a collection of dominical

[53] The question of how the canonical gospels were compiled poses massive problems for NT scholarship; the evidence, however, indicates that the compositional histories behind these documents are probably far more complicated than either the traditional two-source or the four-source theories allow. A glance at K. Aland's *Synopsis quattuor evangeliorum*, 13th ed. (Stuttgart: Deutsche Bibelgesellschaft, 1985) illustrates well something of the complexity of the problem: section 59 (pp. 83–85), to take one example, presents various pericopes (from Matthew, Luke, the Didache, Justin's *Apology*, etc.) dealing with the theme "loving one's enemies." Parallel sayings appear in each pericope, but the *order* in which these sayings are found within their respective collections differs considerably (as does the wording). That any one of these pericopes served as the source for the others must be considered very unlikely; it seems far more probable that the editors of these materials were drawing upon different collections of sayings that were circulating independently in their respective communities.

[54] V. Taylor, *The Formation of the Gospel Tradition* (London: Macmillan, 1935), p. 178. See also M. Albertz, *Die synoptischen Streitgespräche* (Berlin: Trowitzsch und Sohn, 1919), pp. 5–16.

[55] H. D. Betz, *Essays on the Sermon on the Mount* (Philadelphia: Fortress Press, 1985). Compare G. Stanton's critique in "The Origin and Purpose of Matthew's Sermon on the Mount," in *Tradition and Interpretation in the New Testament*, Essays in honor of E. E. Ellis, ed. G. Hawthorne and O. Betz (Grand Rapids: Eerdmans, 1987), pp. 181–192.

sayings that may also have had an independent textual history prior to its incorporation in the gospel.[56] It is only loosely related to its context and forms an intelligible unity on its own.

But even after the first evangelists finished the compilation of the materials in their possession, their gospels continued to grow. Later scribes brought their own traditional materials and added them to the circulating gospels. It is clear, for example, that short traditional "units" were added to the texts of the gospels. Many of these "floating" traditions, some of very ancient origin, have been preserved through this editorial activity. A Jesus saying, for example, has been inserted into the Western texts of Matt. 20:28 (D and, with minor variations, Φ, it, syr^c):

> But seek to increase from that which is small and from the greater to become less. When you enter a house and are invited to dine, do not recline in the prominent places, lest perchance one more honorable than you comes in, and the host come and say to you, "Go farther down"; and you will be put to shame. But if you recline in the lower place and one inferior to you comes in the host will say to you, "Go farther up"; and this will be advantageous to you.[57]

Another later addition, this time a short Jesus saying, appears at Matt. 18:11:

> For the son of man came to seek and to save the lost.

This saying is omitted by the earliest witnesses and has been relegated to the apparatus of Nestle–Aland's 26th edition.[58]

The editor of codex Bezae has added a short Jesus saying to the text at Luke 6:5:

> On the same day [Jesus] saw a man working on the sabbath and said to him, "Man, if you know what you are doing you are blessed, but if you do not know, you are accursed and a transgressor of the law."

---

[56] J. Moffatt (*An Introduction to the Literature of the New Testament*, rev. 3rd ed. [Edinburgh: T. & T. Clark, 1920], pp. 207–209) calls the unit "a written fly-leaf of early Christian apocalyptic prophecy" (p. 207). A survey of the critical literature (up to 1956) is provided by G. R. Beasley-Murray in *Jesus and the Future* (London: Macmillan, 1954), pp. 33–167.

[57] Compare with shorter version of Luke 14:8–10.

[58] The saying is omitted by codices Sinaiticus, Vaticanus, and other witnesses representing several textual types (Alexandrian, pre-Caesarean, Egyptian, Antiochian).

A traditional saying, attested by Aleph, B, C, L, and others, has been incorporated into Matt. 27:49:

> And another took a spear and pierced his side, and out came water and blood.

The tradition recording Jesus' anguished prayer in the garden and the angel's ministry to him (Luke 22:43–44) is absent from such ancient and widely diversified witnesses as papyri 69 and 75, Aleph, A, B, T, W, syr^s, cop$^{sa, bo}$, arm^{mss}, Marcion, Clement, and Origen. Family 13 adds these verses to Matthew's gospel (after 26:39). B. M. Metzger thinks that the verses were "added from an early source, oral or written, of extra-canonical traditions concerning the life and passion of Jesus."[59]

The fact that some of these isolated sayings were added to the gospels at a much later date is especially significant, for if scribes added to documents that had already achieved a certain "fixed" form (by their use within the churches), it is even more likely that they would have added to texts that had not yet received widespread attention!

The gospel MSS also reflect the scribal tendency to add larger blocks of traditional materials to a "received" text. The story of Jesus' encounter with the woman caught in adultery (John 7:53–8:11), for example, is a traditional Jesus story that was added to the text of John at a later date.[60]

Similar scribal activity is evident in the textual witnesses to the longer endings to Mark's gospel (16:9–22).[61] This ending was clearly not a part of the earliest record of this gospel. It may have originally functioned as a second-century summary giving grounds for belief in Jesus' resurrection. In any case, it is not surprising that a scribe would wish to preserve such valuable traditional material. To attach it to the end of Mark's gospel would secure its survival.

The literary difficulties presented by ch. 21 of John's gospel are

---

[59] B. M. Metzger, *The Textual Commentary of the Greek New Testament* (New York: United Bible Societies, 1971), p. 177.

[60] The story is omitted by papyri 66 and 75, codices Aleph and B, and numerous other early MSS. It is also lacking in the works of Tertullian and Origen. The same story appears in later manuscripts between John 7:36 and 37 (codex 225), after John 21:25 (*f*1), after Luke 21:38 (*f*13), and after Luke 24:53 (codex 1333).

[61] The earliest manuscripts end with Mark 16:8 (so Aleph, B, 304); others add 16:9–20 directly following 16:8 (so A, C, D, W, O, et al.); still others include an additional brief paragraph between 16:8 and 16:9–20 (so L et al.). In one manuscript (k), 16:9–20 is lacking, but 16:8 is followed by the brief paragraph (mentioned above) that concludes the gospel.

considerable, and have led most commentators to conclude that the chapter is an appendix, probably added at a later stage in the transmission of the gospel.[62] R. Bultmann has argued persuasively against the unity of the postscript itself, suggesting that it too is a compilation, consisting of an independent Easter story (21:1–14) and two conversations of Jesus with Peter (21:15–23).[63]

These representative examples demonstrate how ancient Christian documents could and did grow. The MS evidence enables us, in the above cases, to observe something of the stages of growth to which the gospels were clearly subject. The gospels seem to have been treated by scribes as repositories of traditional materials. As W. Sanday has observed,

> Possessors of copies did not hesitate to add little items of tradition, often oral, in some cases perhaps written, which reached them.[64]

But what about the remaining NT documents? Were they also subject to interpolation and expansion during transmission?

The textual history of the book of Acts certainly seems to reflect a complicated process of editorial activity. The additions as well as the "non-interpolations" of the Western recension (D, Old Latin, Old Syriac) throw considerable light on early scribal practices.[65] Additions to the text seem to derive from a variety of traditional, apocryphal, or other non-biblical sources.

An additional "regulation," for example, appears in the Western version of the Apostolic Decree (see Acts 15:20 and 15:29); it takes the form of the negative golden rule:

---

[62] C. K. Barrett (*The Gospel according to St. John*, 2nd ed. [Philadelphia: Westminster Press, 1978], pp. 576–588) reckons that no fewer than 28 words in ch. 21 are absent from chs. 1–20. In Barrett's view the appendix must be from a different hand since "it is extremely unlikely that an author, wishing to add fresh material to his own book, would add it in so clumsy a manner" (p. 576). See also the discussion in R. Bultmann, *The Gospel of John: A Commentary*, ET by G.R. Beasley-Murray (Philadelphia: Westminster Press, 1971), pp. 700–718.

[63] Bultmann, *The Gospel of John*, pp. 702ff.

[64] W. Sanday, *Inspiration*, Bampton Lectures of 1893 (London: Longmans, Green, 1894), p. 295.

[65] According to the reckoning by F. G. Kenyon (*The Western Text in the Gospels and Acts*, Proceedings of the British Academy, 24 [London, 1939], p. 26) the Western text is 8.5 percent longer than the Alexandrian. But when the two recensions are compared it is evident (from the Western "non-interpolations") that the Alexandrian text has also been enlarged by scribal additions.

> And whatever you would not wish to be done by others, do not do to another.

A confessional statement has been added to the Western version of Acts 8:37:

> Philip said, "If you believe with all your heart, you may [be baptized]." The official answered, "I believe that Jesus Christ is the son of God."[66]

The texts of the Pauline letters also bear the marks of editorial activity. In the letter to the Romans, for example, there is unmistakable evidence that some textual alteration has occurred. A benediction ("the grace of our Lord Jesus Christ be with you all, amen") appears in various MSS in different contexts; some MSS (papyrus 46, Aleph, B, 1881 et al.) place the benediction at Rom. 16:20b; others (D, G, it[d*], [g], et al.) place it at Rom. 16:24, while in still others (P, 33, 104, et al.) it follows 16:27.

The doxology of Rom. 15:25–27 also appears at various places within the MS tradition, and has been widely recognized as a non-Pauline addition to the text.[67]

The regulations concerning women's conduct that appear at I Cor. 14:33b–35 are marked by the kind of textual disturbance that suggests the presence of a later interpolation into the text,[68] as C. K. Barrett and others have argued.[69]

Other blocks of material in the Pauline letters appear to be scribal interpolations on the basis of internal considerations (such as their literary character, use of language, and content). But the lack of hard textual evidence makes the non-Pauline authorship of such texts much more difficult to prove. J. Moffatt, however, cautions against a hasty dismissal of strong internal evidence in such cases:

[66] This material is not found in papyri 45 and 74 ℵ, B, C, and other early witnesses.

[67] The doxology also appears after Rom. 14:23 in a number of MSS (A, P, 5, 33), while papyrus 46 and a few others place it after Rom. 15:33. According to W. Kümmel (*Introduction*, p. 317) "it should be regarded as certain that the doxology does not originate with Paul and was created originally as a conclusion following 14:23."

[68] Some MSS (for example, D, F, G) place I Cor. 14:34–35 after verse 40. In codex Fuldensis the verses appear twice: in the margin after verse 33 as well as in the text following verse 40.

[69] C. K. Barrett, *A Commentary on the First Epistle to the Corinthians*, 2nd ed. (London: Adam & Charles Black, 1976), p. 333. So also G. Fee, *The First Epistle to the Corinthians* (Grand Rapids: Eerdmans, 1987), p. 705. *Pace* W. F. Orr and J. A. Walther, *I Corinthians* (New York: Doubleday, 1976), p. 312.

Even where the extant text does not suggest any break, the possibility of interpolations cannot be denied outright; the distance between the oldest MSS, or even the oldest versions, and the date of composition, leaves ample room for changes to have taken place in the interval between the autograph and the earliest known text.[70]

More than a little internal evidence suggests that Rom. 13:1–7 has been added to Paul's original letter to the Romans.[71] the text has a self-contained unity and appears to be both independent of, and interruptive of, its context.[72] More importantly, the thoughts presented here are in tension with several basic Pauline ideas.[73] And the fact that no Christian writer refers to Rom. 13:1–7 prior to AD 150 (or perhaps even as late as AD 180) lends credence to the idea that the text was added to the letter by a later hand.[74] J. C. O'Neill regards the unit as a collection of eight injunctions that "was probably ancient at the time of its incorporation."[75]

The Pauline authorship of II Cor. 6:14–7:1 has also been widely doubted on internal grounds.[76] It is hard to deny that the passage

[70] Moffatt, *Introduction*, p. 38.

[71] This position is by no means universally accepted. C. E. B. Cranfield (*Romans IX–XVI* [Edinburgh: T. & T. Clark, 1979], Vol. II, pp. 651ff.) argues against it, although he concedes that "the relation of 13:1–7 to its context remains for us to some extent problematical" (p. 653). See also the arguments defending Paul's authorship of this text by M. Black, *Romans* (Grand Rapids: Eerdmans, 1973), p. 159.

[72] So C. K. Barrett, *A Commentary on the Epistle to the Romans* (London: Adam & Charles Black), 1962 [1957]), p. 244. Although Barrett does not think the passage an interpolation, he does recognize the problems it presents: "The new paragraph, a self-contained treatment of a special theme, appears at first to be introduced somewhat abruptly."

[73] J. Kallas ("Romans XIII.1–7: An Interpolation," *NTS* 11 [1964–1965], 365–374) observes four basic contradictions running through Rom. 13:1–7: (1) there is a lack of any sense of Jesus' immediate return; (2) the term "exousia" is employed to denote earthly human powers, whereas in Paul the term refers to spiritual powers; (3) the powers (exousiai) in this passage are regarded as loyal servants of God, whereas in Paul they always depict evil cosmic figures; (4) the passage reflects the Pharisaic view of retribution – quite different from Paul's view of the suffering of the innocent.

[74] So, E. Barnikol, "Römer 13: Der nichtpaulinische Ursprung der absoluten Obrigkeitsbejahung von Römer 13:1–7," in *Studien zum Neuen Testament: Erich Klostermann zum 90. Geburtstag dargebracht*, Texte und Untersuchungen 77 (Berlin: Akademie-Verlag, 1961). See his summary, pp. 129–133.

[75] J. C. O'Neill, *Paul's Letter to the Romans* (Harmondsworth: Penguin, 1975), p. 209.

[76] But, again, the authorship of this section is much debated. Its authenticity is upheld by many. See, for example, C. G. Moule, *The Second Epistle to the Corinthians* (London: Pickering & Inglis, 1962); F. F. Bruce (*I and II Corinthians*

fits poorly into its present context, or that 7:2 follows excellently upon 6:13.[77] Differences in vocabulary are also evident; six words appearing in 6:14–7:1 do not appear elsewhere in the NT.[78]

The literary relationship between the letter of Jude and II Peter (especially ch. 2) is very complex and difficult to untangle. But the striking similarities between these two documents suggest either that a common document has been incorporated within both letters or that a dependent literary relationship exists between Jude and II Peter.[79] In either case it is clear that preexisting materials have been incorporated into at least one of these documents without any indication that such editorial activity has occurred.[80]

The Apocalypse of John also reflects the marks of a composite document;[81] in its present form it is made up of many diverse traditional elements (including letters, hymns, doxologies, prayers, etc.).[82] The seven letters of the Apocalypse (2:1–3:22) show marked differences in form, language, and theological ideas from the

[London: Marshall, Morgan and Scott, 1971], p. 214) regards the section as a Pauline digression.

[77] Many commentators think that the section is an interpolation; some regard it as a non-Pauline (but Christian) writing, while others think it has a pre-Christian (perhaps Qumranic?) origin. See the discussion by H. D. Betz, "2 Cor. 6:14–7:1: An Anti-Pauline Fragment?," *JBL* 92 (1973), 88–108; J. A. Fitzmyer, "Qumran and the Interpolated Paragraph in 2 Cor. 6:14–7:1," *CBQ* 23 (1961), 271–280. R. Bultmann (*Der zweite Brief an die Korinther* [Göttingen: Vandenhoeck & Ruprecht, 1976], pp. 181–182) regards the text as "typical Jewish (parenetic teachings)," and compares it to the Testament of the Twelve Patriarchs (especially T. Levi 19, T. Naph. 3). He wondered if it had been "revised from a Christian viewpoint."

[78] These are: ἑτεροζυγεῖν, βελιάρ, μετοχή, συμφώνησις, συγκατάθεσις, μολυσμός.

[79] Most modern scholars argue for the latter alternative, giving the priority to Jude. See Kümmel, *Introduction*, pp. 428ff. See also the discussion on the question of literary dependence in C. Bigg's *Commentary on the Epistles of St. Peter and St. Jude* (Edinburgh: T. & T. Clark, 1910), pp. 216ff.

[80] This is clearly to over-simplify a complex problem, for it seems likely that the compiled materials were also modified by the compiler. But even if this were the case, it would still represent a significant example of a compiler who added preexisting materials (*mutatis mutandis*) into his text without any indication that such compilation had occurred.

[81] J. Moffatt (*The Historical New Testament* [Edinburgh: T. & T. Clark, 1901], pp. 677ff.) presents a detailed overview of earlier studies on this apocalypse. For Moffatt, "the composite character of the writing is no longer a hypothesis, it is a postulate, of critical study." See also the more cautious, but similar, conclusion of W. Kümmel, *Introduction*, p. 464.

[82] This is not to suggest that the various preformed traditions within Revelation have simply been thrown together without regard to order or structure. There is obvious structural unity, but it is not of the kind that one would expect from an author; it seems, rather, to be a carefully combined compilation of disparate sources.

materials in chs. 4–22. These distinctive features suggest the previously independent character of these letters.[83]

The fact that NT texts were subjected to significant editorial reworking is not only revealed by a close examination of the MS evidence and of the internal features of the texts themselves. It is attested also by the frequent complaints of the church fathers that the sacred writings of the second-century church were being freely edited and manipulated.

Tertullian, for instance, complained that various heresies were tampering with the sacred texts, each one perverting them "with both additions and subtractions to suit its own teaching."[84] Marcion's critical edition of the Pauline letters is probably the best-known example of this. But it must be remembered that Marcion claimed to be restoring these letters to their original form; in seeking legitimacy for his work, he appealed to what he thought was a generally recognized fact: that the Pauline letters had been considerably edited during transmission. Since the church possessed no standardized NT text, Marcion's tendentious arguments were all the more difficult to refute.

Celsus also accused Christians of editing the sacred texts; Origen quotes him as saying that,

> some believers, as though from a drinking bout, go so far as to oppose themselves and alter the original text of the gospel three or four times over, and they change its character to enable them to deny difficulties in face of criticism.[85]

If the practice of interpolating texts had not been a widespread phenomenon in this period, such accusations would have carried little weight. As J. Moffatt has observed, such a charge "would not have been worth making unless the fact on which it rested had been at least a popular and highly credible habit."[86]

---

[83] The literary integrity of Revelation in general, and of the seven letters in particular, is a matter of dispute. J. Massyngberde Ford (*Revelation*, Anchor Bible Series [Garden City, NY: Doubleday, 1975], pp. 43–45, 55–56) presents a detailed examination of the linguistic differences between chs. 1–3, 22:16b, 20–21, and chs. 4–22, and concludes that chs. 1–3 must have been added by a later writer. Ramsay, *Letters to the Seven Churches* (London: Hodder & Stoughton, 1904), argues that the letters circulated independently. But compare the objections to such theories in M. Kiddle's *The Revelation of St. John* (London: Hodder & Stoughton, 1940).

[84] Tertullian, *Prescription against Heretics* 17.

[85] Origen, *Contra Celsum* II. 27.

[86] Moffatt, *The Historical New Testament*, p. 609.

Eusebius reports that Tatian "ventured to paraphrase (μετα-φράσαι) some words of the apostle [Paul], as though correcting their style."[87] Eusebius also records that Dionysius, the bishop of Corinth, complained that his own letters had been mutilated by "the apostles of the devil," who "have filled them with tares by tearing out some things and putting in others." Dionysius goes on to say,

> it is no wonder that some have gone about to falsify even the scriptures of the Lord when they have plotted against writings so inferior.[88]

To what these "scriptures of the Lord" refer is unclear, but it may be that in the mind of the earliest readers they included both the gospels and the Pauline letters.

A great body of evidence, then, suggests that the earliest NT texts were liable to extensive interpolations, glosses, and other sorts of textual modifications. It would be surprising, in fact, if that were not the case, for it is unlikely that scribes only began to gloss and interpolate the NT writings after the appearance of the church's published edition of collected Christian writings. The texts were undoubtedly more vulnerable to editorial reworking in the earliest period, before the general church editions became available and the scrutiny of the ecclesiastical authorities could be brought to bear upon the shape of the text.[89]

Conclusions and relevance for the Pastorals

The compositional survey above covers an enormously diverse range of Jewish and early Christian writings; almost every major genre of religious literature is represented, including historical narrative, prophetic writings, wisdom collections, apocalyptic works, community manuals, epistolary writings, and gospel accounts. Chronologically, the dating of the various documents

---

[87] Eusebius, *Ecclesiastical History* IV.xxix.6.

[88] Ibid., IV.xxiii.12.

[89] For further discussion of this point see J.C. O'Neill's article, "Glosses and Interpolations in the Letters of St. Paul," in *Texte und Untersuchungen* 126, *Studia Evangelica* 7 (Berlin: Akademie-Verlag, 1982), pp. 379ff. Also, H. Koester, *Introduction to the New Testament* (2 vols., Philadelphia: Fortress Press, 1982), Vol. II, p. 41: "textual corruptions are most frequent during the first decades of the transmission, that is, in the period between the autograph and first edition."

covers the equally expansive period of over one thousand years, from the age of Jeremiah (*circa* 750 BC) to that of the redactor of the Ignatian corpus (AD 400?).

The selection of this mass of literary documents is open to immediate objections, especially since few of the writings examined seem to provide close literary parallels to the Pastorals. Many of the works have been compiled over long periods of time; none of them seems to offer a precise parallel to the Pastorals.

In defending the selection of documents, it must first be conceded that not all of the above documents have an equal contribution to make to our understanding of the Pastorals. It is highly unlikely, for example, that the Pastorals have a compositional history at all like that of II Baruch or the Mishnah. Closer literary parallels to the Pastorals may be afforded by documents like the Didache and the longer recension of the Ignatian corpus. It is fair to say that such texts probably offer more clues about the origin of the Pastorals than, say, I Enoch or the Mishnah.

So why include the more "remote" literature in this survey? Why not collect only the documents that seem to offer the closest literary parallels to the Pastorals and examine them? There are several reasons: first of all, the primary aim of this investigation has not been so much to search for precise literary analogies to the Pastorals, but to provide a broad overview of the compositional histories of Jewish and early Christian literature – that is, to set the backdrop, as it were, of the literary environment out of which the Pastorals emerged. To achieve this aim, the types of literature examined have intentionally been kept very broad; no attempt has been made to focus upon any particular genre or form of writing, or to limit the survey to documents that show some "likeness" to the Pastorals. The most important results of the survey depend in many respects upon the widespread and diverse selection of the materials examined.

Secondly, it cannot be assumed that documents showing close literary parallels share similar compositional histories. In fact, the above survey of the wider literature suggests that the literary history behind each Jewish and early Christian document is a unique one. Editors apparently did not follow any set schema as they went about their task of compilation. The additions to Isaiah's original oracles, for example, show some editorial parallels to those that appear in Jeremiah, but the differences in the way these materials were compiled are equally pronounced. Even among closely related Christian texts a remarkable diversity is apparent in the compositional techniques that were employed. The Gospel of Thomas, for example, like the canonical gospels, includes various collections of Jesus *logia*, but, unlike those gospels, Thomas does not place the *logia* into any narrative framework.

This means that literary relatedness in genre, form, content, etc. is not necessarily all that important in the comparison of the compositional histories of documents. Certain editorial techniques employed by the redactor of Sirach may be reflected in the texts of other composite documents of very different genres and purposes. The Pastorals may not show many literary similarities to I Enoch, but this does not make the compositional history of I Enoch irrelevant. For not only does I Enoch add its witness to the widespread practice of editorial compilation, but the text also shows certain literary marks (like awkward transitions and abrupt breaks in thought) that help clarify, together with the evidence from other documents, certain characteristic features of composite documents.

Consequently, the documents that may seem further removed from the Pastorals by virtue of their different genres, forms, times of origin, compositional histories, etc. still make an important contribution to this study by revealing the remarkable diversity of the editorial activity. In light of such diversity, it would appear to be gross over-simplification of the compiling processes to suggest that the Pastorals (if composite) were compiled *like* the Didache, or *like* the gospels, or *like* the Gospel of Thomas, or *like* the longer recension of the Ignatian corpus. Compilers seem to have followed no specific pattern; hence, the search for precise parallels may be a futile one.

Regarding the time factor, it is true that some of the documents examined above were compiled over hundreds of years, but this does not necessarily negate their relevance as witnesses to the compiling process. In fact, they provide important testimony for the fluidity of the ancient text – the original form of which was not regarded as sacrosanct by later editors. The Pastorals are often presumed to be precisely in the form that Paul, or a pseudo-Paul, wrote them. But the evidence from ancient sacred documents, showing that they have been modified, enlarged, updated, etc. over time, may indicate that the Pastorals underwent a similar process.

It is possible, in fact, that the Pastorals themselves were compiled over a fairly long period of time, perhaps over one hundred years. Such a conjecture cannot be ruled out and might help explain why the Pastorals were apparently so slow to gain recognition within the churches. C. K. Barrett observes in this regard that,

> Any account ... that we may give of [the Pastorals'] origin must if possible explain the fact that up to the middle of the second century, or indeed somewhat later, they were by no means widely known.[90]

The relevance of the survey for this book may, perhaps, best be presented by listing the significant features that are thrown into clear relief by this diverse collection of literary witnesses:

1   A massive array of religious documents held sacred by both Jews and Christians show complicated histories of compilation.

No matter where we look in the literary landscape of which the NT documents are a part, we find texts that exhibit clear marks of frequent and substantial editing. In their present form, the majority of these documents cannot be attributed to any single author. Most are composite works, produced from diverse collections of various materials, and woven together by scribes acting as editors. The effects of this editorial activity can be seen across diverse genres of literature; prophetic books, wisdom collections, apocalyptic writing, community manuals, letters from religious leaders, etc. all show signs of significant editorial influence. It is clear from this survey that the literary circles within which the Pastorals were transcribed were engaged in the editorial redaction of sacred texts on a massive scale.

2   Judging by the ways in which the sacred texts were edited and compiled, it is evident that scribes did not regard their collections of traditional materials as permanently "fixed" or delimited.

Ancient texts grew. This fundamental fact is easily forgotten by modern NT students living in an age that prints books and protects the integrity of its literature through the application of rigid copyright laws. Jewish and early Christian scribes plainly did not

---

[90] C. K. Barrett, *The Pastoral Epistles* (Oxford: Clarendon Press, 1963), p. 2. The first undisputed reference to the Pastorals is by Irenaeus (*Adv. Haer.* 3.14.1), writing around AD 180.

hesitate to add collected traditions to preexisting collections of traditions. From Jeremiah to Proverbs, from the gospels to the letters of Ignatius, it is clear that scribes freely enlarged existing collections of materials by adding their own materials.

The motives behind such editorial activities were undoubtedly varied. But certain basic aims can be discerned: the scribal editors regarded themselves as guardians of the community's sacred traditions; as such, they had as their chief task to protect and preserve the literary heritage which had been passed down to them. Instructions to preserve the wisdom of the ancients is scattered throughout Jewish and early Christian writings; in the book of Sirach (39:1–2), for example, the man who is devoted to the study of the law is described as one "who will seek out the wisdom of all the ancients, and will be concerned with prophecies; he will preserve the discourse of notable men." Such teaching spurred on the process of collecting and compiling traditional materials.

3   The editorial methods used in the preservation of these materials took many forms. Compiling, interpolating, appending, and prefixing – all of these techniques were frequently and freely employed.

Our investigation into the literary histories of Jewish and early Christian texts reveals a remarkable diversity in the editorial methods that scribes, intent upon preserving traditional materials, employed.

Sometimes scribal editors simply "stitched" together formerly independent and loosely related documents. The composite book of I Enoch, the collection of Daniel stories, the fusion of the Epistle of Jeremiah to the end of Baruch all illustrate this editorial method of compilation.

Frequently, large blocks of traditional materials were added to existing collections, often without any suggestion that such editorial activity had occurred. The Sibylline Oracles provide numerous instances of such interpolations, the clearest, perhaps, being the large parenetic section (an extract from Pseudo-Phocylides?) that has been inserted at 2:55ff. The inclusion of the "Two Ways" material in the Didache and the Epistle of Barnabas offers other examples.

Small collections of traditional materials were also brought together and combined, resulting occasionally in much larger collections. Many of the prophetic books, for example, probably grew in this way. Regarding the book of Jeremiah, S. R. Driver remarks:

> The large amount of variation between the *LXX* and the Massoretic text constitutes an independent ground for supposing that, in some cases, the writings composing the Book of Jer. circulated for a while in separate small collections, in which variations might more easily arise than after they were collected into a volume.[91]

Collections of wisdom materials also provide clear examples of this editorial technique.

Existing documents were also enlarged by the inclusion of sometimes very short traditional pieces. Isolated wisdom sayings, for example, have clearly been added to existing texts (cf. Sirach 1:5, 7, 21; Pseudo-Phocylides verses 116–117, 144; et al.). Similar evidence of this activity can be found in the gospel MSS; isolated Jesus *logia*, for example, have been editorially added at Matt. 18:11 and Luke 6:5. In all probability, a short regulation on women's conduct has been added by an editor following I Cor. 14:33a.

4   Scribes appear to have treated existing texts as repositories, or "collecting points," to which they brought their own storehouse of sacred traditions.

It is clear from the survey above that existing documents frequently served as literary vehicles upon which scribes felt free to load other traditional materials. Documents were sometimes enlarged by the addition of similar materials; psalms, for example, were added to existing collections of psalms (11QPs[a]); collections of wisdom sayings were added to the LXX version of Proverbs (compare the MT).

Traditional materials were also collected and editorially combined out of interest in a common theme, or a great leader or religious hero. Non-canonical collections of Daniel stories, for instance, have been collected and added to the canonical Daniel traditions in the LXX. Several post-resurrection stories have been gathered together and added to the end of Mark's gospel (and John's?) by a later editor.

---

[91]   S. R. Driver, *An Introduction to the Literature of the Old Testament*, 9th rev. ed. (Edinburgh: T. & T. Clark, 1920), pp. 271–272.

5   In the compilation of traditional materials, scribes did not only add "like" to "like." Existing documents served as vehicles onto which diverse literary forms were added.

Compilers of sacred traditions were clearly not concerned about mixing formally unrelated materials. Preformed hymns, prayers, letters, wisdom sayings, apocalyptic warnings, farewell addresses, etc. were editorially imbedded within all sorts of literary genres. The book of Sirach, for instance, is a collection of wisdom sayings, but a sixteen-verse psalm has been added to the text (following 51:12) of the codex Vaticanus. A number of disparate elements have apparently been added at some stage to the Community Rule of Qumran, including a "Messianic Rule" (IQS^a) and a collection of blessings (IQS^b). On stylistic and linguistic grounds there is reason to believe that the seven "letters" imbedded within the Apocalypse of John were added to chapters 4–22 by a later editor.[92]

6   The compilation of diverse literary elements frequently resulted in documents that are marked by abrupt transitions and logical discontinuities.

This assessment applies to many of the documents examined in the above survey. A lack of coherence and logical progression is especially prominent in the collections of wisdom materials such as Proverbs, the book of Wisdom, Sirach, etc. But many other Jewish and early Christian documents show similar marks of logical discontinuity. The miscellaneous exhortations that have been added to the book of Tobit (4:7–18) have only a loose connection with the surrounding narrative, and even less (except formally) with each other. The materials within the Didache and the Epistle of Barnabas show no sustained development of thought. Nor do the canonical gospels – or at least certain sections within the gospels; it is not easy, for example, to find any logical sequence in the collected instructions that appear in Mark 9:42–50.

Literary coherence and development of thought may be important to an author, but it does not seem to have been the prime concern of compilers. What the compiler receives he transmits; his task is to preserve. Consequently, the flow of thought and logical progression within composite documents is often lost to view.

[92] See Massyngberde Ford, *Revelation*, pp. 43–45. But see the objections of Kümmel, *Introduction*.

7 Scribes employed a variety of editorial techniques in the linking together of preformed traditions.

We have observed that compilers often connected sayings or collections together almost mechanically by means of verbal links (cf. Pseudo-Phocylides verses 35–36); this helps explain the lack of logical coherence that appears throughout many composite documents. The passage from Mark's gospel just mentioned (Mark 9:42–50) is clearly an artificial collection of sayings strung together on the basis of catch-words: (9:42, ἕνα τῶν μικρῶν, cf. 9:37; 9:48, πῦρ; 9:49, πυρί; 9:49, ἁλισθήσεται; 9:50, ἅλας; compare also the "seed" sayings in Mark 4:26–32). There is reason to think that Mark took over these sayings as he found them in an already existing collection, with little or no attempt to provide them with a chronological or topographical setting.[93]

Editors also arranged materials together by topics or themes. Sirach 3:1–16, for example, presents us with a loosely connected group of sayings on "Honoring your father"; in 4:1–10 several groups of sayings have been gathered together around the topic "On treating the less fortunate."

Occasionally compilers appear simply to have juxtaposed their sources, making little effort to smooth out the logical inconsistencies and abrupt transitions that naturally arise from such compilation. As R. Kraft has noted, this kind of editorial compilation is pervasive throughout ancient Jewish and early Christian writings.[94]

Editors frequently made a combined use of these and other methods in their compiling work. Most composite works show varying kinds of editorial redaction.

8 Authorial activity is frequently absent from composite documents.

It is a remarkable fact that most of the documents examined in the above survey show very little authorial activity. This is not to say that they lack intentionality, or purpose, or even structure; the

---

[93] On this point, V. Taylor (*The Gospels: A Short Introduction*, 3rd ed. [London: Epworth, 1935], p. 32) remarks: "That we are justified in speaking of a 'collection,' and probably a written collection, is suggested by the fact that these sayings are often loosely strung together like similar sayings in Proverbs and other Jewish books."

[94] Kraft, *The Apostolic Fathers*, Vol. III, *Barnabas and the Didache*, p. 20. Kraft suggests that the awkward juxtapositions within many ancient Jewish and early Christian texts may indicate that the compilers worked from within "school" settings. This point is addressed more fully in chapter 6.

compilers clearly had aims in mind when they put disparate materials together, and they show varying degrees of interest in structuring their materials along certain lines. But, in spite of this, most composite documents read more like collections than compositions.

Authors write with a plan in mind, and their writing is usually reflective of this; their paragraphs show logical progression and order; their various concerns are connected by carefully crafted transitional sentences; seldom do authors allow their writing to move forward without some driving train of thought. But as we have seen, most composite literature reads very differently. This suggests that the compilers did not normally regard themselves as literary authors; they were not interested in writing anything novel. Nor did they function as mere copyists; they were principally collectors, protectors of tradition, editors, to whom fell the great responsibility of preserving the community traditions.[95]

These conclusions, if valid, have a fundamental contribution to make to our study of the Pastorals. First of all, they serve to warn against a too hasty acceptance of the literary integrity of authorial unity of these letters. It is clear from the overview that no genre of literature was exempt from Jewish and early Christian scribal redaction; sacred documents of all sorts were treated as "collecting points" or vehicles upon which other cherished traditions were loaded; even genuine epistles could function as depositories to which editors would add other materials (cf. the Ignatian letters).[96]

[95] It must be granted, however, that compilers did at times engage in authorial activity. The Epistle of Aristeas is probably a composite work, the various materials of which have been woven carefully together and expanded by an author desiring to make a certain case. To an extent, the same can be said for such documents as the Testament of the Twelve Patriarchs and Luke–Acts. But the number of the composite documents that show signs of having been written by self-conscious authors is small. And even in such documents many of the "seams" remain visible where preexisting sources have clearly been taken over (without any apparent revision) and incorporated into the text. In the production of *most* composite documents, it seems right to conclude that scribes usually functioned "passively," as collectors, rather than "actively," as authors.

[96] The long recension of the Ignatian letters was probably produced around AD 350, long after the emergence of the Pastorals. But the relevance of the Ignatian corpus for understanding the textual history of the Pastorals is not, for that reason, diminished. They conclusively show that the radical compilation of genuine epistles by scribes did occur; and if such widely circulated and highly valued letters like those of Ignatius (cf. Eusebius) could be redacted as late as the fourth century, then we must be open to the possibility (if not the likelihood) that the Pastorals were subject to a similar treatment – especially given the fact that

Secondly, the survey highlights certain literary features that are characteristic within composite documents, including: obscure and awkward transitions between topics or themes; the lack of sustained argument and logical development of thought; the appearance of ideas or arguments that have no connection with the immediate context; the presence of loosely related sayings, connected together by artificial catch-word devices. If an ancient document (like the Pastorals) exhibits features like these, there is added reason to suspect that editorial compilation may have occurred.[97]

Thirdly, the survey provides us with evidence that authentic documents were often enlarged by the addition of related, but non-genuine, materials. The prophetic books provide the clearest examples of this. Most prophetic literature is composite; no one author can be ascribed to these prophecies in their present form; they are disparate collections. But a small core of authentic oracles probably lies imbedded within each book, and served as the original structure upon which other collections of related (though "inauthentic") materials were added. Authentic oracles of Jeremiah, for example, are preserved in the book that goes by his name; but his prophecies make up a relatively small portion of the text in its present form. Other oracles, written by different prophets, have been added, as well as other related materials. Still, the original ascription to Jeremiah has been retained by the religious community out of which it emerged.

In the same way, the canonical texts of Psalms and Proverbs contain genuine collections of Davidic psalms and Solomonic proverbs, to which later editors added psalms and proverbs composed by others and cherished by both Jews and early Christians. These original collections served as the core around which other materials were collected. The long Ignatian recension illustrates how a core of authentic letters could be similarly enlarged.

This information suggests that authentic texts frequently stand behind (or imbedded within!) composite documents. The question of whether a similar process occurred to the Pastorals is of obvious significance to our study, and must be examined in more detail in the analysis which follows (chapters 3–5).

---

the Pastorals would have been redacted prior to the church's general acceptance (or canonization) of these documents!

[97] An author, of course, could incorporate preexisting materials into his text, but he would presumably refashion them to ensure that their insertion would not break his flow of argument.

Finally, the compositional histories of the above literature indicate that scribes treated these documents as living traditions, and that the traditions were still being collected within the early Christian communities. As a scribe went about his work, he was strongly disinclined to allow any sacred traditions within his grasp to be lost. And the most effective way to preserve such materials was to add them to an existing text during the process of copying.

As J. Moffatt has observed,

> the conception of an early Christian writing as a necessarily inviolate, rigid, and rounded whole, is entirely misleading ... It is plainly a matter for increased delicacy and exacter scrutiny to fix the period of composition for the substantial part of a writing which ... may have been retouched and enlarged by the author, or ... may have been subjected to revision by other and later hands.

The Pastorals are commonly read by commentators as an "inviolate, rigid, and rounded whole." Yet we have already observed (see chapter 1) something of the difficulties they pose to interpreters who presume that they have a simple literary history.

The above examination suggests that the editorial reworking of sacred texts was common within early Christian communities, and that most Jewish and early Christian documents have complex compositional histories. It now remains to examine the texts of the Pastorals themselves to see what marks of editorial activity may have survived in the texts as we now possess them.

3

I TIMOTHY: A COMPOSITIONAL ANALYSIS

1:1–2 Epistolary salutation

This salutation (like those in II Timothy and Titus) follows the ancient Greek (and Pauline) epistolary form: A to B, greeting. The style of the greeting is in many respects similar to that of the other Pauline letters, but a number of oddities appear that make its authenticity doubtful. The formality and elaborateness of the salutation as well as the solemn emphasis on Paul's apostolic authority seem a surprising way to begin a personal letter, especially between two close and intimate friends.[1]

Several un-Pauline expressions appear in the salutation; the phrase κατ' ἐπιταγὴν θεοῦ σωτῆρος ἡμῶν (1:1), for example, has only one close NT parallel (Titus 1:3): κατ' ἐπιταγὴν τοῦ σωτῆρος ἡμῶν θεοῦ. Nowhere in Paul's letters is God referred to as the savior; σωτήρ, in fact, is a term Paul rarely employs; it is only found at Phil. 3:20 (cf. Eph. 5:3), where it refers to Jesus. In the Pastorals, however, the use of σωτήρ is common; it appears ten times, six referring to God and four to Jesus.[2] That the phrase may have a liturgical origin is suggested by the use of a similar expression in the non-Pauline doxology at the end of Romans (16:26):

---

[1]   The oddity of the salutation was noted by John Calvin (*Commentary on the Epistles to Timothy and Titus*, ed. D. Torrance and T. Torrance [Edinburgh: Oliver & Boyd, 1964], p. 187), who observed that Paul would have had "no need to set forth his titles and reassert his claims to apostleship, as he does here, for the name alone would certainly have been enough for Timothy." Calvin concluded that the Pastorals must have been intended for a wider audience than just Timothy. But if that were the case, one would expect Paul to include some reference to the larger community in the salutation as he did, for example, in his semi-personal letter to Philemon (see 1:1).

[2]   I 1:1, 2:3; 4:10; Titus 1:3; 2:10; 3:4 refer to God as savior; II 1:10; Titus 1:4; 2:13; and 3:6 link the term with Jesus.

κατ' ἐπιταγὴν τοῦ αἰωνίου θεοῦ. The same idea occurs in the doxology that concludes Jude 24: μόνῳ θεῷ σωτῆρι ἡμῶν.

The phrase Χριστοῦ 'Ιησοῦ τῆς ἐλπίδος ἡμῶν is another that finds no parallel in the NT. In Col. 1:27 Jesus is called ἡ ἐλπὶς τῆς δόξης, but here in this salutation the term ἐλπίς seems to function as a fixed title for Jesus. The use of such a title (outside of the Pastorals) is not attested in early Christian literature before the Ignatian letters.[3] A. T. Hanson regards it as a "mark of third-generation Christianity."[4]

If the formulaic expression "an apostle according to God our savior, and Christ Jesus our hope" is removed, the salutation appears far less formal, and the major difficulties in ascribing it to Paul fall away. It may be that these fixed liturgical expressions were added at a later date to a brief but authentic Pauline salutation.[5] We know that pious interpolations were added to many Jewish and early Christian texts; the Sibylline Oracles, for instance, were clearly "Christianized" by such additions. And if, as many scholars argue, the sixteen prayers scattered among books VII and VIII of the Apostolic Constitutions are of Jewish origin, then the process of "enhancing" the text with liturgical language is even more evident.[6] The same phrase, "through Christ Jesus our hope" (cf. I 1:1 above), has apparently been added to one of the hellenistic synagogal prayers taken over by the early church.[7]

The greeting at 1:2 is identical to that which appears in II Tim. 1:2, but it differs from the characteristic form found in all the genuine Pauline letters.[8] All of Paul's letters contain the two-part formula: χάρις καὶ εἰρήνη. The addition here (and in II Timothy) of ἔλεος is particularly striking, not only since Paul's greetings are remarkably uniform,[9] but also because he so rarely uses the term

---

3   See Ign. Trall. Insc. 2:2; Ign. Mag. 11:1; Ign. Eph. 21:2; Ign. Phil. 11:2.
4   A. T. Hanson, *The Pastoral Epistles*, The New Century Bible Commentary (Grand Rapids, MI: Eerdmans, 1982), p. 55.
5   Paul's original greeting may have begun simply: "Paul to Timothy, my true child in faith ..." Compare the discussion at II 1:1–2; Titus 1:1–4.
6   See the article by K. Kohler, "Didascalia," in *The Jewish Encyclopedia*, ed. Isidore Singer (New York: Funk and Wagnalls, 1903), Vol. IV, pp. 588–594. The sixteen prayers are published as a collection in *The Old Testament Pseudepigrapha*, ed. J. Charlesworth (London: Darton, Longman & Todd, 1985), Vol. II, pp. 671–697.
7   See the text "Hellenistic Synagogal Prayers" (3.27) in Charlesworth's *OT Pseudepigrapha*, Vol. II, p. 680.
8   The same triple formula also appears in II John 3. Cf. Jude 2.
9   There is verbatim agreement in the following Pauline greetings: Rom. 1:7; I Cor. 1:3; II Cor. 1:2; Gal. 1:3; Phil. 1:2; II Thess. 1:2; Philem. 3; cf. Eph. 1:2. The

ἔλεος.[10] It seems very possible, therefore, that an original Pauline greeting has been expanded, perhaps, as C. K. Barrett has suggested, as a result of liturgical usage.[11]

The original greeting may have read simply:

> Paul to Timothy, my true child in faith. Grace and peace from God our Father and Christ Jesus our Lord.

1:3–7 Epistolary motive

Significant formal and literary problems emerge at this point. Instead of the customary Pauline thanksgiving, the letter moves immediately to a rehearsal of the commission given by Paul to Timothy.[12] As we have seen (in chapter 1 above), this omission is a dramatic deviation from the Pauline letter form and presents difficulties, not only for those who accept the authenticity of the letter in its present form, but also for those who argue that the letter was carefully crafted by a pseudonymous author imitating the Pauline style. Why would an imitator omit such a basic Pauline epistolary feature? The omission suggests that whoever put I Timothy in its present form was not concerned to imitate Paul's epistolary customs.[13]

The grammatical construction of the larger paragraph (I 1:3–11) also poses problems. The extent of the difficulties is reflected in the remark by Blass–Debrunner–Funk that the construction is "reduced to utter chaos by interminable insertions and appended clauses."[14] G. Holtz attributes the confusion to hurried speech or rapid dictation and compares Gal. 3:6, but the problems here can scarcely be resolved by appealing to haste in dictation.[15] The paragraph as a whole reflects little sequence of thought, and is

---

precise form of the greetings found in I Thess. 1:1 and Col. 1:2 is debated because of variations in ancient MSS.

[10] Excluding the Pastorals, ἔλεος appears only five times in the Pauline corpus: Rom. 9:23, 11:31, 15:9; Gal. 6:16; Eph. 2:4. In the Pastorals it also occurs five times: I 1:2; II 1:2, 16, 18; Titus 3:5.

[11] C. K. Barrett, *The Pastoral Epistles* (Oxford: Clarendon Press, 1963), p. 39.

[12] Of all Paul's letters, only Galatians lacks a thanksgiving. Even Philemon, the most personal of Paul's letters, contains the customary thanksgiving.

[13] Compare, for example, the imitation thanksgiving that appears in the pseudapostolic Epistle to the Laodiceans.

[14] F. Blass and A. Debrunner, *A Greek Grammar of the New Testament*, trans. and ed. R. Funk (Chicago: University Press, 1961), p. 245 (#467).

[15] G. Holtz, *Die Pastoralbriefe*, 2nd ed. (Berlin: Evangelische Verlagsanstalt, 1972), p. 33.

characterized throughout by abrupt and puzzling transitions (see the analysis below). The difficulties have led some commentators to conjecture that 1:3–11 must be a later editorial interpolation.[16] But it seems more likely that an original Pauline note has been expanded.

The authenticity of 1:3–4 has been doubted on the grounds that Timothy would not need to be told why he was to remain in Ephesus. But this argument can cut both ways; why would a pseudonymous author include such a sentence if it were so obviously inappropriate? It seems far more likely that 1:3–4 was part of Paul's original note, functioning as an "official" reminder of an earlier agreed-upon resolution. O. Roller has commented on the well-known style of this form of literary instruction:

> The contextual introductions [sc. from I Tim. and Tit.] with their repetition of the instructions previously given to both recipients orally … are utterly official … (and) were well known as part of classical official style.[17]

Paul is simply reminding Timothy that his earlier charge to remain in Ephesus and to direct the affairs there still stands. The remark may also serve as a sort of "authorization" note for Timothy, certifying that his special task in Ephesus (see below) has direct apostolic backing.

Paul's original note to Timothy began by instructing him to continue directing (παραγγέλλω, 1:3) the leadership in Ephesus. No detailed instructions were required, since Paul's recent visit to Ephesus (1:3) would have enabled him to discuss at length with Timothy matters of specific concern facing the church there, and since Paul expected a speedy return (3:14). The lack of any thanksgiving is understandable as a Pauline omission, given the relatively informal nature of the note; it is not easy to see why a pseudonymous author would omit such an obvious Pauline epistolary characteristic.

Paul's major concern (1:3–7) has to do with the problem of false

---

[16] For example, R. Falconer, *The Pastoral Epistles* (Oxford: Clarendon Press, 1937), p. 123; A. Hilgenfeld, "Die Hirtenbriefe des Paulus neu Untersucht," *ZWTh* 40 (1897), 15ff.

[17] O. Roller, *Das Formular der Paulinischen Briefe*, Beiträge zur Wissenschaft vom Alten und Neuen Testament 4:6 (Stuttgart: Kohlhammer, 1933), p. 148; compare also p. 302. Roller gives only two examples of this popular form of epistolary address, but others have been adduced by M. Wolter, *Die Pastoralbriefe als Paulustradition* (Göttingen: Vandenhoeck & Ruprecht, 1988), p. 181.

teachers who are threatening the stability of the church in (and around?) Ephesus. The information given was certainly not news to Timothy but, as the note was probably used to "authorize" his activity in Ephesus, it was no doubt useful to him, giving as it does apostolic identification of the community's problems.

1:8–11 Traditional sayings (on the law)

It is difficult to identify any clear development of thought between 1:7 and that which follows. J. Calvin tried to make sense of the transition by suggesting that the apostle is here anticipating "a false accusation being brought against him"; J. N. D. Kelly regards the unit (1:8–11) as a "digression about the place and function of the law."[18] A logical connection, at any rate, is hard to see; it seems more likely that the mention of the νομοδιδάσκαλοι in 1:7 suggested to a scribe a brief collection of material on the νόμος which he then included.

Two introductory formulas (οἴδαμεν δὲ ὅτι, εἰδὼς τοῦτο ὅτι) appear which, according to W. Bauer, are frequently employed to "introduce a well-known fact that is generally accepted." Such expressions seem to function throughout the Pastorals as "markers," signaling the presence of preformed traditional materials.[19] Similar markers of preformed materials appear elsewhere in Jewish and early Christian literature; in Polycarp's letter to the Philippians (4:1), for example, the formula εἰδότες οὖν ὅτι introduces the proverbial saying: "we brought nothing into the world and we can take nothing out of it" (cf. I Tim. 6:7).[20] A similar formula (τοῦτο γὰρ ἴστε γινώσκοντες) precedes the vice list that appears in Eph. 5:5.[21]

The lack of any logical connection between 1:8 and 1:9ff. is a

---

[18] J. N. D. Kelly, *A Commentary on the Pastoral Epistles* (London: Adam & Charles Black, 1963); Calvin, *Commentary*, pp. 192–193.

[19] A. T. Hanson (*The Pastoral Epistles*, p. 59) observes that 1:9 begins with an anacoluthon and suggests that the formula "understanding this" may be a "technique for introducing an already existing vice-list."

[20] So K. Lake (*The Apostolic Fathers*, LCL [London: W. Heinemann, 1965], p. 291) on Polycarp, Phil. 6:1: "The introductory formula 'knowing that' renders it probable that these words are a quotation, but the source is unknown." See also II Tim. 3:1, where it introduces a traditional apocalyptic piece; in Acts 2:30 it precedes an OT citation.

[21] Paul, of course, could have used this formula himself, but the un-Pauline remarks about the law that follow in 1:8 make this unlikely (cf. the reference to C. F. D. Moule on p. 1 above).

further indication that the two pieces were at one time independent of one another.[22] From the thrust of 1:8, one would naturally expect a further exposition on the meaning of the "lawful" use of the law; but, instead, another popular saying is quoted that leads in a very different direction. The resulting confusion has been noted by S. Wilson:

> The argument seems to be a curious combination of a Pauline catch-phrase, and the Stoic view that the law is directed only at the lawless .... There is something of a confusion between Torah and natural law or, at least, the use of a Stoic principle as a means of understanding the purpose of the Torah.[23]

Wilson attributes the confusion to the "Pastor" who "knew a Pauline phrase, perhaps from oral tradition, but did not fully understand the way Paul would have used it."[24] It seems odd, however, that a disciple of the apostle would be confused on such a key Pauline issue. It is far more likely that a scribe, more concerned about the preservation of traditional material than about logical consistency, has brought together two originally independent sayings on the law.

A catalogue of vices follows (1:9b–11), the traditional character of which has been widely recognized;[25] some, in fact, who argue for the authenticity of the Pastorals allow that Paul may have taken over this material and incorporated it into his letter.[26] But in light

---

[22] M. Dibelius and H. Conzelmann (henceforth D–C), *The Pastoral Epistles* (Philadelphia: Fortress Press, 1972), p. 22, recognize the tension between the two units: "V 9 introduces instead a further, well-known principle, which implies something entirely different from the preceding clause."

[23] S. G. Wilson, *Luke and the Pastoral Epistles* (London: SPCK, 1979), pp. 91–92.

[24] Ibid., p. 92. For a similar assessment of the problem, see E. F. Scott, *The Pastoral Epistles*, The Moffatt New Testament Commentary Series (London: Hodder & Stoughton, 1936), p. 11.

[25] See, for example, B. S. Easton, "New Testament Ethical Lists," *JBL* 51 (1932), 1–12; S. Wibbing, *Die Tugend- und Lasterkataloge im Neuen Testament und ihre Traditionsgeschichte unter besonderer Berücksichtigung der Qumran-Texte* (Berlin: Topelmann, 1959); E. Schweizer, "Traditional Ethical Patterns in the Pauline and Post-Pauline Letters and their Development (Lists of Vices and House-tables)," in *Text and Interpretation: Studies in the NT presented to Matthew Black*, ed. E. Best and R. Mcl. Wilson (Cambridge: University Press, 1979), pp. 195–209.

[26] On the traditional character of this list, J. N. D. Kelly (*The Pastoral Epistles*, p. 49) writes: "the early Church soon amassed a substantial body of hortatory material which could be brought into play on the appropriate occasion." See also: E. E. Ellis ("Traditions in I Corinthians," *NTS* 32 [1986], 484): "the

of the un-Pauline nature of 1:8, and the verbal link between 1:8 and 1:9ff., it seems better to attribute the insertion to a later editor. Two facts are especially significant: (1) of the fourteen terms which make up this list, only three (πόρνοι, ἀρσενοκοίται, and ψεῦσται) appear elsewhere in the NT;[27] and (2) the list follows the order of the Decalogue.[28] It is possible that the catalogue was taken over from a preexisting hellenistic-Jewish source.

The bland proviso attached to the conclusion of the catalogue ("anything else contrary to sound doctrine") comes unexpectedly in light of the serious offenses listed in the catalogue. D. Guthrie calls it a "surprise" and attributes it to "a transference of thought from teaching mainly designed for criminals to teaching intended as the normal rule of life."[29] It seems more likely that the proviso signals a break in the traditional material, a "transference," not of thought, but of source; it may be a scribal gloss, added to cover all other deviations from the accepted teaching.

The patchwork nature of this collection of disparate materials is further evident from the expression that concludes the unit (1:11). C. K. Barrett observes that "it is not clear how v. 11 is attached to what precedes," and it cannot be denied that the connection seems rather odd.[30] The phrase is grammatically awkward, and its meaning in the present context is obscure. It seems to function here almost as a summarizing formula, tying together the materials that have been gathered.

1:12–17 Autobiographical material

This unit takes the form of an "autobiographical" account of Paul's conversion, the recounting of which would surely be un-

---

probability that these catalogues ... were transmitted as fixed traditions is strengthened ... by the presence of introductory formulas."

[27] See the evidence in S. Wibbing, "Die Tugend- und Lasterkataloge im Neuen Testament," *ZNW* 25 (1959), 87.

[28] Excluding the fourth and the tenth commandments. See the detailed examination of the catalogue provided by W. Nauck, "Die Herkunft des Verfassers der Pastoralbriefe," Th.D. thesis, Göttingen, 1950, pp. 9ff.

[29] D. Guthrie, *The Pastoral Epistles* (Leicester: Inter-Varsity Press, 1958), p. 62.

[30] So Barrett, *The Pastoral Epistles*, p. 43. N. Brox (*Die Pastoralbriefe*, Regensburger Neues Testament VII.2 [Regensburg: F. Pustet, 1969], p. 108) notes the "strongly formalized" character of the verse and adds that "the interpretation of the forced word order is not at all simple." E. Hesse (*Die Entstehung der neutestamentlichen Hirtenbriefe* [Halle: C. A. Kaemmerer, 1889], p. 96) calls the link between 1:10 and 1:11 "unsatisfactory" and thinks that it reflects a seam where materials have been added.

necessary for the historical Timothy. The sudden outburst of thanksgiving comes unexpectedly at this point in the letter, following the extended vice list of 1:9–11.[31] The addition of καί (codex D, the majority text, et al.) at the beginning of 1:12 indicates that early editors also sensed the rough transition between this verse and 1:11.[32]

Phrased in edifying and stylized language, the passage echoes the schema of the autobiographical discourses that appear frequently in Jewish literature.[33] Such narrative materials often function paradigmatically, offering a patriarch's past experiences as an example to be followed or avoided.[34]

The traditional character of this unit has been elucidated further by M. Wolter, who compares its various elements to those that appear within the "thanksgiving hymns" of Judaism:

> Essential and specific elements of this nature are to be found in this text: introductory formulae ... with declaration of the reason (v 12); a look back at the past which corresponds to the accounts of affliction in the thanksgiving songs of individuals in the Old Testament (v 13); an account of salvation (v 14); closing hymnic confession (v 17).[35]

Wolter finds the closest analogy to this material in the "Teachersongs" from Qumran: (IQH 2:1–19; 2.20–30; 4.5–5.4; 5.5–19, 20–36; 7.6–25; 8.4–40).[36]

In its present form the material in I Tim. 1:12–17 is clearly a unit, but this must not be taken to mean that originally it was the product of one hand. Various literary "seams," in fact, may still be seen within the passage, suggesting that it is made up of several

---

[31] C. K. Barrett (*The Pastoral Epistles*, p. 46) calls it a "personal digression"; so also Guthrie, *The Pastoral Epistles*, p. 63.

[32] Regarding the addition of καί, H. J. Holtzmann (*Die Pastoralbriefe kritisch und exegetisch behandelt* [Leipzig: Wilhelm Engelmann, 1880], p. 298) writes: "it was added (D), so that the connection could be made."

[33] See, for example, T. Judah 19:1–5, in which the patriarch Judah gives a stylized account of his sinful past to which he adds: "But the God of my fathers, who is compassionate and merciful, pardoned me because I acted in ignorance." Compare a similar "confession" in the Assumption of Moses 12:7. Also, T. Reuben 1:5–10; T. Simeon 2:6–13; T. Issachar 3:1–8.

[34] K. Baltzer (*The Covenant Formulary*, ET by D. Green [Philadelphia: Fortress Press, 1971], p. 144) calls such pieces "biographical confessions or examples for admonition."

[35] Wolter, *Die Pastoralbriefe*, p. 63.

[36] Ibid.

previously independent pieces; the most obvious of these is the "faithful saying" which is formally introduced in 1:15. Even those who uphold the Pauline authorship of the Pastorals recognize the likelihood that traditional material is being cited here.[37]

Another "seam" is evident in 1:17, where a fixed, liturgically styled doxology appears, the contents of which have little connection with the immediate context. The doxology contains no specifically Christian elements and most likely had its origins within the Jewish synagogue.[38]

In addition to these literary markers, the content of the passage also suggests its composite nature. It is not easy to reconcile the two portraits of Paul presented here, since one who received mercy because he "acted in ignorance" (1:13) can hardly be considered "the chief of sinners" (1:15c). Perhaps two traditional accounts of Paul's conversion (1:12–15 and 1:15c–16) have been combined to form this *Dankhymnus*.

On the basis of such disparities in form and content, it seems right to conclude that 1:12–17 was not written by any single author, but is a collection of traditional materials dealing with Paul's conversion and the majesty of God's grace. The loose tie that 1:12–17 has to its context suggests that it was probably added as a preformed block of traditional material by the editor of the Pastorals.

1:18–20 An apostolic charge

This material seems to be part of the original Pauline note and probably followed originally on 1:7. In its present context the section presents many difficulties; the sudden reference to the charge (ταύτην τὴν παραγγελίαν, 1:18) is confusing and seems out of place. Commentators who accept the unity of the text are divided on its meaning; some think that the charge refers back to 1:3,[39] while others follow Chrysostom in identifying it with what

---

[37] E. K. Simpson (*The Pastoral Epistles* [London: Tyndale Press, 1954], pp. 34–35), for example, thinks that Paul has taken over one of the λόγοι πνευματικοί which were circulating in his time. J. N. D. Kelly (*The Pastoral Epistles*, p. 54) thinks the saying derives from "early catechetical or liturgical material."

[38] The expression "king of the age" appears frequently within Jewish writings; see, for example, Tobit 13:6, 10. W. Lock (*The Pastoral Epistles* [Edinburgh: T. & T. Clark, 1924], p. 17) suggests that the doxology "is probably a semi-quotation from some Jewish liturgical formula." D–C, *The Pastoral Epistles*, p. 30, calls it a "Jewish cultic formula."

[39] See, for example, B. Weiss, *Die Briefe Pauli an Timotheus und Titus* (Göttingen: Vandenhoeck & Ruprecht, 1902), p. 100.

follows in 1:18 ("fight the good fight");[40] still others understand it
to include the instructions within the epistle as a whole.[41]

The lack of precision is brought about by the loose connection
between 1:18–20 and its surrounding context. The passage does not
follow smoothly after 1:17, nor does it provide an easy transition to
2:1. The discontinuity between 1:17 and 1:18 leads N. Brox to
conjecture that 1:12–17 must be an interpolation.[42]

2:1–3:16 Community regulations

A remarkable change in the literary "atmosphere" is apparent in
this section.[43] The personal remarks to Timothy (1:18–20) give way
to an unexpected collection of formal community regulations and
duties (2:1–3:16).[44] The legislative nature of this material has often
been noted,[45] as has the discontinuous and sometimes illogical
arrangement of the various regulations.[46]

2:1–7 On prayer

The previously independent character of this unit is clear from the
way it is introduced. The introductory formula does not seem to fit
the context; the function of οὖν (2:1), for example, is puzzling; to
what does it refer? And what is meant by the unusual phrase
πρῶτον πάντων (only here in the NT)? In its current context it is
clearly not the first charge (see 1:3), nor is there any clear
corresponding "second." Even if the phrase is taken to mean "most
important of all," it is hard to see how the regulations of 2:1ff.

[40] C. Ellicott, *An Official Critical and Grammatical Commentary on the Pastorals*
(London: J. Parker and Son, 1856), p. 20.
[41] So D–C, *The Pastoral Epistles*, p. 32; F. Gealy, *The First and Second Epistles to
Timothy and the Epistle to Titus*, The Interpreter's Bible, Vol. XI (New York:
Abingdon Press, 1955), p. 393.
[42] Brox, *Die Pastoralbriefe*, p. 117.
[43] The abrupt change in topic does not, in itself, prove that the author of 1:18–20
was not the author of 2:1, since we know that authors are capable of such
transitions. But the arguments (see below) against the unity of authorship here
are compelling and have a cumulative force.
[44] H. J. Holtzmann (*Die Pastoralbriefe*, p. 305), following Schleiermacher, notes the
"*immediate*" transition between 1:20 and 2:1.
[45] H.-W. Bartsch (*Die Anfänge urchristlicher Rechtsbildungen* [Hamburg: H. Reich,
1965], pp. 160ff.) thinks that the Pastorals incorporate three kinds of community
regulations: (1) rules for worship; (2) rules for community offices; and (3) general
house rules (*Haustafeln*).
[46] C. K. Barrett (*The Pastoral Epistles*, p. 49) observes, for example, that "it is not
always possible to find links between the paragraphs."

connect in any way with the concerns over false teaching that predominate in chapter 1 (1:3, 1:19–20). A. Hilgenfeld's recognition of this tension led him to conclude, correctly, I think, that

> whoever wrote II, 1 ... can have written neither I, 3–11 nor I, 18–20.[47]

The transitions within the paragraph (2:1–7) are also hard to follow (cf. 2:7); the discontinuities once again seem best attributed to the originally independent character of the materials included. Several traditional pieces appear to have been gathered together to make up this unit on prayer:

2:1–2   A regulation on prayer
2:3   A literary marker
2:4   Creedal fragment
2:5–6   Creedal fragment
2:7   Apostolic authorization.

(2:1–2) Community rule: on prayer

The regulation on prayer (2:1–2) contains seven words found nowhere else in Paul's writings.[48] The instruction to pray for "kings and all those in authority" with its appeal to self-interest ("that we might lead a quiet and peaceful life") has a striking parallel in the counsel of Rabbi Hanina:

> Pray for the peace of the kingdom; for except for the fear of that we should have swallowed up each his neighbor alive.[49]

The fixed character of this instruction can also be seen in the parallel that appears in Polycarp's letter to the Philippians (12:3):

> Pray also for the Emperors, and for potentates, and princes.

It can scarcely be doubted that the regulation here has been

---

[47]   Hilgenfeld, "Die Hirtenbriefe des Paulus," *ZWT* 40 (1897), p. 17.

[48]   ἔντευξις, ἤρεμος, ἡσύχιος, βίος, διάγω, εὐσέβεια, σεμνότης.

[49]   *Pirque Aboth* 3.2. Prayer for authorities was regarded within Judaism as a duty. In Baruch 1:11ff., for example, an instruction is given to "pray for the life of Nebuchadnezzar king of Babylon." See also: Ezra 6:10; I Macc. 7:33; Philo, *In flaccum* 49.

incorporated from another source, be it a church order, or an ancient liturgy, or a Jewish prayer manual.[50]

(2:3) Literary marker

The conjunction γάρ appears in some MSS (Aleph [corrected], D, F, G, et al.) and was probably added by later editors who failed to see a sufficient logical connection between 2:3 and that which precedes.[51] The connection, in fact, is formal rather than logical.

The phrase is a formulaic "marker" of traditional materials, signaling here the inclusion of a community rule in 2:1–2, and declaring its validity. It seems to be functioning here in much the same way as the "faithful words" formula found elsewhere in the Pastorals (see I 1:15).

A similar link to traditional materials appears in I Clem. 7:2–3, where a reference to the "venerable rule of our tradition" is followed by the exhortation:

> Let us see what is good and pleasing and acceptable in the sight of our Maker.[52]

Similar expressions occur in the LXX, suggesting that the phrase was not composed by the author of the Pastorals but is, instead, a formulaic saying that has been taken over from Judaism.[53] The same phrase (with minor modifications) also occurs at I Tim. 5:4, where it signals the citation of a regulation on widows.

(2:4–6) Creedal fragments

Two creedal fragments follow, apparently linked to the preceding material on thematic grounds (that is, God's universal concern; cf. 2:1, "prayers for *all* men"; 2:4, "God desires *all* men to be saved"; 2:6, "a ransom on behalf of *all*"). The first fragment (2:4) consists

---

[50] See D–C's excursus (*The Pastoral Epistles*, pp. 37–39) on "Prayer for Pagan Authority."

[51] E. K. Simpson (*The Pastoral Epistles*, p. 41) is aware of the logical discontinuity here and observes that it is "requisite to associate this verse with the preceding."

[52] In I Clement the traditional material has been incorporated by an *author*, not a compiler. Why not here? The answer seems to be that throughout the larger context of I Timothy 2, there is no real development of thought or logical progression – a feature that points to the work of a compiler, not an author.

[53] So, for example, Deut. 12:25 reads: ἐὰν ποιήσῃς τὸ καλὸν καὶ τὸ ἀρεστὸν ἐναντίον τοῦ κυρίου τοῦ θεοῦ σου. See also Deut. 12:28; 13:18; 21:9, and the discussion in Bartsch, *Die Anfänge*, pp. 30–31.

of two lines which, if we replace the relative pronoun ὅς with θεός (probably the original subject), are both twelve syllables in length.

The second fragment (2:5–6) is a balanced unit containing four rhythmical clauses; its compact literary style is notably different from that of the materials surrounding it. The fact that it is a set form is confirmed by its inclusion of ideas that appear unmotivated by the context (for example, the mention of monotheism, and the reference to Jesus' mediatorial role). C. Spicq, following F. Gealy, observes that the last phrase, τὸ μαρτύριον καιροῖς ἰδίοις (2:6), is so elliptical as to be almost unintelligible.[54] The obscurity of the phrase may derive, not so much from its condensed style (so E. K. Simpson)[55] as from its lack of genuine (that is, original) context.

(2:7) Apostolic deposition

The fact that Paul never refers to himself as a preacher (κῆρυξ) or a teacher (διδάσκαλος) in his earlier letters counts against the genuineness of this text. On the other hand, it is equally difficult to explain why an imitator would set such a vehement apostolic assertion here in an otherwise impassive context.

The problem is lessened when the formal literary character of this passage is observed. The deposition seems to be functioning almost as a "seal of authorization," marking off a collection of traditional materials and affirming their continuing validity. The parallel in II 1:11 seems to confirm this reading of the text. There the saying (in an abbreviated but verbatim form) appears again at the end of a traditional creedal or hymnic fragment.

2:8–15 Community rules: on conduct, dress, submission

A collection of traditional regulations regarding the conduct of men and women within the worshiping community follows. The previously independent character of the material is especially evident from the abrupt and sudden transitions that occur within the paragraph itself. The admonition to women (2:9), for example, is only loosely connected to 2:8 and presents significant translation problems owing to its lack of any main verb.[56] J. H. Bernard

---

[54] C. Spicq, *St. Paul: Les Epîtres Pastorales*, Etudes Bibliques (Paris: Gabalda, 1969), p. 368.

[55] Simpson, *The Pastoral Epistles*, p. 44.

[56] See A. Schlatter's discussion (*Die Kirche der Griechen im Urteil des Paulus*

attributes the interpretive difficulties in 2:9 to a sudden change of mind by the author:

> St. Paul, beginning his sentence ... as if he were going to add directions about the public devotions of women, goes off in a different direction and supplies principles for their general deportment and dress.[57]

But no single author is to blame for such confusion; it is, rather, a genuine mark and a natural consequence of composite documents.

This cluster of regulations probably owes its place here in I Timothy to the catch-word προσεύχεσθαι (2:8), and seems to be addressing the general issue of "Directions for Public Worship."[58]

The cluster includes four rules and a collection of haggadic-like sayings:

2:8	On the conduct of men
2:9–10	On the dress of women
2:11	On women's subordination
2:12	On women's subordination
2:13–15	A midrashic (haggadic) piece.

(2:8) On the conduct of men

This regulation directed to men is formally introduced by the technical term βούλομαι;[59] the term signals the presence here of legislative materials and affirms their continuing apostolic validity. The same phrase βούλομαι οὖν appears in I 5:14, where it again introduces a regulation, this time pertaining to widows.

The duty to pray with uplifted hands was well known within Judaism (cf. Ps. 141:2; 143:6; Lam. 3:41; II Macc. 14:34), and it is possible that this regulation has come from a preexisting Jewish

---

[Stuttgart: Calwer Vereinsbuchhandlung, 1936], p. 83). Regarding 2:9ff., Schlatter writes: "It is, however, not certain how Paul combined the words."

[57] J. H. Bernard, *The Pastoral Epistles* (Grand Rapids, MI: Baker, 1980 [1899]), p. 44.

[58] So, N. Brox (*Die Pastoralbriefe*, p. 129), who entitles the section (2:8–15) "The prayers of the men and the behavior of the women during the worship service."

[59] See, for example, the letter from King Antiochus to an officer in Josephus, *Antiquities* 12.150. Compare the discussion by Bartsch, *Die Anfänge*, pp. 47ff., and Spicq, *Les Epîtres Pastorales*, p. 372. Spicq notes that βούλομαι was a technical term within hellenistic circles denoting a "decision of the legislature, the will of a sovereign."

source. Clement shows an awareness of the same custom (and may employ the same source!) when he exhorts the Corinthians:

> Let us then approach him in holiness of soul, raising pure and undefiled hands to him, loving our gracious and merciful father. (I Clem. 29:1)

(2:9–10) On the dress of women

A diverse collection of traditional regulations on women begins at this point. The first rule (2:9–10) seeks to limit women's devotion to fashion, and in so doing reflects a commonplace of the time; similar instructions appear within Jewish, Christian, and pagan circles:

> [The holy woman] must not wear any gold ornament, nor put on rouge, nor white paint, nor a wreath, nor braid her hair; nor put on shoes.[60]

The introductory ὡσαύτως serves to link 2:9 with 2:8, but only in a formal (and not a consecutive) sense. That is, it must not be interpreted as somehow carrying over "to women all that has been said about men [in 2:8]."[61] It is possible, of course, that ὡσαύτως simply marks the transition (as it often does in tables of *Haustafeln*) between one group of sayings and another. But it may be functioning here as a literary device that serves to link together previously independent materials. The term appears at least five times in the Pastorals:

I 2:9	on women
I 3:8	on deacons
I 3:11	on deaconesses
Titus 2:3	on aged women
Titus 2:6	on young men.[62]

The synonym ὁμοίως seems to function in a similar way to mark off traditional materials:

---

[60] From the mystery inscriptions of Andania. See Dittenberger, *Orac. Syll.* II. 736.22ff. (cited by D–C, *The Pastoral Epistles*, p. 46); see also the references in Strack–Billerbeck, *Kommentar zum NT* (Munich: C. H. Beck), Vol. III, p. 645, 428ff.

[61] So Lock, *The Pastoral Epistles*, p. 31.

[62] It is noteworthy that ὡσαύτως appears only twice in Paul's letters: see Rom. 8:26; I Cor. 11:25.

I Pet. 3:1	on women
3:7	on husbands
5:5	on young men
Poly. Phil. 5:2	on deacons
5:3	on young men.

(2:11) On the subordination of women

C. Spicq and others have noted the abrupt shift in thinking that occurs here.[63] The discontinuity between 2:11 and that which precedes, in fact, led G. Holtz to conclude that in 2:11–15,

> the strong suspicion strikes us of a later addition or disfigurement.[64]

Holtz is correct in observing that the text here reads oddly, but, in attributing the oddity to a later interpolator, he fails to take into consideration the composite nature of this document. If the regulations collected in 2:9–15 derive, as I think, from different sources, then abrupt and unusual shifts in thinking and emphasis are to be expected.

Three features suggest that 2:11 originated within a different context from that of 2:9–10: (1) the differences in literary style between the two rules;[65] (2) the sudden and unmotivated switch from the plural γυναῖκας (2:9) to the singular γυνή (2:11); and (3) the change from the infinitive (κοσμεῖν, 2:9) to the third-person imperative (μανθανέτω, 2:11).

(2:12) On the subordination of women

Another traditional regulation concerning the role of women in the community follows, this time using the authoritative first-person

---

[63] Spicq, *Les Epîtres Pastorales*, p. 379. Spicq tries to explain the abruptness by suggesting that the author is returning to the original subject of the section: "The asyndeton indicates that one has switched to another plan." R. Karris (*The Pastoral Epistles* [Wilmington, DE: Michael Glazier, 1979], p. 66) observes that 2:11–12 "occur almost without warning."

[64] Holtz, *Die Pastoralbriefe*, pp. 72–73. Holtz gives three reasons for this suspicion: (1) that 2:11–15 breaks the flow of chs. 2–3; (2) that the rigid attitude expressed here toward women parallels that of I Cor. 14:34–35 (which Holtz thinks is an interpolation); and (3) that the earliest sources suggest that women (far from being excluded) were very active in the worship and service of the church.

[65] The compact, epigrammatic style of 2:11 contrasts with the more elaborate style of 2:9–10.

singular ἐπιτρέπω.[66] The phrase ἐν ἡσυχίᾳ in its present context seems unnecessary in light of its appearance in 2:11. In all likelihood this redundancy is due to the linking together (by word association?) of two formerly independent regulations on women.

(2:13–15) Midrashic material

An haggadic-like collection of "sayings" on women (cf. Gen. 3:13, 16) concludes this unit of materials. The unit presents a number of exegetical difficulties; the context of 2:14 leads one to expect the aorist tense of γίνομαι instead of the perfect γέγονε ("has come to be in transgression"), which seems to read awkwardly in the present context. The oddity led W. Lock to conjecture that the saying ('Αδὰμ γὰρ ... γέγονε) is "a quotation from some Jewish Apocrypha, scornful of women."[67] Parallels are not difficult to find; the book of Sirach, for example, includes a number of collected sayings "on women," one of which incorporates the following:

> From a woman sin had its beginning, and because of her we all die.[68]

The meaning of the second saying (2:15) is very obscure; contextual difficulties (among others) led C. Spicq to conclude that the verse must be a gloss.[69] The ambiguity of the singular subject (to whom is "she" referring?) and the puzzling plural verb (μείνωσιν) are odd features, and become especially problematic if one author is assumed responsible for this document. It is easier to accept the difficulties as owing to the fact that the material is no longer in its original context; in fact, it may be that 15a and 15b have been combined from two different sources, thus resulting in the bizarre grammatical construction.[70]

---

[66] ἐπιτρέπω was often used to introduce an authoritative decision: see John 19:38 (of Pilate); Acts 21:40 (of a centurion); I Cor. 16:7 (of the Lord). Compare the use of ἐπιτρέπω in I Cor. 14:34–35.

[67] Lock, *The Pastoral Epistles*, p. 33.

[68] Sir. 25:24. Compare the collections of material: Sir. 25:16–26 ("on evil wives"); Sir. 26:1–4 ("on good wives"); Sir. 26:6–9 ("on evil wives"). Note the long addition in some MSS of another collection of sayings on women in Sir. 26:19–27.

[69] Spicq, *Les Epîtres Pastorales*, p. 382. "If the textual tradition were not unanimous one would have seen in this verse a gloss, it is so poorly adapted to its context."

[70] So Bartsch, *Die Anfänge*, p. 72.

(3:1a) Literary marker

If the "faithful word" formula signals a solemn citation,[71] its appearance here is very odd. Neither that which precedes nor that which follows can easily be regarded as a citation. E. K. Simpson thinks that the remark "looks somewhat superfluous" in its present context.[72]

It seems better to take the expression as a formulaic marker, signaling the end (or the beginning?) of a collection of traditional materials, and marking them off as authoritative within the community. The appearance of this marker at the end of traditional material occurs also in Titus 3:8 (and perhaps I 4:9).[73]

3:1b–13 Qualities of leaders

The transition from the preceding materials is once again sudden and abrupt. There is no development of thought that links 2:15 with 3:1b; another collection of traditional materials simply appears, this time introduced by a proverbial saying.

This block of materials (3:1b–13) is unified by its concern for establishing proper leadership standards within the community. No specific duties are listed; rather, catalogues of virtues and vices serve to describe the qualities required of an overseer (3:2–7), deacons (3:8–10, 12–13), and deaconesses (3:11).

The qualities required of the leaders are remarkable for their general (that is, not specifically Christian) character.[74] No exceptional virtues are required of these leaders; on the contrary, those aspiring to "Christian" leadership are told that they must not be drunkards, given to violence, or contentious (cf. 3:3, 8). These features suggest the likelihood that preexisting (perhaps pre-Christian?) lists of leadership qualities have been taken over and employed here in a new context.

---

[71] So, for example, J. Calvin (*Commentary on Timothy and Titus*, p. 221) considers the expression as "a preface to a statement of some importance."

[72] Simpson, *The Pastoral Epistles*, p. 50.

[73] The variant reading πιστὸς ὁ ἀνθρωπίνος (D* b m) is probably a scribal emendation of the "faithful word" formula, the change being made because 3:1b seemed an odd "faithful saying."

[74] D. Guthrie (*The Pastoral Epistles*, p. 80) finds the lack of specifically Christian standards "surprising" but tries to account for the difficulties by asserting that "the majority of converts probably came from a background of low moral ideals." It seems far more likely that general parenetic materials have been taken over here and put to new use.

The varieties of literary style, the unusual vocabulary, and the odd arrangement of some of the materials (see below) indicate that more than one traditional source has been collected and incorporated here. The entire passage, in fact, seems to consist of loosely connected, conventional virtues relating to "the qualities of leadership." It is remarkable that, except for the concluding phrase, ἐν πίστει τῇ ἐν Χριστῷ 'Ιησοῦ (3:13), there is nothing particularly Christian within the entire collection.[75]

The collection of materials includes:

3:1b	An introductory proverbial saying
3:2–7	Lists of qualities of an overseer
3:8–13	Lists of qualities of a deacon/deaconess.

(3:1b) Introductory maxim

The precise meaning and function of this proverb in its present context remains unclear.[76] On the basis of the peculiar style and vocabulary of the saying, G. Knight (who affirms the authenticity of the Pastorals) concludes that the expression cannot have originated with Paul, but probably derives from a Christian community.[77] T. Zahn is also aware of the alien character of this text, concluding that the saying must be "a proverb of rather broad significance and non-Christian origin."[78] Whatever its origin, it is most likely that originally independent material has been taken over here. The general phrase εἴ τις may indicate that a regulative source is being quoted.[79]

---

[75] The insertion of not specifically "Christian" sources into the Pastorals points to a compiler who drew from a wide collection of traditional materials.

[76] See F. Gealy (*The Epistles to Timothy and Titus*, pp. 408–409) for a survey of five different attempts to clarify the meaning and function of this saying. Gealy himself thinks that the saying "is obviously a quotation. But what its original meaning was or just why it is quoted here is uncertain" (p. 408).

[77] G. W. Knight, *The Faithful Sayings in the Pastoral Letters* (Grand Rapids, MI: Baker, 1979), pp. 59–61. Knight notes the puzzling (and un-Pauline) use of ἐπισκοπή, ὀρέγομαι, and καλὸν ἔργον.

[78] T. Zahn, *Introduction to the New Testament*, ET by J. Trout et al. (3 vols., Edinburgh: T. & T. Clark, 1909), Vol. II, p. 124.

[79] Compare Ellis, "Traditions," pp. 244–245. Ellis suggests that the conditional sentence may serve as a marker of traditional materials in the Pastorals (cf. I 1:8; 5:4).

(3:2–7) Qualities required of an overseer

The use of δεῖ plus the infinitive may be a signal here (as in 3:7; Titus 1:7) that traditional materials have been taken over.[80] The phrase introduces a virtue/vice list (3:2–3) composed of twelve items, ten of which are found nowhere else in Paul's letters. The list is uniform in style, in clear contrast to the requirements that follow (3:4ff.). Not only does the style change, but the content of 3:5ff. is also markedly different from that which precedes. In Brox's words:

> at this point a bridge is expressly built from the general rule of virtue to the specific qualification of office.[81]

These changes in style and content suggest the likelihood that different sources have been combined here. The strange repetition of the phrase ἐμπέσῃ τοῦ διαβόλου in 3:6 and 3:7 supports this conjecture.

(3:8–13) Qualities required of a deacon/deaconess

This cluster of material shows the same kind of sudden stylistic changes as does that of 3:1–7; it begins with a virtue/vice list composed of four items, followed by a series of individual regulations directed to deacons and deaconesses. The introductory ὡσαύτως (3:8) signals the presence of traditional materials (cf. 2:9) and serves to link this cluster to that which precedes.

The poor arrangement of the material does not indicate (*pace* Easton) "that it is the Pastor's composition."[82] It is, in fact, just this kind of discontinuity that makes it difficult to ascribe this material to one author; development of thought is expected from an author. R. Falconer conjectures that the text has "suffered by displacement" and suggests that the correct order was 2:8, 9, 12, 10, 13, 11, but such a desperate solution is not required;[83] apparent displacement of materials is a hallmark of composite documents.

The confusion over the identity of the women referred to in 3:11 (wives of deacons/deaconesses?) is another indication that pre-

---

[80] So Bartsch (*Die Anfänge*, p. 13). Other formal indicators noted by Bartsch include: third-person imperatives; authoritative verbs (like βούλομαι and διατάσσομαι); and conditional clauses beginning with εἰ or εἰ δέ.

[81] Brox, *Die Pastoralbriefe*, p. 144.

[82] B. S. Easton, *The Pastoral Epistles* (London: SCM, 1948), p. 133.

[83] Falconer, *The Pastoral Epistles*, p. 136.

existing materials have been taken over here and placed in "non-native" contexts. This conjecture gains support from the reappearance of the formal ὡσαύτως in 3:11, which serves again to signal the introduction of a traditional virtue/vice list.

3:14–15 Epistolary motive

The community regulations are interrupted here by a puzzling autobiographical note. The abruptness of the transition was observed as long ago as 1807 by F. Schleiermacher, who noted the lack of any logical connection:

> Thus we are at a loss to find the connection between our verse and the previous and following ones, but even the internal order of the verse is no better.[84]

It appears likely that this passage was part of the original Pauline note sent to Timothy; it is difficult to imagine why a pseudonymous author would include the remark on Paul's intended speedy return (3:14; cf. 4:13) since such a scenario would run the risk of making the elaborate instructions of I Timothy seem unnecessary.

But if the passage is authentic, it can hardly be in its original context. The instructions given in chs. 2–3 are too elementary to require Timothy's attention; and if they are intended for the sake of the larger Christian community (so Jeremias), it is difficult to understand why the expression "in order that you may know" is in the singular (ἵνα εἰδῇς). In its present context, the passage fits awkwardly both in tone and subject matter with that which immediately precedes (on deacons) and that which follows (a confessional fragment).

If we accept the note's authenticity, we find that it fits well enough following the previous cluster of genuine Pauline material (cf. 1:18–20). The remarks regarding "how one ought to behave in the church of God" (3:15) probably referred originally to the problem of the false teachers and insubordinate members within the church (cf. 1:3–7, 18–20).

---

[84] F. Schleiermacher, "Ueber den sogenannten ersten Brief des Paulos an den Timotheos [*sic*]," in *Sämmtliche Werke* (32 vols., Berlin: G. Reimer, 1836), Vol. I, part 2, p. 304. Cf. F. Gealy (*The Epistles to Timothy and Titus*, p. 418): "This passage is without grammatical or doctrinal connection with the material which immediately precedes or follows."

3:16 Confessional fragment

A formulaic saying (3:16a) introduces the creedal or hymnic fragment of 3:16b. The term ὁμολογουμένως appears as part of a fixed expression three times in IV Maccabees: "it must be admitted (ὁμολογουμένως) that devout (εὐσέβεια) reason is sovereign over the emotions" (cf. 6:31; 7:16; 16:1). The fact that the term in IV Maccabees appears within a context of "piety" (as it does in I Tim. 3:16a) is striking, and leads A. T. Hanson to conclude that the author of the Pastorals is "deliberately copying 4 Maccabees."[85] There is too little evidence either to verify or to deny such a claim; an important thing to note, however, is that the term ὁμολογουμένως appears as part of a formulaic saying in IV Maccabees, and serves there, as in I Timothy, to provide a transition to a new block of materials.

The independent and preformed character of the fragment has long been recognized.[86] The introductory ὁμολογουμένως, the abruptness of ὅς (with its resulting variant readings), the three rhythmically equal couplets, and the fact that the content of the passage occasionally exceeds its immediate context all suggest that this is cited material.

The origin of the fragment is unclear. The fact that there is no explicit reference to Christ's death or resurrection is very striking; its vagueness requires that we allow for the possibility that a pre-Christian hymn has been taken up here and applied to Christ.[87]

4:1–5 Eschatological polemic

An abrupt transition leads to a series of polemical sayings, framed in apocalyptic language (cf. II 3:1ff.). The introductory expression (τὸ δὲ πνεῦμα ῥητῶς λέγει), and the (recitative?) ὅτι, suggests that some authoritative material is being cited;[88] perhaps the material that follows was originally a floating collection of prophetic

---

[85] A. T. Hanson, "An Academic Phrase: I Timothy 3:16a," in *Studies in the Pastoral Epistles* (London: SPCK, 1968), p. 23.

[86] The suggestion was put forward at least as early as 1817 by Rambach in his *Anthologie christlicher Gesänge*, Vol. I, p. 33. Cited by Holtzmann, *Die Pastoralbriefe*, p. 329.

[87] C. K. Barrett (*The Pastoral Epistles*, p. 66) observes that "it is probable that the hymn rests to some degree on pre-Christian models."

[88] J. Calvin (*Commentary on Timothy and Titus*, p. 236) calls the expression a word of "solemn assurance." D–C (*The Pastoral Epistles*, p. 64) notes that ὅτι is found in prophecies, and cites Justin's *Apology* 1.35.10; 63.10.

sayings.[89] Similar collections are common within apocalyptic Judaism; the Testament of the Twelve Patriarchs, for example, contains such eschatological polemics:

> I know, my children, that in the last times your sons will turn their backs on simplicity and become obsessed with greed; they will abandon innocence and resort to cunning; and forsaking the Lord's commands, they will attach themselves to Beliar. And they will give up farming and follow their own wicked inclination. (*T.Iss.* 6:1–2)

> For I know that in the last days you will defect from the Lord ... you will live by every evil deed, committing the revolting acts of the gentiles, chasing after wives of lawless men, and you are motivated to all wickedness by the spirits of deceit among you. (*T. Naph.* 5:4–5)

The eschatological polemic in I Tim. 4:1–5 is not unlike these examples. The language is typically vague and broadly aimed; the opponents are only identified as "some" people (τινες, 4:1) who engage in a variety of clearly evil activities.

It is noteworthy that the false teachings identified in 4:1–3 (immorality and asceticism) are very different from the heresies mentioned earlier in 1:3b–7 (myths and genealogies). Such variations are not surprising if the various blocks of material derive from different sources.

4:6–10 Traditional admonitions

"These things" (ταῦτα) occurs frequently in the Pastorals, but it is often difficult to ascertain its reach. Does it refer to the principles laid down in 4:4–5 (Bernard), or to the preceding paragraph (Scott), or to the material between 3:16 and 4:5 (Chrysostom), or to the entire first four chapters (Parry)? The term is equally vague in its other appearances within the Pastorals (cf. I 4:11; 6:2; II 2:14; Titus 2:15).

The imprecision suggests that ταῦτα may not be intended as a specific designation of reference; it may be serving, rather, as a formal literary marker, signaling the end of one collection of traditional materials and the beginning of another. This use of

---

[89] R. Falconer (*The Pastoral Epistles*, p. 139) suggests that both this passage and II 3:1ff. may predate the Pastorals.

ταῦτα can be seen in the letter of Barnabas, where the term appears both at the beginning and at the end of the traditional "Two Ways" material:

> 17:2   ταῦτα μὲν οὕτως.
> 21:1   ὁ γὰρ ταῦτα ποιῶν ἐν τῇ βασιλείᾳ τοῦ θεοῦ
> δοξασθήσεται.

The poem of Pseudo-Phocylides begins with the word ταῦτα,[90] indicating that the term does not ·always refer to that which precedes, but can serve to mark off that which follows as well.[91] Equally significant is the fact that ταῦτα also brings this collection of proverbial sayings to a close.[92]

A collection of traditional materials incorporated into the Sibylline Oracles (2.66–148) is also referred back to by ταῦτα:[93]

> 149f.   οὗτος ἀγών, ταῦτ' ἐστὶν ἀέθλια,
> ταῦτα βραβεῖα, τοῦτο πύλη ζωῆς
> καὶ εἴσοδος ἀθανασίης.

In the Pastorals the word is also linked to collections of traditional materials. Here at I Tim. 4:6, for example, it seems to signal the beginning of a cluster of miscellaneous admonitions and proverbial sayings. No thread of logic drives this unit along; only the loosest thematic link (training in godliness?) holds the diverse materials together.[94]

The vocabulary is distinctive, including five words which occur nowhere else in the NT (outside of the Pastorals).[95] The unit includes the following elements:

> 4:6   Introductory admonition to leaders
> 4:7a   Admonition to avoid tales

[90] Ps.-Phoc. 1–2: "These counsels (ταῦτα) of God by this holy judgment Phocylides the wisest of men sets forth, gifts of blessing."

[91] *Pace* E. E. Ellis ("Traditions in the Pastoral Epistles," pp. 243f.), who argues that ταῦτα signals the conclusion of preformed materials.

[92] Ps.-Phoc. 229–230: "These are the mysteries of righteousness (ταῦτα δικαιοσύνης μυστήρια); living thus may you live out a good life, right up to the threshold of old age."

[93] The material has been taken from Pseudo-Phocylides (see the discussion in chapter 2 above).

[94] The seemingly unnecessary and abrupt appearance of 4:6–7a led R. Falconer (*The Pastoral Epistles*, p. 142) to conclude that these verses must be editorial insertions; but the composite nature of the material is sufficient to account for the apparent "interruption."

[95] ἐντρέφω, γραῴδης, γυμνασία, ὠφέλιμος, ἀποδοχή.

4:7b   Admonition to train for godliness
4:8   Proverb on physical/spiritual training
4:9   Faithful word formula
4:10   Concluding saying.

The proverb-like quality of the whole section makes it difficult to determine with any precision what the "faithful saying" mentioned at 4:9 actually is.[96] The lack of cohesiveness within the unit suggests that each of the admonitions and sayings could have originally been independent of the rest. The reference to myths, for example, in the Letter of Aristeas (168) shows how the admonition in I Tim. 4:7a could have had a proverbial character within certain circles in Judaism:

> Nothing absurd or mythical is related in our scripture.
>
> (L. Arist. 168)

The two sayings of 4:7b and 4:8 are plainly linked by the reference to εὐσέβεια, but the logical transition is not nearly so clear.[97] It may be that two formerly independent sayings touching on the same theme have been strung together here. The general epigrammatic quality of 4:8 is evident from the many Stoic parallels that can be adduced; in *Ad Demonicum* (21), for example, Pseudo-Isocrates writes:

> Train yourself in self-imposed toils, that you may be able to endure those which others impose upon you.[98]

The meaning of the opening phrase (εἰς τοῦτο γάρ) in 4:10 is obscure; it does not easily link up with that which precedes (4:8) or that which follows 4:10b.[99] Calvin tries to clarify the development of thought by suggesting that 4:10 anticipates an objection, but this is impossible to verify.[100] It seems better to accept the miscellaneous

---

[96] See Knight, *Faithful Sayings in the Pastoral Letters*, pp. 62f. Knight notes the confusion and surveys the commentators' opinions: many think that the "faithful sayings" refers to 4:8, while some link it to 4:10, and others to 3:16.

[97] F. Gealy (*The Epistles to Timothy and Titus*, p. 429) notes the uncertain connection between I 4:7b and 4:8.

[98] Cited by D–C (*The Pastoral Epistles*, p. 68), who think that 4:8 has the ring of a Greek aphorism that has been taken over by Jews or Christians.

[99] Commentators have long debated the intended reference of 4:10a. See the discussion by Ellicott, *Grammatical Commentary on the Pastorals*, p. 59.

[100] Calvin, *Commentary on Timothy and Titus*, p. 245.

nature of the material and take 4:10 as a formerly independent saying that has been incorporated from a different context.

4:11–16 Traditional admonitions

Παράγγελλε ταῦτα signals another collection of loosely connected admonitions and sayings that seem to be strung (like beads on a string) around the theme of "commands to Timothy." The accumulation of ten imperatives, the vague use of ταῦτα (4:11, 15) and τοῦτο (4:16), and the lack of any internal cohesion suggest that the material has been gathered from various sources.

A close parallel to this cluster of personal parenesis appears in Tobit 4:1–19, where, in the form of a testament, Tobit gives a collection of traditional admonitions to his son Tobias. The mixture of personal and general parenesis,[101] the lack of continuity between admonitions, the use of conventional language,[102] the heaping up of imperatives, the emphasis upon personal discipline and fidelity to the traditions that have been handed down[103] – all of these formal literary features appear both in Tobit 4:1–19 and I Tim. 4:11–16. The parallels reflect the use of a traditional schema that was frequently employed in the collection of parenetic materials.

Tobias' role as an exemplary Jew is clear. The personal admonitions directed to him, consequently, are not meant to have a limited validity; they are of value to anyone desiring to be a good Jew. The same sort of significance seems to have been given to the personal admonitions that appear in I 4:11–16. In this case, traditional Pauline teachings (4:12–14) may have been gathered together and incorporated with non-Pauline traditions (see 4:16b) in the belief that they were all of general validity for leaders within the community. The formulaic ταῦτα in 4:15 may signal the inclusion of another block of previously independent (non-Pauline?) materials (4:15–16). Included in this collection of admonitions are:

---

[101] For example, the "personal" admonition in Tobit 4:14 ("Watch yourself, my son, in everything you do, and be disciplined in all your conduct") is followed by the negative golden rule in 4:15.

[102] Compare the conventional phrases: "Remember the Lord ... my son" (Tobit 4:4); "beware, my son" (Tobit 4:12); watch yourself (πρόσεχε), my son" (Tobit 4:14c); "my son, remember" (Tobit 4:19c); "do not be afraid, my son" (Tobit 4:21).

[103] See, for example, Tobit 4:5, 14, 19.

4:11	Introductory marker of traditional materials
4:12	Admonition to be exemplary
4:13	Admonition to attend to traditional worship customs
4:14	Admonition to employ one's gift
4:15	Introductory marker of traditional materials
4:16a	Admonition to attend to the traditions
4:16b	Concluding promise to the faithful.[104]

5:1–22 Community rules

This block of traditional materials is loosely held together by concern for the care of various groups within the community. That the collection derives from various sources is apparent from the discontinuity both among and within the collected traditions (see below).

(5:1–2) On the treatment of community members

Kelly observes that "at this point the tone and content of the letter change abruptly."[105] The independent character of 5:1–2 can hardly be denied. The discussion on the proper treatment of members of the community appears unexpectedly and is just as suddenly left off. As a general "household rule" it seems to parallel, both in structure and content, traditional rules popular within pagan and Jewish circles.[106]

A faint sketch of this rule may be reflected in I Clem. 1:3, where the Romans are commended for their treatment of the rulers and the aged (πρεσβύτεροι); these remarks are then followed (1:3b) by regulations concerning the conduct of various groups within the community: the young (νέος), the wives, and the husbands. The passage closes with a mention of the "rule of obedience" (κανὼν τῆς ὑποταγῆς, 1:3c), which may indicate the use of a fixed catechetical source by the early church.

---

[104] The saying promises "salvation" to the one who faithfully obeys the traditional admonitions. A similar promise appears in Tobit 4:9: "So [by following the admonitions on charity] you will be laying up a good treasure for yourself against the day of necessity." See also the close parallels in II Clem. 15:1; 19:1.

[105] Kelly, *The Pastoral Epistles*, p. 109.

[106] A striking parallel appears in the Greek inscription cited by D–C (*The Pastoral Epistles*, p. 72): "continually honoring older men as parents, peers as brothers, and younger men as sons."

In its original setting, at any rate, the rule that appears at I Tim. 5:1–2 probably had its place among many others, in a context similar, perhaps, to the collection of "household rules" found in Sirach chs. 7–8.[107]

(5:3–16) On the care of widows

This unit comprises a cluster of materials relating to the care of widows in the community. The frequently rough and obscure transitions within the passage give rise to major exegetical questions. The extent of the difficulties is reflected in R. Parry's suggestion that the "curiously ill-arranged" materials in 5:3–8 must have been displaced and should be read as follows: 3, 4, 8, 7, 5, 6.[108] Other commentators find the placement of 5:16 problematic, and conjecture that it must have strayed from its original place (following 5:4 and 5:8?).[109] B. S. Easton notes the apparent redundancies within the passage and attributes them to the "anxiety of the writer."[110]

There is considerable evidence, however, to suggest that the obscurities within this section are not due to displacement or editorial addition but to the fact that the unit is a collection of previously independent sayings on the care of widows. The formulaic τοῦτο γάρ ἐστιν ἀπόδεκτον ἐνώπιον τοῦ θεοῦ (5:4b, cf. 2:3) signals, in all likelihood, that the regulation of 5:4a is a citation. Another "marker" indicating the likely presence of traditional materials appears in 5:7: καὶ ταῦτα παράγγελλε.

The lack of linguistic precision also suggests that materials have been removed from their original context. The admonition at 5:4 begins with a singular subject ("if any widow," 5:4a) which changes abruptly to an unexpressed plural (μανθανέτωσαν, 5:4b). That subsequent copyists sensed the confusion is evident from the

---

[107] The collection of rules on the treatment of community members in Sirach is remarkable for its diversity: it includes children (7:23), daughters (7:24), wives (7:26), fathers (7:27), mothers (7:27), priests (7:29), the poor (7:32), the sick (7:35), the powerful (8:1), the rich (8:2), the ill-bred (8:4), and the old (8:6).

[108] R. Parry, *The Pastoral Epistles* (Cambridge: University Press, 1920), p. 31. See also Falconer (*The Pastoral Epistles*, pp. 147–148), who thinks that the confusion in the order "may have arisen from the process of additions to what was a church manual."

[109] See, for example, Scott, *The Pastoral Epistles*, p. 63; Spicq (*Les Epîtres Pastorales*, p. 538) notes that in its context "la tonalité de cette exhortation surprend."

[110] Easton, *The Pastoral Epistles*, p. 151. Easton notes the repetition that occurs in 5:4 and 5:8.

change in some MSS from the plural verb to the singular.[111] The Vulgate and Chrysostom take the subject to be the "widows," although "children" or "grandchildren" would appear to fit the present context better.

It seems best to attribute the confusion within the passage, not to a careless or inattentive author, but to the composite nature of this material. Once again, the absence of the original context contributes to the confusion that is all too apparent throughout this unit.

The sayings may be divided as follows:

5:3	Superscription on widows (cf. 3:1)
5:4	On widows with families
5:5–7	On "real" widows
5:8	On the neglect of widows
5:9–10	On enrolling older widows
5:11–15	On young widows
5:16	On widows with families

(5:17–21) On elders

This series of collected admonitions concerning elders may owe its placement here in the immediate context to the catch-word τιμή (cf. 5:3, 6:1). The unit as a whole lacks any internal development of thought, and the disjointed sequence of the materials causes considerable exegetical difficulties.[112] The present collection seems to incorporate the following regulations and sayings:

5:17	On the care of elders
5:18a	Traditional citation (Deut. 25:4; cf. I Cor. 9:9)
5:18b	Proverbial saying[113]
5:19a	On accusations against elders
5:19b	Traditional citation (Deut. 17:6; 19:15)
5:20	On discipline of elders
5:21	Summary marker of traditional materials.

There is little logical development within this section, but a thematic thread is again visible: a number of diverse regulations

---

[111] MSS 945 d, f, m, et al. read μανθανέτω.

[112] R. Falconer (*The Pastoral Epistles*, p. 149) considers the possibility that materials have become displaced here, as in 5:3–16.

[113] Compare Luke 10:7; Matt. 10:10; Did. 13:1–2. The fact that in I Tim. 5:18 no appeal is made to Jesus' authority suggests that the saying probably circulated as a common proverbial expression.

pertaining to elders (some of them complete with stock proof-texts
– cf. 5:17–18, 19) have been gathered together.

The sudden appearance of the solemn oath in 5:21 is surprising.
Barrett suggests that it "shows the earnestness of the author's
feelings," while Guthrie thinks that it reflects the weak character of
Timothy, who needed "stiffening up."[114] But such attempts to
explain the psychological motives behind the oath miss the formulaic character of the expression; it is functioning here simply as a
marker of the traditional materials which precede it (5:17ff.).

Outside of the Pastorals the term διαμαρτύρομαι and the fixed
expression ταῦτα φυλάξῃς both serve to signal the presence and to
underscore the importance of collected traditional sayings. In the
LXX version of Deut. 31:28, for example, διαμαρτύρομαι occurs at
the conclusion of a lengthy collection of traditional Mosaic teachings. In Deut. 32:46 (LXX) the same word appears at the end of the
preformed Song of Moses (32:1–43).

The ταῦτα formula is linked in I Tim. 5:21 to the verb φυλάσσω,
a term which had long been employed within Judaism to signify the
transmission and preservation of religious traditions.[115]

5:22–25 Miscellaneous admonitions

The order of the following admonitions defies attempts at system-
ization and had given rise to numerous conjectures. H. J. Holtzmann, for example, puzzled by the seemingly unmotivated
admonition to "keep yourself pure" in 5:22b, thinks that the verse
may be misplaced and suggests that it may have originally followed
5:2.[116] Similar doubts surround the peculiar admonition to drink
some wine in 5:23; J. Calvin notes how it interrupts the train of
thought and suggests that it may have been a marginal note that
found its way into the text through a scribal error.[117]

Such attempts to account for the discontinuity of this material
reflect the seriousness of the problems facing the interpreter. How
can such lack of order and coherence be explained?

Many who assume that one author is responsible for this document are driven to the desperate expedient of postulating textual

---

[114] Barrett, *The Pastoral Epistles*, p. 80; Guthrie, *The Pastoral Epistles*, p. 107.
[115] See the frequent use of φυλάσσω in the Testament of the Twelve Patriarchs:
T. Reub. 3:9; T. Sim. 3:1; 4:5; T. Jud. 16:1; T. Iss. 5:1; T. Zeb. 5:1; 10:2 et al.
[116] Holtzmann, *Die Pastoralbriefe*, p. 356.
[117] Calvin, *Commentary on Timothy and Titus*, p. 266.

displacement. But such a conjecture is nothing less than a tacit admission that the text as we have it does not read like the product of a single mind. No "author" would write in this way.

It seems better to accept the composite nature of this material and thereby allow for the diversity and discontinuities that characterize it.

The collection of admonitions includes:

5:22a   Admonition on the restoration of a penitent
5:22b   Admonition on purity
5:23   Admonition on asceticism
5:24–25   Proverbial sayings on judgment.

The lack of genuine context explains the difficulty in assessing the precise meaning of these admonitions. For example, 5:22a may refer to the laying on of hands in ordination,[118] or to the restoration of penitents to fellowship,[119] but in the present context no clear decision between these two options is possible. The admonition on purity (5:22b) seems unmotivated by its present context, as does the instruction to "drink some wine" (5:23).

The general proverbial character of 5:24 is underscored by the double use of the indefinite pronoun τις ("the sins of some men"). The idea that one's good deeds or evil works would "go before" (προάγω) him into judgment was a commonplace:

> Each will receive according to his deeds. If he be good his righteousness will lead him, if he be evil the reward of iniquity is before him.   (Barn. 4:12)

The formulaic ὡσαύτως introduces another proverb (5:25) presenting a similar view.

6:1–2 On the conduct of slaves

Another sudden transition brings the reader without warning or introduction to a unit that deals with the proper conduct of slaves.[120] A small cluster of admonitions on the treatment of slaves in Pseudo-Phocylides (223–227) shows how collections of pre-

---

[118] So D. Daube, "The Laying on of Hands," in *The New Testament and Rabbinic Judaism* (London: Athlone Press, 1956), pp. 224ff. Daube argues that within Judaism the laying on of hands was part of a rabbi's ordination service.

[119] See, for example, Eusebius, *Ecclesiastical History* VII. 2 (LCL): "It was the ancient custom that [repentant heretics] should receive only the laying on of hands with prayers." Cf. the Syriac Didascalia II.41.

[120] See K. Weidinger, *Die Haustafeln: Ein Stück urchristlicher Paränese* (Leipzig:

viously unrelated admonitions could be brought together, connected only by a general theme:

223:    Provide your slave with the tribute he owes to his stomach.
224:    Apportion to a slave what is appointed so that he will become as you wish.
225:    Insult not your slave by branding him.
226:    Do not hurt a slave by slandering him to his master.
227:    Accept advice also from a kindly disposed slave.

These admonitions are concerned with the proper treatment of slaves by their masters; but there is evidence that the conduct of slaves toward their masters was also a part of Jewish *Haustafeln*.[121] Perhaps the most striking parallel to the material on slaves in I Tim. 5:1–2 comes from the Mishnah tractate 'Aboth:

> Antigonus of Soko received [the law] from Simeon the Just. He used to say: Be not like slaves that minister to the master for the sake of receiving a bounty, but be like slaves that minister to the master not for the sake of receiving a bounty; and let the fear of heaven be upon you.   (1:3)

The placement of this domestic rule fragment at I Tim. 6:1–2 may be due to the catch-words πάσῃ τιμῇ (see 5:3, 17). The regulative nature of this material is apparent from the third-person plural imperatives ἡγείσθωσαν (6:1), καταφρονείτωσαν (6:2), and δουλευέτωσαν (6:2).

The material is separated from the traditional instructions that follow by the formulaic ταῦτα δίδασκε καὶ παρακάλει.

6:3–21 Miscellaneous injunctions

It is no easy task to outline the remainder of chapter 6. Most

Hinrichs, 1928). See also Bartsch, *Die Anfänge*, pp. 144f. Bartsch thinks that a preexisting document on the duties of Christian slaves to their owners lies behind this passage. Many parallels to this kind of *Haustafel* survive: compare, for example, Eph. 6:5–9; Col. 3:22–4:1; I Pet. 2:18–20; Titus 2:9; Did. 4:10f.; Barn. 19:7; Ign. Poly. 4:3.

[121] See, for example, Philo's *De Decalogo* 165–167: "There are many other instructions given, to the young on courtesy to the old, to the old on taking care of the young, to subjects on obeying their rulers ... to servants on rendering an affectionate loyalty to their masters ... to masters on showing the gentleness and kindness by which inequality is equalized" (LCL). The same concern is touched upon in the Sibylline Oracles (2:278), where servants who rise up against their masters are listed among the godless.

commentators simply regard the section as a miscellany of diverse materials. D. Guthrie, for example, observes that

> the concluding portion of the Epistle contains no clear sequence of thought, and it is best therefore to deal with it in self-contained sections.[122]

This is a remarkable admission by Guthrie, for it indicates that his attempt to read I Timothy as a typical letter has failed. He finds the sequence of thought in chapter 6 to be so disjointed as to necessitate a fundamental modification in his hermeneutical method: each unit of material must be dealt with separately, with little regard to its immediate or particular context.

It is, of course, precisely this understanding of the text that must be applied, not just to chapter 6, but to the whole of the Pastorals.

(6:3–5) Polemic against false teachers

This section returns abruptly to the subject of the false teachers (cf. 1:3f.; 4:1–5). It is unmotivated by what precedes and is followed by an apparently unrelated proverbial saying (6:6). The admonition consists of one long sentence, and incorporates a number of stock polemical expressions,[123] a conventional vice list, and a cluster of rare and unique NT words.[124]

The construction of the opening subordinate clause (εἰ followed by the negative μή) is odd, both because it appears so rarely in the NT and because elsewhere in the Pastorals εἰ is followed by οὐ (cf. I 3:5; 5:8).[125] This remarkable deviation can hardly be attributed to the whim of the author. Such grammatical constructions belong to the "tissue" of language and flow from an author's pen without thought. It is a stylistic feature. The fact that the style here contrasts

---

[122] Guthrie, *The Pastoral Epistles*, p. 110.

[123] R. Karris ("The Background and Significance of the Polemic of the Pastoral Epistles," *JBL* 92 [1973], 549–564) thinks that a traditional polemical schema lies behind this collection of charges against false teachers. Compare, for example, Philo's stock criticisms of those who quibble with words (*Congr.* 53) and those whose actions are motivated by greed (*Vit. Mos.* 2.209–216; *Migr. ab.* 171).

[124] Five words within this sentence are NT *hapax legomena*: νοσέω, λογομαχία, ὑπόνοια, διαπαρατριβή, πορισμός. Six others appear nowhere else in Paul's writings: ἐτεροδιδασκαλέω, προσέρχομαι, ὑγιαίνω, εὐσέβεια, ἐπίσταμαι, ζήτησις.

[125] See Blass and Debrunner, *A Greek Grammar of the New Testament*, p. 221 (#428). The construction (in 6:3) is regarded by Blass as a remnant of classical Greek. The only other NT occurrence is in the codex Bezae reading of Luke 6:4.

with similar constructions elsewhere in the Pastorals may indicate the diverse origin of this material.

It is striking that here (as in 1:3f.) the false teachers are never clearly identified; the content of their teaching is never described. The use of the indefinite pronoun τις, the lack of any specific charges, and the conventional denunciations against those who deviate from the "sound teaching" give the admonition an almost universal validity.

A similar admonition appears in the Didache (6:1) at the end of the "Two Ways" material:

> Ὅρα, μή τίς σε πλανήσῃ ἀπὸ ταύτης τῆς
> ὁδοῦ τῆς διδαχῆς, ἐπεὶ παρεκτὸς θεοῦ
> σε διδάσκει.

There is no reason to think that this was directed towards any specific heretical group; it seems, rather, to be serving as a general warning, the aptness of which was limited by neither circumstances nor time. The admonition is similar to that which appears in I Tim. 6:3–5 in two important respects: both are concerned with a falling away from "the way of the teaching" (= "the godly teaching," I 6:3); and both are notably vague in their references to the false teachers (employing the indefinite pronoun τις).

It seems likely that the editor of I Timothy has incorporated at 6:3 a general warning against apostasy (similar to that which appears in the Didache). The link with 6:2c may be the catchword δίδασκε (cf. ἑτεροδιδασκαλεῖ, 6:3).

(6:6–10) Proverbial sayings

This cluster of loosely connected epigrammatic sayings on moderation is linked to 6:5 by the catch-word πορισμός. Logically, however, 6:5 and 6: have little in common. In 6:5 πορισμός appears with εὐσέβεια to describe the impure motives of the false teachers; in 6:6 the same words reappear but take on the opposite meaning, and the thought begun in 6:5 is suddenly discontinued.

That preexisting materials have been taken over and incorporated here is indicated by the fact that the ideas introduced in 6:6–10 are essentially unrelated to the concerns of the immediate context; nothing is said about the false teachers (6:3) or their corruptible influences (6:4–5). The literary style also changes suddenly, with short and pithy sayings replacing the flowing style of 6:3–5.

The sayings have a quasi-philosophical ring about them, and carry no specifically Christian message; A. T. Hanson suggests that the author has concentrated into this paragraph "more general maxims drawn from pagan philosophy than in any other passage in the three letters."[126] But one need not turn to pagan philosophers for parallels in language and thought; Jewish writings offer equally striking parallels. For example:

> (cf. 6:6)
> You have great wealth if you fear God and refrain from every sin. (Tobit 4:21)

> (cf. 6:7)
> Naked I came from my mother's womb, and naked I shall return. (Job 1:21; cf. Eccl. 5:14 LXX)

> (cf. 6:8)
> The essentials for life are water and bread and clothing and a house to cover one's nakedness. (Sir. 29:21)

> (cf. 6:9)
> Those who amass gold and silver; they shall quickly be destroyed. Woe unto you, O rich people! For you have put your trust in your wealth. You shall ooze out of your riches. (I Enoch 94:7b–8; cf. Ps.-Phoc. 44–45)

> (cf. 6:10)
> The love of money is mother of all evil.
> (Ps.-Phoc. 42; cf. Sib. Or. 2:111; *T. Sim.* 5:3; Philo, *Spec. Leg.* I. 24.281)

(6:11–16) A commissioning charge

The relation of this parenetical unit to its context is problematic.[127] There is no logical connection either with that which precedes or that which follows. And the internal order of the unit itself is equally puzzling.

Both the content and the form of this unit suggest that it contains

---

[126] Hanson, *Studies in The Pastoral Epistles*, p. 107.
[127] Some commentators think that it may be a later editorial addition: see, for example, D–C, *The Pastoral Epistles*, p. 87; Brox, *Die Pastoralbriefe*, p. 212.

preformulated materials. The expression "man of God," for example, never appears in Paul's earlier letters, and seems a somewhat peculiar title by which to address a personal friend.[128] The reference to Pilate in the creedal fragment (6:13) is hardly prompted by the context; and the solemn adjuration (6:13–14) and rhythmic doxology (6:15–16) also appear better suited to a liturgical context than a personal letter.

More tellingly, the formulaic Σὺ δέ (with variations) often serves to introduce blocks of preformed materials within the Pastorals. In II Tim. 3:10, for example, it precedes a traditional virtue list; in II Tim. 4:5, σὺ δέ introduces a duty list, and in Titus 2:1 the same expression precedes a collection of community rules.[129]

The fixed expression ταῦτα φεῦγε, δίωκε δὲ ... also seems to signal the presence of traditional materials. The same phrase occurs again at II Tim. 2:22, where it serves to introduce a virtue list similar to that which appears in this unit (6:11).[130] The personal "confession" of II Clem. 18:2 includes a reference to fleeing (φεύγω) temptation and pursuing (διώκω) righteousness. In I Clem. 30:1 φεύγω introduces a lengthy vice list and is followed by κολλάω and a virtue list. Similar injunctions to "flee" from evil and "pursue" or cling to the good are widespread within Judaism: in the *T. Gad* 5:2, for example, Gad says, "And these things (ταῦτα) I speak to you from experience, my children, that you may flee (φεύγω) from hatred and cling (κολλάω) to the love of the Lord."[131]

Some commentators think that this passage (I Tim. 6:11–16) draws upon an adult baptismal address;[132] others suggest an ordination liturgy.[133] The precise origins of the unit remain

---

[128] The phrase only appears in the Pastorals within the NT (compare II 3:17). In both contexts it carries a conventional ring, designating in general terms a leader.

[129] See also II 2:1; 2:3 (v.l.); 3:14. Compare the use of a similar phrase (ὑμεῖς οὖν) in the Testament of the Twelve Patriarchs: for example, T. Ben. 8:1; T. Ash. 3:1.

[130] Three of the four virtues occurring in II 2:22 also appear in I 6:11: δικαιοσύνη, πίστις, ἀγάπη.

[131] Compare T. Dan. 6:10; T. Ben 8:1. In T. Ash. 3:2, note the variant reading φεύγω for ἀποτρέχω.

[132] So Gealy, Jeremias, Falconer, Easton, Spicq, Holtz, Kelly, H. Windisch, "Zur Christologie der Pastoralbriefe," *ZNW* 34 (1935), 213–238.

[133] So D–C, Barrett, Brox, Hanson. See especially E. Käsemann, "Das Formular einer neutestamentlichen Ordinationsparänese," in *Neutestamentliche Studien für Rudolph Bultmann* (Berlin: A. Töpelmann, 1954), pp. 261–268. Käsemann makes incisive observations on the preformulated character of this material, and discusses the author's apparent use of certain stereotypical expressions as "markers" (see p. 262).

shrouded, but there can be little doubt that this passage was not composed ad hoc by the author of this letter.

(6:17–19) Admonition to the wealthy

This admonition is problematic for two reasons: it abruptly returns to the theme just addressed in 6:6–10, and it breaks any thread of continuity between 6:16 and 6:20. Commentators have offered all sorts of conjectures in hopes of resolving the apparent discontinuity; A. von Harnack, for example, argues that it is an interpolation, added around AD 150, "according to the needs of the time."[134] Others think that the text must have been accidentally displaced from its original context.[135] Jeremias notes the difficulty and tries to account for it by labeling the piece a "postscript" (*Nachtrag*).[136]

These proposed remedies are neither convincing nor necessary. They serve, however, to reveal anew the seriousness of the problems facing those who maintain that a single author is responsible for this document.

J. N. D. Kelly's suggestion that "a later editor would have surely chosen a more appropriate place for inserting new material of this kind" is clearly in danger of over-simplifying the editorial process.[137] Composite documents, almost by definition, possess complicated editorial histories. The Didache, for example, owes its present form to the work of editors, but the materials it contains are not arranged in any clear and systematic order. Instructions on almsgiving, for instance, do not appear neatly grouped together, but are scattered throughout the manual in a less than "appropriate" fashion (cf. Did. 1:5–6; 4:5–8; 11:12; 13:4; 15:4).[138] The present form of the Didache (as well as that of the Pastorals) suggests that the

---

[134] A. von Harnack, *Geschichte der altchristlichen Literatur bis Eusebius* (4 vols., Leipzig: Zentralantiquariat, 1958 [1893–1904]), Vol. I, p. 482. For similar conjectures, compare Falconer, *The Pastoral Epistles*, p. 158; Easton, *The Pastoral Epistles*, p. 170.

[135] For example, Lock, *The Pastoral Epistles*, p. 73.

[136] J. Jeremias, *Die Briefe an Timotheus und Titus* (Göttingen: Vandenhoeck & Ruprecht, 1953), p. 40.

[137] Kelly, *The Pastoral Epistles*, p. 147. Kelly's way out of the problem is to label 6:11–16 a Pauline "digression," but this fails to appreciate the extent of the differences in form, content, and style that separate 6:11–16 from its surrounding context.

[138] R. Kraft (*The Apostolic Fathers*, ed. R. Grant [6 vols., New York: Thomas Nelson, 1965], Vol. III, *Barnabas and the Didache*, p. 64) suggests that the subsequent history of "church manual" materials (like the Apostolic Constitu-

earliest editors were more concerned about the preservation of traditional materials than they were about literary order.

It is hard to see how R. Falconer can assert that the source of the admonition in 6:17 "may be in the circle Luke–Acts."[139] The saying here seems to have all the marks of a conventional piece of Jewish parenesis on the dangers of wealth. The connection between wealth, arrogance, the uncertainty of riches, and the need to trust in God is traditional and can be paralleled in many Jewish writings; Philo, for example, commenting on Deut. 10:21, writes:

> Let God alone be thy boast and thy chief glory, [Moses] continues, and pride thyself neither on riches nor on reputation nor dominion nor comeliness nor strength of body, nor any such thing, whereby the hearts of the empty minded are wont to be lifted up. Consider in the first place that these things have nothing in them of the nature of the true good; secondly, how quickly comes the hour of their passing.[140]

Other Jewish proverbial sayings parallel the admonitions in 6:18–19 to share one's wealth and lay up a good foundation (or "treasure") for the future. A striking parallel to these verses appears in the parenetical section of Tobit (4:8–9):

> If you have many possessions, make your gift from them in proportion ... So you will be laying up a good treasure for yourself against the day of necessity.

These parallels show the proverbial character of this admonition in I Tim. 6:17–19. On the basis of the unusual vocabulary (six NT *hapax legomena*),[141] and the awkward setting in the context, it is likely that the piece came "ready-made" to an editor of the Pastorals who incorporated it here into the letter.

(6:20–21a) Concluding admonition

Paul's original note to Timothy ended with this concluding charge

---

tions and the Apostolic Traditions of Hippolytus) clearly reflects complex editorial activity within early Christian circles.

[139] Falconer, *The Pastoral Epistles*, p. 159. Falconer points to the gospel parallels, especially Luke 12:21 and 16:1–12. Cf. Jeremias, *Die Briefe an Timotheus und Titus*, p. 40.

[140] Philo, *Spec. Leg.* I.311 (LCL); Cf. Philo, *De Josepho* X.43; Jer. 9:23; Ps. 52:7.

[141] ὑψηλοφρονέω, ἀδηλότης, ἀγαθοεργέω, εὐμετάδοτος, κοινωνικός, ἀποθησαυρίζω.

to "guard the tradition." The comment seems aptly directed to Timothy in light of the false teachings that are filtering into the Ephesian church. The lack of any personal greetings is not unusual in light of the brief and personal nature of the note.

4

II TIMOTHY: A COMPOSITIONAL ANALYSIS

1:1–2 Epistolary salutation

The authoritative claim to apostleship that inaugurates this letter (ἀπόστολος Χριστοῦ Ἰησοῦ διὰ θελήματος θεοῦ) parallels verbatim that which occurs at the beginning of II Corinthians (cf. I Cor. 1:1);[1] in the Corinthian correspondence, Paul's solemn claims to authority seem fitting in light of the serious disputes that had erupted over his apostleship. But here, at the beginning of a personal letter, the formality appears misplaced. The second phrase (κατ' ἐπαγγελίαν ζωῆς τῆς ἐν Χριστῷ Ἰησοῦ), linked grammatically to ἀπόστολος, adds to the peculiarity by underscoring the aim and purpose of Paul's apostleship.[2]

The formality of this salutation (like those of I Timothy and Titus) poses problems for those who wish to maintain the Pauline authorship of this letter.[3] D. Guthrie, for example, observes that the letter opening "seems rather stiff when addressed to Paul's closest associate," but goes on to argue that Paul writes this way because "he can never forget the noble work to which he was so impressively called."[4] The problem with this response is that Paul's salutations in Philippians, I and II Thessalonians, and Philemon make no mention of his apostleship and carry none of the solemnity that makes the opening of II Timothy appear so odd.

It seems better to argue either that the salutation is the production of an imitator, or that Paul's original salutation was much

---

[1] Compare also the verbatim salutation of Col. 1:1.

[2] So J. H. Bernard, *The Pastoral Epistles* (Grand Rapids, MI: Barker, 1980 [1899]), p. 107. C. K. Barrett, *The Pastoral Epistles* (Oxford: Clarendon Press, 1963), p. 91, also notes the emphasis here on Paul's apostleship.

[3] B. S. Easton, *The Pastoral Epistles* (London: SCM, 1948), p. 37, calls the salutation "unthinkable in a letter to Paul's tried and true lieutenant."

[4] D. Guthrie, *The Pastoral Epistles* (Leicester: Inter-Varsity Press, 1947), p. 121.

shorter than the solemn form that has come down to us. Although the latter conjecture is not supported by surviving textual evidence, it gains considerable credibility on other grounds. We know from the surviving recensions of the Ignatian corpus, for example, that expansion of epistolary salutations did occur. In the longer recension of Ignatius' letter to Polycarp an editorial addition appears that was intended no doubt to complete Ignatius' own self-designation:

Short recension	Long recension
Ignatius, who is also called Theophorus, to Polycarp ...	Ignatius, bishop of Antioch, and a witness for Jesus Christ, to Polycarp ...[5]

If the phrases that serve to enhance Paul's apostolic authority in II Timothy are removed (beginning with ἀπόστολος and ending at the final 'Ιησοῦ (1:1), the difficulties surrounding this salutation are greatly lessened, and a warm and intimate greeting emerges:

> Paul to Timothy, my beloved child. Grace and peace from God our Father and Christ Jesus our Lord.

Perhaps the solemn expressions of authority were added after Paul's death by an editor who wished to give the apostle his full due, or to enhance the official character of this apparently personal letter.

1:3–5 Thanksgiving

II Timothy is the only one of the Pastorals that includes a thanksgiving. But in its present form this "thanksgiving," consisting of one long and involved sentence, poses difficulties, both to those who think the Pastorals genuine, and to those who regard this piece as a carefully crafted imitation.[6] The material clearly echoes Paul's thought (cf. Rom. 1:8–11), but it does so in markedly un-Pauline language; χάριν ἔχω appears in the place of Paul's frequent εὐχαριστέω (Rom. 1:8; Phil. 1:3; I Thess. 1:2, et al.);[7] ἔχω

---

[5] A. Roberts and J. Donaldson (eds.), *The Writings of the Apostolic Fathers* (Edinburgh: T. & T. Clark, 1867), Vol. I, p. 257.

[6] P. Dornier (*Les Epîtres Pastorales* [Paris: Gabalda, 1969], p. 181) notes the crucial role played by this passage: "These three verses (3–5) are interesting because they illustrate in themselves alone the whole problem of the authenticity of the Pastorals."

[7] The seriousness of this deviation from the Pauline style is underscored by

τὴν περὶ σοῦ μνείαν occurs instead of the Pauline μνείαν ὑμῶν ποιοῦμαι (Rom. 1:9); the usual Pauline ἐπὶ τῶν προσευχῶν μου (Rom. 1:10) is replaced by ἐν ταῖς δεήσεσιν μου; and instead of Paul's preferred adverb ἀδιαλείπτως (Rom. 1:9, I Thess. 1:2) the thanksgiving in II Timothy employs the adjective ἀδιαλείπτος.

The construction of the text raises other difficulties; in Paul's thanksgivings the verb εὐχαριστέω is usually followed by a pronoun object phrase ("for you") and frequently by the causal conjunction ὅτι (see, for example, Rom. 1:8–11). All of these stylistic features are missing in II Tim. 1:3–5.

Such linguistic and formal differences make it unlikely that Paul was the author of this material. But the dissimilarities also count against the hypothesis that a pseudonymous author, intent on imitating Paul, was responsible for this piece. The commonly held view that the author of II Timothy modeled his thanksgiving upon that of Romans (1:8–11) is especially vulnerable at this point.[8] Why would a Paulinist diverge so widely, not only in language but also in form, from his Pauline model?[9]

The thanksgiving also presents other difficulties. The grammar of the long sentence is jumbled and clumsy, the main verb being overburdened by a string of seven loosely connected subordinate clauses. No clear train of thought drives the sentence on (the object of the thanksgiving is never expressed!), and the connections between the various clauses are not easily followed.[10] The meaning

---

P. Schubert (*Form and Function of the Pauline Thanksgivings* [Berlin: A. Töpelmann, 1939], p. 34): "The formal and functional homogeneity of the Pauline εὐχαριστέω thanksgiving is clearly demonstrated by the invariable occurrence of the initial principal clauses in which εὐχαριστέω is the characterizing verb."

8   Advocates of this theory include H. J. Holtzmann, *Die Pastoralbriefe kritisch und exegetisch behandelt* (Leipzig: Wilhelm Engelmann, 1880), p. 378; M. Dibelius and H. Conzelmann (henceforth D–C), *The Pastoral Epistles* (Philadelphia: Fortress Press, 1972), p. 98; N. Brox, *Die Pastoralbriefe*, Regensburger Neues Testament VII.2 (Regensburg: F. Pustet, 1969), p. 225. For a more recent proponent see M. Wolter, *Die Pastoralbriefe als Paulustradition* (Göttingen: Vandenhoeck & Ruprecht, 1988), p. 204: "the giving thanks in 2 Tim. 1,3 links up with the Pauline texts that have been referred to [Rom. 1:8–10; Eph. 1:16; I Thess. 1:2; Philem. 4] and would imitate the custom of the (Pauline) letter style."

9   J. N. D. Kelly (*A Commentary on the Pastoral Epistles* [London: Adam & Charles Black, 1963], p. 155) is only half correct in his assertion that "the structure of this passage strikingly resembles that of the normal Pauline thanksgiving, including in 4 a participial clause followed by a final clause." It is true that six of the seven syntactical units that make up the Pauline thanksgiving (cf. Schubert, *Form and Function*, p. 15) do occur here; nevertheless, the variations from the Pauline style within these units are even more striking than the similarities.

10   Many commentators have noted the confused construction (for example, Holtzmann, Lock, Barrett). Few, however, have attempted to explain the cause of the

and function of the conjunction ὡς, for example, is not easily determined. Is it intended to have a causal sense here, or a temporal one, or some other?[11] And what does ἀδιάλειπτον modify, ἔχω μνείαν or ἐπιποθῶν σε ἰδεῖν?[12]

Some commentators try to account for the cluttered syntax by appealing to Paul's strained emotional condition;[13] others argue that 1:4 should be regarded as a parenthetical comment, and bracketed off from the rest of the sentence. But such explanations fail to take into consideration the peculiarities of the thanksgiving as a whole.

No completely satisfying solution to the problems within this thanksgiving is at hand. The material seems strangely fragmented and discontinuous; to use L. Houlden's expression, it almost seems like "a catena of allusions to personal, heartfelt passages in [the Pauline] letters."[14]

The diversity of the solutions put forward reflects something of the difficulties inherent in this unit of material:

1. the thanksgiving is a clumsy forgery by a writer recalling phrases from other Pauline letters;[15]
2. the thanksgiving is genuine Pauline material (written by an amanuensis?); the apparent confusion derives from our lack of understanding of the grammatical conventions.
3. the thanksgiving is a collapsing of two previously independent Pauline fragments.[16]

confusion. E. F. Scott (*The Pastoral Epistles*, The Moffatt New Testament Commentary Series [London: Hodder & Stoughton, 1936], p. 88), for example, simply observes that "the sentence is never properly finished, and runs off into a digression."

[11] J. Chrysostom (*Homilies on the Epistles of St. Paul to Timothy, Titus and Philemon*, ET by J. Tweed [Oxford: J. H. Parker, 1843], p. 168) takes ὡς to mean ὅτι (cf. the Vulgate, AV), but this results in the rather strange idea that Paul's thanksgiving is due to his repeated prayers for Timothy. J. Calvin (*Commentary on the Epistles to Timothy and Titus*, ed. D. Torrance and T. Torrance [Edinburgh: Oliver & Boyd, 1964], p. 290) gives the conjunction a temporal meaning: "as often as I remember you in my prayers, as I do continually, I give thanks" (cf. RSV). But there is no evidence that ὡς ever follows χάριν ἔχω in this way.

[12] C. K. Barrett (*The Pastoral Epistles*, p. 92) opts for the latter.

[13] J. N. D. Kelly (*The Pastoral Epistles*, p. 156), for example, attributes the break in thought to "Paul's pent-up affection." R. Parry (*The Pastoral Epistles* [Cambridge: University Press, 1920], p. 48) suggests that the odd construction is due to Paul's anxiety and haste.

[14] L. Houlden, *The Pastoral Epistles* (Harmondsworth: Penguin, 1976), p. 108.

[15] For example, Holtzmann, *Die Pastoralbriefe*, pp. 111f.

[16] F. Hesse (*Die Entstehung der neutestamentlichen Hirtenbriefe* [Halle: C. A. Kaemmerer, 1889], pp. 175ff.) argues that two Pauline letters are combined

The peculiarity of the thanksgiving makes it hard to assess questions pertaining to its origin. Perhaps it is enough simply to highlight this unit as problematic by any reading of the letters.

1:6–14 Miscellaneous admonitions to hold to the traditions

This section is loosely held together by its emphasis on the need to persevere and hold fast to the traditions. Traces of genuine Pauline instructions to Timothy may be incorporated here, but in its present form the unity of the text is suspect on several grounds: the miscellaneous and disjointed nature of the materials (see below); the sudden changes in literary style (cf. 1:9–10); the inclusion of materials unmotivated by, and unrelated to, the context (see 1:9, πρὸ χρόνων αἰωνίων).

C. K. Barrett suggests that it is necessary to segment the section in order to follow its logic:

> it is difficult to summarize this section under a title, for the writer passes from Paul to Timothy, and from summaries of the Gospel and its gifts to claims laid by the Gospel upon those who believe, and especially upon ministers. It must be followed from point to point.[17]

The wisdom of Barrett's advice becomes evident to anyone who attempts an outline of this material. One looks in vain for any sustained development of thought; the material is constantly disrupted by changing subject matter, variations in literary style, and the presence of seemingly unnecessary expressions. In short, it reads poorly as a literary unit.

The composite nature of the material is once again apparent. Traditional Pauline teaching has been combined with a number of community materials, including a traditional saying (1:7), a creedal/hymnic fragment (1:9–10), and three sayings on guarding the "good deposit" and keeping the sound words (1:12–14).

1:6 Admonition to an ordinand

The phrase "for this cause" (δι᾽ ἥν αἰτίαν) is commonly taken as a

within II Timothy, and that II 1:3–5 is a composite block of two sayings that were wrongly put together by an editor: (1) I 1:3a, 5; and (2) I 3b, 4.

[17] Barrett, *The Pastoral Epistles*, p. 93.

connecting phrase, linking the thought of 1:6ff. with that of the preceding thanksgiving. But the admonition given here does not readily follow from what is said in 1:3–5: there Timothy's heritage is extolled; here the topic is ordination. It appears that the link between the two sections may owe more to word association than to logic: compare ἀναμιμνῄσκω (1:6 or the variant ὑπομιμνῄσκω?) and ὑπόμνησις (1:5).

If this be so, the function of the phrase δι' ἥν αἰτίαν must be reevaluated. Rather than serving as a logical connecting link between 1:5 and 1:6, the phrase may serve here to introduce traditional materials that have been collected from various sources; this conjecture gains credibility when it is observed that the same phrase introduces a catena of three citations in Heb. 2:11 (Ps. 22:2; Isa. 8:17; Isa. 8:18), while in Titus 1:13 it appears in close association with the citation about "all Cretans" (1:12). It may also be functioning to introduce traditional materials in II Tim. 1:12 (see below).

The contrast between the picture of ordination portrayed here and that which appears in I 4:14 poses problems that cannot be easily dismissed; here the rite seems to be the responsibility of one man, but in I 4:14 the "laying on of hands" is clearly an act of the presbytery. P. Trummer thinks the tension arises from

> the intermingling of two conceptions of ordination: the probable contemporary practice of the author in I Tim 4:14, and the back-dating to the supposed historical ordination of Timothy by Paul in 2 Tim 1:6.[18]

Although Trummer recognizes the tension, his solution is less than convincing; it is hard to see why a pseudonymous author would mix two concepts of ordination in this way. It seems more likely that the differences between the two passages stem from the composite nature of the Pastorals, and the fact that two distinct sources have been taken up and incorporated into the Pastoral corpus.

The admonition cited in 1:6 may derive from a traditional

---

[18] P. Trummer, *Die Paulustradition der Pastoralbriefe* (Frankfurt: P. Lang, 1978), p. 77. D–C, *The Pastoral Epistles*, p. 71 suggests that the presbyterial emphasis in I 4:14 is due to the "congregational character" of I Timothy, while the personal touch in II 1:6 stems from the testamental character of II Timothy. Such an interpretation requires that the Pastorals be thought of as carefully designed, pseudepigraphical writings. Evidence of careful design, however, is precisely what the Pastorals lack.

account of Timothy's commissioning by the hands of Paul. The account is reminiscent of Joshua's commissioning by Moses (Num. 27:18–20):

> And the Lord said to Moses, "Take Joshua the son of Nun, and lay your hands upon him; cause him to stand before Eleazar the priest and all the congregation, and you shall commission him in their sight. You shall invest him with some of your authority.

1:7 Proverbial saying

The conjunction γάρ loosely links 1:7 to 1:6. The connection is disrupted, however, by a number of seemingly unmotivated changes in the mode of address: the personal admonition in 1:6 takes on a generalized, almost proverbial, character; the three present-tense verbs (ἀναμιμνήσκω, ἀναζωπυρεῖν, ἐστίν 1:6) give way to an aorist (ἔδωκεν, 1:7); and the second-person singular pronoun becomes a first-person plural.

E. K. Simpson attributes this oddity to "the apostle's penchant for generalizations,"[19] but this does not adequately explain the sudden change in thought or the non-Pauline language (πνεῦμα δειλίας ... δυνάμεως ... ἀγάπης ... σωφρονισμοῦ).[20]

It seems more likely that γάρ is serving here as an introductory conjunction, signaling the inclusion of a traditional saying. That γάρ can function in this manner is evident from its use elsewhere; in Rom. 10:13, for example, it introduces a verbatim citation from Joel 3:2 (LXX). In Rom. 13:9 it signals a citation from Deut. 5:17–21 (LXX).[21]

The traditional piece cited here carries the ring of a wisdom saying. For the sense, compare Sirach 34:14: "He who fears the Lord will not be timid, nor play the coward (δειλιάω), for he is his hope."

---

[19] E. K. Simpson, *The Pastoral Epistles* (London: Tyndale Press, 1954), p. 123.

[20] The differences in language also count against Holtzmann's suggestion (*Die Pastoralbriefe*, p. 112) that we have before us an "obvious modification of Rom. 8, 15."

[21] See also OT citations introduced by γάρ at I Cor. 2:16 (Isa. 40:13); 10:26 (Ps. 24:1), 15:27 (Ps. 8:7). Cf. I Tim. 6:7, 10; Poly Phil. 7:1 (I John 4:2–3). See the discussion by E. E. Ellis, "Traditions in the Pastoral Epistles," in *Early Jewish and Christian Exegesis: Studies in Memory of William Hugh Brownlee*, ed. Craig Evans and W. Stinespring (Atlanta: Scholars Press, 1987), p. 246, nn. 54–55.

1:8 Traditional admonition

The opening phrase echoes the concern of Rom. 1:16, but the verbal dissimilarities (τὸ εὐαγγέλιον, Rom. 1:16; τὸ μαρτύριον here) argue against literary dependence. This admonition may be a genuine piece of Pauline teaching that was incorporated at an early stage into this traditional material on perseverance and holding fast to the traditions.

1:9–10 Creedal/hymnic fragment

Here the style of the writing suddenly changes; the admonition of 1:8 gives way to a flowing, hymn-like passage. The rhythm and balance of these verses, as well as the fact that they contain elements unnecessary to the context, indicate that preformulated materials have been employed.[22] Although commentators are divided as to the classification of this material,[23] most believe that these verses constitute a preformed fragment of some kind.[24]

The use of ἐπιφάνεια is striking here as it seems to contrast with the meaning of the word used elsewhere in the Pastorals. In all of the other NT occurrences (I 6:14; II 4:1, 8; II Thess. 2:8) the word refers to Jesus' apocalyptic return, but here it clearly signifies his incarnation.[25] It seems unlikely that the same writer would use a significant technical term in such contrasting ways without any mention of the fact. This may be another indication that the material has been taken from a different source.

1:11 Apostolic authorization

B. S. Easton notes that for the historical Timothy "no assertion

---

[22] See the discussion on the formulaic characteristics of this fragment in E. Norden, *Agnostos Theos* (Berlin/Leipzig: Teubner, 1913), pp. 201ff., 381.

[23] On the problem of categorizing this fragment, see E. Norden, *Die antike Kunstprosa* (2 vols., Stuttgart: Teubner, 1958 [1909]), Vol. II, pp. 852ff.

[24] Compare, for example, the following suggestions: a eucharistic prayer (A. T. Hanson, *The Pastoral Epistles*, The New Century Bible Commentary [Grand Rapids, MI: Eerdmans, 1982], p. 122); a Christian hymn (Easton, *The Pastoral Epistles*, p. 40); a confession of faith (Dornier, *Les Epîtres Pastorales*, p. 189); a baptismal confession (F. Gealy, *The First and Second Epistles to Timothy and the Epistle to Titus*, The Interpreter's Bible, Vol. XI [New York: Abingdon Press, 1955], p. 467); a kerygmatic formula (D–C, *The Pastoral Epistles*, p. 99).

[25] The verb ἐπιφαίνω appears with a similar meaning at Titus 3:4, but there it is the "goodness and loving kindness" of the Lord that is said to appear.

could be more superfluous" than this autobiographical comment.[26] For the reasons discussed above (see chapter 3, p. 69 above) the saying cannot be regarded as a genuine Pauline remark; it seems to be functioning, however (both at I 2:7 and here), as a literary device, signaling the validity of traditional materials. In both contexts the expression follows a creedal fragment.

1:12a A literary signal

The formulaic phrase δι' ἥν αἰτίαν (see 1:6) may be functioning here to "bracket" the traditional materials collected within the section (1:6–1:11), or (and this appears more likely) it may be introducing the cluster of sayings which follow, all loosely tied to the theme of perseverance and fidelity to the "deposit."[27]

1:12b–14 A confessional statement and two admonitions

These three verses have only a superficial connection to one another; they all refer in some way to the "deposit" (1:12, 14) or the need to hold to the "sound words" (1:13), but when they are examined more closely it becomes clear that in substance they have little in common.

Perhaps the most significant indication of this is the different meaning of the term παραθήκη in 1:12 and 1:14. Because most commentators assume the integrity of this passage, they think it necessary to harmonize the meaning of παραθήκη in II 1:12 with its other occurrences in the Pastorals (II 1:14 and I 6:20, where it plainly means the "sound words" given to Timothy to preach). Such harmonization is useful, for it avoids the difficulty of the same word being used by the same author in the same passage to mean two quite different things.[28] But the natural reading of 1:12 and 1:14 does not seem to allow such an interpretation.[29] In 1:12 we

---

[26] Easton, *The Pastoral Epistles*, p. 44.

[27] It is striking that the phrase both here and in Hebrews is closely associated with the ideas of suffering (see πάθημα, Heb. 2:10), shame (ἐπαισχύνομαι, Heb. 2:11), and trust (πείθω, Heb. 2:13).

[28] See, for examples, the remarks of C. Spicq (*St. Paul: Les Epîtres Pastorales*, Etudes Bibliques [Paris: Gabalda, 1969], p. 720): "It is indeed difficult to think that an expression as technical and as exceptional in the New Testament as that of *guarding the παραθήκη* should change its signification at a distance of two verses."

[29] N. J. D. White (*The First and Second Epistles to Timothy, the Epistles to Titus*, The Expositor's Greek Testament [London: Hodder & Stoughton, 1910], p. 158)

have a confessional statement affirming that God will guard the παραθήκη (one's life?) entrusted to him.[30] In 1:14 the term appears in a catechetical-like admonition and refers to the "deposit of the faith" entrusted to someone.

It seems better to accept that an inherent tension exists between these two texts, and to attribute the differences in meaning to the fact that the passages probably originated within different contexts; in all likelihood, they were gathered together because of their mutual reference to the παραθήκη.[31]

1:15–18 Personalia

The shift from the catechetical-like admonition in 1:14 to this autobiographical section is sudden and unexpected; there is nothing in the immediate context that can be said to prompt the reference to apostasy (1:15) or the remarks about Onesiphorus (1:16–18).[32] C. K. Barrett calls the passage a "digression," while J. Moffatt regards it as an "erratic boulder" in its present setting.[33] The unit as a whole parts easily from its context, both in content and in form. The particularity of the section (with its references to

---

notes that "nothing but a desire to give παραθήκη the same meaning wherever it occurs ... could have made Chrys. explain it here as 'the faith, the preaching of the Gospel.'"

[30] So the AV, JB translations. The parallel with II Maccabees 3:10ff. gives the literal context to the metaphorical use of the term in II 1:12. Referring to the widow's and orphan's deposit left in the temple, the text reads: "The priests prostrated themselves ... and called toward heaven upon him who had given the law about deposits (παρακαταθήκη), that he should keep them safe (διαφυλάσσω) for those who had deposited them" (II Macc. 3:15).

[31] R. Falconer (*The Pastoral Epistles* [Oxford: Clarendon Press, 1937], p. 78) thinks that the different use of παραθήκη in 1:14 and the break in the connection between 1:12 and 1:14 "point to a later editorial insertion by the same hand as in I Tim. i.18, 19, vi. 20, 21."

[32] Typical of attempts to show the relevance of this section in its present context is J. N. D. Kelly's suggestion (*The Pastoral Epistles*, p. 168) that Paul's references to Phygelos and Hermogenes (1:15) are intended as "warning examples" to Timothy, while his description of Onesiphorus is meant as a "comfort example." N. Brox ("Zu den persönlichen Notizen der Pastoralbriefe," *BZ* 13 [1969], 83), arguing a slightly different line (and assuming a pseudonymous author) writes: "the whole passage [1:15–18] is formed precisely to provide an illustration of the warning in 1, 8, which is characteristic of the contents and intentions in 2 Tim. 'Do not be ashamed of the witness of our Lord, nor of me his prisoner.'" Such suggestions seem to attribute far too much subtlety to the author of the Pastorals.

[33] Barrett, *The Pastoral Epistles*, p. 100; Moffatt, *Introduction*, p. 403.

individuals) contrasts with the general parenetic nature of the materials that precede and follow (1:12–14; 2:1ff.).

All of these features suggest the likelihood that this material did not originate within the present context; but there is no compelling reason to deny its authenticity. P. N. Harrison argues persuasively for the genuineness of 1:16–18, but his exclusion of 1:15 is less compelling.[34] The whole block of personalia distinctively protrudes within its context (as elsewhere in the Pastorals) and must be recognized as a unit.

2:1–13 Collection of personal admonitions

The miscellaneous character of this section can scarcely be overlooked. C. K. Barrett simply observes that the material "spreads diffusely."[35] The unit comprises several diverse elements, including a collection of proverbial admonitions on discipline (2:3–7), a creedal fragment (2:8), an autobiographical unit (2:9–10), and another creedal fragment (2:11–13).

The composite character of this section is suggested not only by the abrupt changes in subject matter, but also by the various formulaic markers that appear (see below).

2:1–2 Personal admonitions

Commentators have put forward many suggestions as to how 2:1 (cf. οὖν) links with the material which precedes, but the sheer diversity of their proposals reflects the obscurity of the connection.[36] It seems better to take the particle οὖν as a part of the formulaic expression Σὺ οὖν, τέκνον μου and regard it as an introductory marker of traditional materials. We have already observed

---

[34] P. N. Harrison, *The Problem of the Pastoral Epistles* (London: Oxford University Press, 1921), p. 125. Harrison apparently excludes 1:15 because the reference to Asia seems to fit poorly with the clearly Roman context of 1:16–18. But this assumes the unity of the fragment! Perhaps 1:15–18 is a collection of two formerly independent Pauline notes.

[35] Barrett, *The Pastoral Epistles*, p. 100.

[36] So, for example, C. J. Ellicott (*An Official Critical and Grammatical Commentary on the Pastoral Epistles* [London: J. Parker and Son, 1856], p. 113) thinks that the reference is to 1:15; B. S. Easton (*The Pastoral Epistles*, p. 46) prefers 1:16–18; R. Falconer (*The Pastoral Epistles*, p. 80) suggests that 2:1 resumes the thought of 1:6–7; while W. Lock (*The Pastoral Epistles* [Edinburgh: T. & T. Clark, 1924], p. 93) thinks that it takes up the concern of 1:14.

how the phrase σὺ δέ can function in this way (see I 6:11; Titus 2:1), and σὺ οὖν seems to be a variation of this formula.

The appearance of the formulaic τέκνον μου lends support to this interpretation.[37] This phrase appears as an introductory marker of traditional materials within both Jewish and early Christian literature.[38] Its formulaic character is especially evident from its use in the Didache, where it serves to introduce traditional proverbial admonitions:

> 3:1 My child, flee from every evil man.
> 3:3 My child, be not lustful.
> 3:4 My child, regard not omens.
> 3:5 My child, be not a liar.
> 3:6 My child, be not a grumbler.

These parallels suggest that the phrase σὺ οὖν, τέκνον μου (in II 2:1) may not be intended to develop the thought of 1:16–18, or to serve as an endearment from Paul to Timothy; rather, the phrase may be functioning as a formulaic marker of traditional materials.

The traditional character of what follows seems to confirm this view. Ancient teaching is incorporated at II 2:1–2 on the importance of preserving the community's traditions (παρατίθημι, cf. I 1:18). Similar admonitions are frequent within Jewish testamental literature:

> καὶ ἃ ἠκούσατε παρὰ τοῦ πατρὸς ὑμῶν,
> μετάδοτε καὶ ὑμεῖς τοῖς τέκνοις ὑμῶν.
>
> (*T. Dan.* 6:9)[39]

In light of this, it seems best to take the opening phrase of 2:1 as an introductory marker of the whole collection of traditional teachings which follow.

2:3–6 Proverbial admonitions

Three proverbial sayings (on soldiers, 2:4; on athletes, 2:5; on farmers, 2:6) have been strung together following the opening admonition: "suffer as a good soldier" (2:3a). The loose connection

---

[37] See the discussion in Norden, *Agnostos Theos*, pp. 290f.

[38] The term τέκνον appears frequently within the book of Sirach: cf. 2:1; 3:1 (plural); 3:12; 3:17; 4:1; 6:18; 6:23 and *passim*.

[39] Compare also T. Sim. 7:3; T. Lev. 4:5; 10:1.

among the sayings,[40] and their lack of any specifically Christian content, suggests that they were not written ad hoc but have been taken over from another source.[41] This is also indicated by the distinct vocabulary within this section.[42]

The commonplace character of these sayings makes it risky to assert with A. T. Hanson that the author of this section "has in mind a number of passages from I C. 9."[43] All three images (soldier, athlete, farmer) are commonly utilized metaphors within ancient literature.[44] R. Bultmann has shown how Greek rhetoricians enjoyed piling up such metaphors.[45] It is quite possible that these proverbial sayings were taken over as a unit from a pre-Christian source and inserted here. The fixed character of such proverbs would account for their less than perfect parallelism within II Timothy.[46] And it would make sense of the scribal gloss in 2:4, where the phrase τῷ θεῷ has been added following στρατευόμενος.[47] The gloss appears to be an attempt to make the proverbial saying more suitable to its present religious context.

2.7 Literary marker

The proverbial material is followed by the puzzling clause: νόει ὅ λέγω J. N. D. Kelly calls the verse "almost a parenthesis," and its

---

[40] L. Donelson (*Pseudepigraphy and Ethical Argument in the Pastoral Epistles* [Tübingen: J. C. B. Mohr (Paul Siebeck), 1986], p. 89) struggles to find the continuity within this section. Using the categories defined in Aristotle's *Art of Rhetoric*, Donelson argues that the three proverbial sayings of II 2:3–6 are functioning as the logical premises to the three imperatives in 2:1–2. He is forced to admit, however, that "there is no apparent direct correspondence between the three imperatives and the three maxims ... the logic becomes very general and perhaps not all that easy for the reader to supply."

[41] So N. Brox, *Die Pastoralbriefe*, p. 241.

[42] Eleven words appear that occur nowhere else in Paul's letters: συγκακοπαθέω, πραγματεία, στρατολογέω, ἀθλέω, νομίμως, στρατιώτης, ἐμπλέκομαι, βίος, στεφανόω, γεωργός, μεταλαμβάνω.

[43] Hanson, *The Pastoral Epistles*, p. 128. The parallels in I Cor. 9 (cf. 9:7a, 9:7b; 9:24–27) are not close enough to show the kind of dependency that Hanson suggests.

[44] See, for example: on soldiers, Epict., *Diss.* I.14.15; on athletes, Philo, *Abr.* 35, *Quod omn. prob.* 26.110; Epict., *Diss.* III.10, III.15.2f., IV Macc. 6:10; 16:16; 17:15ff.; on farmers, Deut. 20:6; Prov. 27:18; Sir. 6:19.

[45] R. Bultmann, *Der Stil der Paulinischen Predigt und kynisch-stoische Diatribe* (Göttingen: Vandenhoeck & Ruprecht, 1910), pp. 38f.

[46] The concern for the personal reward due the farmer, for example, does not strictly parallel the point of the other two proverbs. On this point, see F. Gealy's observations, *The First and Second Epistles to Timothy and the Epistle to Titus*, The Interpreter's Bible, Vol. XI (New York: Abingdon Press, 1955), pp. 480f.

[47] τῷ θεῷ appears in F, G, the old Latin MSS, the Vulgate (corrected), Cyprian, Ambrosiaster.

function here is not easy to determine.[48] R. Harris's theory that the phrase is a citation from the Greek poet Pindar lacks supportive evidence, but the fact that Pindar employs the same expression within a poetic work indicates that it may carry a formulaic sense.[49]

The expression here may be serving to signal the end of the preceding collection of traditional materials (2:3–6). Could it be functioning in a formal way like the Hebrew *selah*? W. Lock compares it to the Latin tag *verbum sapienti*.[50]

The clause that follows has a proverbial ring similar to that of Prov. 2:6: "For the Lord gives wisdom; from his mouth come knowledge and understanding (σύνεσις)." The traditional character of the saying here may be signaled by the presence of the introductory γάρ.

2:8 Creedal fragment

An unexpected summary of the gospel follows, unprompted by the immediate context. The balanced rhythmic style has a liturgical quality:

> μνημόνευε 'Ιησοῦν Χριστὸν
> ἐγηγερμένον ἐκ νεκρῶν,
> ἐκ σπέρματος Δαυίδ.

Other features also suggest that this is a creedal or hymnic fragment that has been taken over from another source; the order of the name "Jesus Christ" is very rare, if not unprecedented, in II Timothy. The Nestle–Aland text (26th ed.) accepts the order "Jesus Christ" only at 2:8.[51] The reference to the seed of David seems irrelevant to the present context; the closest parallel to this phrase comes from another creedal fragment that appears in Rom. 1:3f.[52]

2:9–10 Autobiographical material

The creedal fragment is linked directly to an autobiographical unit

48 Kelly, *The Pastoral Epistles*, p. 176.
49 R. Harris, "Pindar and St. Paul," *Exp. T.* 33 (1921–1922), 456f.
50 Lock, *The Pastoral Epistles*, p. 94.
51 Compare the following instances of the name: 1:1 (twice), 1:2, 1:9, 1:10, 1:13; 2:1, 2:3, 2:10; 3:12, 3:15; 4:1, and 4:22 (v. l.). Textual variants appear at 1:2 and 1:10.
52 Both ideas (Jesus' resurrection and his royal lineage) are also present in the Romans creed, but in reverse order. See C. H. Dodd, *The Epistle of Paul to the Romans* (London: Hodder & Stoughton, 1932), pp. 4–5. Compare also Ign. Smyr. 1:1; Ign. Eph. 18:2; Ign. Trall. 9:1.

that may include genuine Pauline traditions. A similar creedal fragment follows the genuine material in I Tim. 3:14–16. The whole block of material (2:8–10) may have come to the editor as a single piece and was inserted here because of the reference to suffering in 2:9 (κακοπαθέω, cf. 2:3, συγκακοπαθέω; 2:11, συναποθνήσκω).

2:11–13 Creedal hymnic fragment

The intended subject of this "faithful word" formula (πιστὸς ὁ λόγος) is disputed. Those who think that the formula always refers to a soteriological saying find the faithful word in 2:10.[53] B. Weiss suggests that it refers back to 2:8–9, while N. White regards the expression as a confirmation of 2:4–11.[54] Others argue that the formula points to the verses that follow (2:11–13).[55]

The view taken here is that the formula simply marks the introduction, or the conclusion, of a collection of traditional materials. The autobiographical unit of 2:8–10 clearly gives way to a different source in 2:11; the singular pronoun (μου, 2:8) and the singular verbs (κακοπαθῶ, 2:9; ὑπομένω, 2:10) suddenly become plural; the symmetry and rhythmic balance of 2:11–13 is unmistakable and differs considerably in style from that which precedes or follows.[56]

Commentators have had difficulty in accounting for the γάρ at the beginning of this fragment (2:11; cf. I 4:9). Some argue that its occurrence here counts against the view that 2:11–13 is a fragment from a hymn or a creed.[57] Others think that the conjunction may have been part of the original fragment that was taken over.[58]

In light of the function of γάρ elsewhere in the Pastorals (cf. I

---

53 See, for example, A. Schlatter, *Die Kirche der Griechen im Urteil des Paulus* (Stuttgart: Calwer Vereinsbuchhandlung, 1936), p. 236. So also W. Nauck, "Die Herkunft des Verfassers der Pastoralbriefe," Th.D. thesis, Göttingen, 1950, pp. 49f. Nauck thinks that the "faithful word" expression is not a citation formula but a confirming word.

54 B. Weiss, *Die Briefe Pauli an Timotheus und Titus* (Göttingen: Vandenhoeck & Ruprecht, 1903), pp. 270f.; N. J. D. White, *The Epistles to Timothy and Titus*, p. 163: "The teaching or saying referred to is 'the word of the cross' as set forth by simile and living example in the preceding verses, 4–11."

55 So, for example, D–C, *The Pastoral Epistles*, p. 109; Barrett, *The Pastoral Epistles*, p. 104. Also, G. W. Knight, *The Faithful Sayings in the Pastoral Letters* (Grand Rapids, MI: Baker, 1979), pp. 112f.

56 The text as printed in Nestle–Aland (26th ed.) clearly reveals this symmetry.

57 So, for example, Ellicott, *Grammatical Commentary on the Pastorals*, p. 120.

58 See Bernard, *The Pastoral Epistles*, p. 120; Scott, *The Pastoral Epistles*, p. 105.

6:7, 10), it seems better to understand it here as a literary device, serving to introduce the cited fragment that follows it.

2:14–26 Polemical admonitions

Once again, a formulaic expression (ταῦτα ὑπομίμνῃσκε, διαμαρτυρόμενος ἐνώπιον τοῦ θεοῦ) introduces an abrupt change in subject matter as well as literary style (cf. I 6:21). C. K. Barrett remarks that "the connexion with the preceding paragraph is indeed not close."[59] Not only is there no clear connection to what precedes, but the logical progression within the passage itself is difficult to follow. This lack of internal cohesion is best attributed to the previously independent character of the materials; a concern over apostasy appears to be the thread that loosely holds these polemical admonitions and proverbial expressions together.

The language throughout is alien both to Paul's other letters and to the NT as a whole; sixteen words do not appear in the other Paulines, and five of these are NT *hapax legomena*.[60]

2:14a Literary signal

The formulaic usage of ταῦτα has been noted several times (see especially I 4:6, 11); here it occurs at the close of a traditional citation (2:11–13), and seems to mark off once again the beginning of a new unit of material.

The expression διαμαρτυρόμενος ἐνώπιον τοῦ θεοῦ is closely linked (as in I 5:21) to the formulaic ταῦτα.[61] Here also the adjuration serves to mark off distinct collections of traditional materials.[62]

The variant readings for θεοῦ in 2:14 seem to be motivated by the desire to adapt fixed (and pre-Christian?) expressions to their new setting within the Christian community. Instead of the reading printed in our text ("charge them before God," 2:14), some MSS

---

[59] Barrett, *The Pastoral Epistles*, p. 105.

[60] The NT *hapax legomena* are: λογομαχέω, χρήσιμος, ἀνεπαίσχυντος, ὀρθοτομέω, γάγγραινα; the other non-Pauline words include: ὑπομιμνήσκω, καταστροφή, βέβηλος, κενοφωνία, περιίστημι, νομή, ἀστοχέω, ἀνατρέπω, μέντοι, στερεός, χρυσοῦς, ἀργυροῦς, ξύλινος, δεσπότης.

[61] The expression in II 2:14, unlike I 5:21 and II 4:1, lacks any reference to Christ. This may reflect an earlier pre-Christian form of the saying; perhaps the literary device as taken over from Judaism (as the OT parallels suggest: cf. Deut. 31:28; 32:46). W. Nauck ("Die Herkunft," pp. 41f.) notes that μαρτυρέω is never constructed with ἐνώπιον in secular literature.

[62] See the discussion on pp. 85–86 above.

read "... before the Lord," while a few late MSS read "... before Christ."[63]

The Nestle–Aland text takes 2:14b as the continuation of 2:14a: "... charge [them] before the Lord to avoid disputing about words"; but on the basis of the parallel in II Tim. 4:1 it seems more likely that a colon should be supplied after θεοῦ, and an independent clause begun, either with μὴ λογομαχεῖν (taking it as an imperatival infinitive, cf. Luke 9:23, Rom. 12:15, Phil. 3:16) or with the variant μὴ λογομάχει.[64] The resulting translation seems to clarify the "list" quality of the admonitions and sayings that follow: "remind [them] of these things, charging [them] before God: stop disputing about words ... etc."[65]

2:14b Admonition on word disputes

The first admonition in this cluster concerns disputes about words. The verb λογομαχέω occurs only here within the NT, but the noun form (λογομαχία) appears, significantly, in the middle of a similar block of polemical admonitions at I Tim. 6:4.[66]

2:15 Wisdom saying on the approved workman

It is not easy to find a logical connection that ties this proverbial saying either to that which precedes or that which follows.[67] R. Falconer's conclusion that 2:15 is "probably displaced" reflects his despair of finding any thread of continuity within these three verses.[68] His conjecture gains force if one assumes that a single

---

63 The variant "Lord" appears, for example, in A, D, Ψ, 048, and the majority text; a few minuscules read "Christ."

64 H. J. Holtzmann (*Die Pastoralbriefe*, p. 415) cites Hoffmann and Ewald as two who take μὴ λογομαχεῖν here as an imperatival infinitive. The reading λογομάχει appears in A, C (uncorrected), 048, 1175, and a few minuscules.

65 It is true that this reading causes a somewhat awkward asyndeton, but the style here is not smooth by any reading.

66 See the discussion on I 6:2b–5 on pp. 89–90 above, and note the formulaic ταῦτα δίδασκε καὶ παρακάλει.

67 R. Karris (*The Pastoral Epistles* [Wilmington, DE: Michael Glazier, 1979], p. 225) notes the apparent lack of consecutive thought in this section but tries to minimize it by suggesting that "the author thinks by means of contrasts." The difficulty with this solution is that the intended contrast between 2:15 and 2:14 is not at all clear.

68 Falconer, *The Pastoral Epistles*, p. 84. Falconer sees serious literary problems throughout the whole of 2:14–3:17.

author is at work here; under such an assumption, it is difficult to account for the logical discontinuity. But if the materials have been collected from disparate sources, the difficulties are greatly lessened. The proverb of 2:15 may not fit precisely with the sayings and citations around it, but such lack of continuity is not surprising given the preformed nature of the materials.

This helps explain why the Pastorals sometimes read like a hellenistic moral handbook;[69] useful bits of advice and wisdom have been collected and put together, but it is a matter of secondary interest how well the materials cohere with one another.

It is probably not coincidental that the only other known occurrences of the word ὀρθοτομέω are to be found within wisdom sayings from the book of Proverbs (3:6; 11:5). The expression here at 2:15 is proverbial, and incorporates ideas well known to us from Jewish writings. In the *T. Joseph* (2:7), for example, Joseph tells of being tested and approved (δόκιμος) by God. The figurative sense of ἐργάτης as a workman for God appears in the *T. Benj.* (11:1, ἐργάτης κυρίου).

It may be that the proverb in II 2:15 has been taken over from Jewish circles; there is nothing specifically Christian about it.

2:16–17a Admonition on profane babblings

The subject returns abruptly to the matter of empty words and profane babblings; the fixed character of the expression τὰς δὲ βεβήλους κενοφωνίας is apparent from its previous occurrence in I 6:20. The verb περιΐστημι occurs again at Titus 3:9 in a similarly polemical context.

The stock character of the admonition is clear from the many parallels that have been adduced.[70] The passage, in R. Karris's words, has the character of a form-letter, the general contents of which can easily be shifted from one context to another.[71]

---

[69] Compare, for example, the collection of gnomic wisdom and advice in the *Enchiridion* of Epictetus (Epictetus, ET by W. A. Oldfather, LCL [London: W. Heinemann, 1928], Vol. II, pp. 483ff.); see also a compilation of 451 ethical and religious aphorisms in the *Sentence of Sextus*, ET by H. Chadwick (Cambridge: University Press, 1959).

[70] A similar thought is preserved, for example, in Epictetus (*Discourses* II.17.8): ἢ κενῶς τὰς φωνὰς ταύτας ἀπηχοῦμεν. Compare R. Karris's charts showing the various polemical *topoi* with examples from Greek literature in "The Function and Sitz im Leben of the Paraenetic Elements in the Pastoral Letters," unpublished Ph.D. thesis, Harvard, 1971, pp. 21, 44.

[71] R. Karris, "The Background and Significance of the Polemic of the Pastoral Epistles," *JBL* 92 (1973), 555.

2:17b–18 Personalia

The sudden reference to specific individuals and their heresy is puzzling; it seems an odd intrusion into this cluster of otherwise general and commonplace admonitions. Perhaps it was coupled to the preceding admonition when the editor of the Pastorals incorporated it; but the reappearance of the phrase ὧν ἐστιν to introduce the personalia raises doubts, for it is the same expression that introduces the mention of Hymenaeus and Alexander in I Tim. 1:20, and Phygelus and Hermogenes in II Tim. 1:15. In each of these passages, the reference to specific individuals seems detached from its context.

W. Lock may be right when he suggests that the personalia here and at I Tim. 1:20 are editorial interpolations;[72] however, it may be that these references are genuine, and the materials surrounding them have been tagged on at a later date. In any case, it appears that the polemic and the personalia were not originally connected; when the personalia are removed, the general polemical character of the cluster is preserved.

2:19 Midrashic-like exposition (on election and apostasy)

The preformed character of this text is apparent from the difficulties that arise when an attempt is made to interpret its meaning; commentators are not sure what the saying means, or what its immediate connection to the context is. Considerable obscurity surrounds the meaning of the terms θεμέλιος and σφραγίς.[73] N. White observes that the metaphor seems confused.[74] But the confusion is not easily ascribed to the work of an author; one would expect an author to clarify his meaning. It seems likely that the difficulties here stem from the fact that language from another context has been incorporated.[75]

[72] See his remarks in *The Pastoral Epistles*, pp. xxxi, 99. Lock thinks that the interpolations were designed to give "an illustration from [the editor's] own time."

[73] The meaning of θεμέλιος is disputed; does it, for example, refer to the facts of Christian belief (Parry), or to the church (Scott), or to faith (Dornier), or to God's election (Calvin), or to Christ himself (A. T. Hanson)? The meaning of σφραγίς varies according to how one interprets θεμέλιος.

[74] N. J. D. White, *The Epistles to Timothy and Titus*, p. 167. White attributes the confusion to "a condensation of expression."

[75] D–C (*The Pastoral Epistles*, p. 112) think that the author is quoting from early Christian poetry, and point to a parallel in the Odes of Solomon (8:14); A. T.

The unit itself is a small cluster of traditional sayings on election and apostasy. An opening saying introduces two quotations, both of which probably have their origin within Judaism (cf. Num. 16:5, 26; Isa. 26:13).

The unit may have been added to the larger cluster of materials (on apostasy) because of its reference to Numbers 16 and the story of Korah's rebellion.

2:20–21 A proverb on useful vessels

Without warning the metaphor suddenly switches to vessels of honor and dishonor, prompting C. K. Barrett to remark that its "connexion with the context is not so clear."[76] Again, the abrupt change in subject matter is probably not due to the whim of an author, but rather to the introduction of another preformed proverbial saying.

The preformed character of the saying is evident from the fact that its meaning does not really fit the tenor of the immediate context; instead of invective against those who have strayed from the truth, the proverb declares that all the "members" of a household are necessary, both the honorable and dishonorable. It is a point that must have been intended for a different purpose and context.[77]

The ambiguity of ταῦτα in verse 21 is again puzzling; does it refer to the false teachers, or their teachings, or did it have a different reference in its native context?

2:22 Admonition to flee vices and pursue virtues

The commentators note the difficulties in attributing this verse to Paul. C. F. D. Moule finds the verse particularly problematic in view of its portrayal of Timothy.[78] The warning to "flee youthful

---

Hanson ("The Apostates: II Timothy 2:19–21," in *Studies in the Pastoral Epistles*, pp. 34f.) thinks that 2:19 is an extract from a Christian baptismal source.

[76] Barrett, *The Pastoral Epistles*, 107.

[77] Compare, for example, the close parallel that appears in Wisdom 15:7: "For when a potter kneads the soft earth and laboriously moulds each vessel for our service, he fashions out of the same clay both the vessels that serve clean uses and those for contrary uses, making all in like manner." See also Rom. 9:21; I Cor. 3:12.

[78] C. F. D. Moule, "The Problem of the Pastoral Epistles: A Reappraisal," *BJRL* 3 (1965), 433f.

lusts" is hardly one that Timothy, who would be nearing forty at the end of Paul's life, would seem to require.

But the origin of this text is better sought by observing its formal characteristics. A parallel to this admonition has already been discussed at I 6:10; the same set expression (φεῦγε ... δίωκε) occurs there, and is followed (as here) by a virtue list. The same pattern appears in I Clem. 30:1 and II Clem. 10:1. These formal features suggest that this text was not written ad hoc, but was a preformed piece of floating proverbial wisdom.

2:23 Admonition against speculations

This stock denunciation of speculations makes a rough transition from the preceding admonition to "pursue righteousness ... with those who call upon the Lord from a pure heart."

The language of this text strangely parallels that of admonitions found elsewhere within the Pastorals. The verb παραιτέομαι, for example, appears at I Tim. 4:7 and at Titus 3:10, both within strongly polemical contexts. The three terms μωρός, μάχη, and ζήτησις are found linked together again in another admonition in Titus 3:9, while ζήτησις and λογομαχία occur within a cluster of polemical admonitions at I Tim. 6:4. Such similarities suggest that the polemical clusters that appear throughout the Pastorals have been drawn from the same treasury of stock terms of derision.

2:24–26 On the conduct of God's servant

This text seems to be linked to that which precedes by the catch-words μάχη (2:23) and μάχεσθαι (2:24). But the ideas presented here contrast with other admonitions that appear in this cluster of sayings. Here the tone is lenient and conciliatory; the emphasis is on patience; and the hope expressed is that God might grant repentance to the opponents, that they might come to their senses. Such sentiments are very distant from the harsh denunciations that have gone before (cf. II 2:14, 16). The earlier admonitions did not call for the "gentle instruction of the opponents," but for their exclusion from the community (2:21). The attitude also changes at the end of the following paragraph (3:5: "avoid such people!"). Such differences in temper seem to indicate the previously independent status of these various sayings.

3:1–5 Eschatological material

A traditional apocalyptic saying followed by an elaborate vice list is introduced by the imperatival phrase τοῦτο δὲ γίνωσκε, ὅτι.[79] A. T. Hanson thinks that the vice list (3:2–5) is modeled on Rom. 1:29–31, but the dissimilarities in vocabulary between these two passages make that most unlikely.[80] Eighteen words in this list are not found anywhere in Paul's writings, and seven of these are NT *hapax legomena*.[81]

The unit begins with the familiar apocalyptic expression ἐν ἐσχάταις ἡμέραις ἐνστήσονται καιροὶ χαλεποί; this traditional saying was attributed at an early date to the apostles (see Jude 18; II Pet. 3:3), but, in view of the many parallels from Jewish literature, it most probably derives from pre-Christian traditions.[82]

The well-attested variant reading γινώσκετε (3:1; note the plural!) may go back to the original form of the prophecy, when it was directed to a wider audience.[83] A later editor, thinking that a plural verb seemed odd within a personal letter to Timothy, might have effected the change to the singular.

The formulaic phrase καὶ τούτους ἀποτρέπου signals the close of one preformed unit (3:1–5a) and the beginning of another. The frequently appearing ταῦτα seems to be serving again to mark off traditional materials.[84]

---

[79] A similar expression, εἰδὼς τοῦτο, ὅτι, appears at I 1:9 (see above), where it introduces a lengthy vice list. In II Pet. 3:8ff. the imperatival phrase τοῦτο μὴ λανθανέτω ... ὅτι signals the beginning of what seems to be a preformed midrash. See also T. Issachar 6:1; T. Levi 4:1.

[80] Hanson, *The Pastoral Epistles* (1982), p. 144. Hanson makes the interesting conjecture that the vices listed here may have been "smartened up by the author's acquaintance with Philo" and compares Philo, *De fuga et inventione* 81. But this assumes that the editor of the Pastorals was also an author, and it is precisely the touch of an author that is missing throughout these letters.

[81] The *hapax legomena* include: φίλαυτος, ἄσπονδος, ἀκρατής, ἀνήμερος, ἀφιλά-γαθος, φιλήδονος, φιλόθεος, ἀποτρέπω. The other non-Pauline words are: φιλάργυρος, βλάσφημος, ἀχάριστος, ἀνόσιος, διάβολος, προδότης, προπετής, τυφόομαι, εὐσέβεια, ἀρνέομαι.

[82] See the discussion on pp. 78–79 above, and compare the following parallels: Jer. 22:20; Isa. 2:2. Also, from the Testament of the Twelve Patriarchs: T. Iss. 6:1; T. Jud. 18:1; T. Zeb. 8:2; T. Dan. 5:4; T. Jos. 19:10.

[83] The plural is read by codices A, F, G, 33, and a few other MSS.

[84] E. E. Ellis ("Tradition in the Pastoral Epistles," p. 243) regards this material as a "cited tradition" and suggests that the conclusion of the preformed material is signaled by the shift to an imperative (ἀποτρέπου) in 3:5c.

3:6–9 Polemic against false teachers

The change from the future tense in 3:1 to the present tense in 3:5b and 3:6 is problematic; if the text is assumed to be Pauline and read as a consecutive narrative, the implication must be that the vicious characters referred to in 3:1–5a are current church members![85] And those who argue for the pseudonymous authorship of this letter are obliged to suggest that in 3:6ff. the "Pastor" must be describing "conditions of his own day."[86] It seems more likely that the change in tense (and emphasis) has been caused by the introduction of a different source.

This unit consists of another string of general invectives against opponents; the denunciation is stinging, but the polemic is completely nameless; that is, the opponents are impossible to identify. Almost any false teacher could fit the stock criticisms.

A distinctive feature within this cluster of materials is the unusual prediction that it includes. The threat of the false teachers seems less than cataclysmic: "the opponents will not advance further" (οὐ προκόψουσιν ἐπὶ πλεῖον, 3:9). This hopeful prediction is in clear contrast to the prophecies about the false teachers that appear elsewhere in II Timothy: in 2:16, for example, it is said about those who indulge in profane chatter that "they will advance further" (ἐπὶ πλεῖον προκόψουσιν) and that "their word will spread like gangrene." And in 3:13 the prediction is that "evil men and sorcerers will advance from bad to worse" (προκόψουσιν ἐπὶ τὸ χεῖρον).

N. Brox recognizes the apparent contradiction, but thinks that it can be resolved by noting the distinction between a "warning" (or parenetic) statement (2:17, 3:13) and a polemical statement (3:9):

> Concerning the phenomenon of heresy, for example, he speaks differently depending on whether he is talking polemically or parenetically, just as he can also fictitiously set the whole issue of heresy in the future as a threat, or in the present as an evil.[87]

Brox's argument relies heavily upon nuance, and his suggestion

---

85 John Calvin (*Commentary on the Epistles to Timothy and Titus*, ed. D. Torrance and T. Torrance [Edinburgh: Oliver & Boyd, 1964], p. 323) notes this oddity: "it is surprising how men who have the great sins that Paul here mentions should be able to keep up an appearance of godliness, as he says they do."

86 So, for example, Easton, *The Pastoral Epistles*, p. 64.

87 Brox, *Die Pastoralbriefe*, p. 256.

that 2:17 and 3:13 are of a different literary character than 3:6 is open to serious doubt.[88]

But if it be accepted that this material is of a composite nature, the need to harmonize or explain away the tensions vanishes. Collections of preformed materials are naturally prone to such tensions.

3:10–13 Personal admonitions

There is no clear development of thought between 3:6–9 and the unit that follows (3:10–13).[89] The connection seems purely formal, resting upon the references in both passages to the "advance" (προκόπτω, 3:9, 13) of evil men.

The new unit is introduced by the formulaic marker of traditional materials σὺ δέ (see I 6:11; II 3:14; 4:5; Titus 2:1). A nine-member virtue list is linked to traditional references to Paul's sufferings in Asia Minor; two general sayings on persecution and the advance of evil men follow; the several pieces, then, that make up this cluster of traditions include:

3:10–11   Virtue list and autobiographical material
3:12   Saying on persecution
3:13   Apocalyptic saying.

In its present form, the unit contains five non-Pauline words, two of which are NT *hapax legomena*.[90]

Transitions within this unit are rough; the personal style of 3:11 is abruptly left off at 3:12, giving way to a general saying on the inevitability of suffering.[91] Perhaps the double mention of διωγμός

---

88   H.J. Holtzmann (*Die Pastoralbriefe*, p. 430), in a characteristically candid assessment, simply says "the contradiction with 2,17; 3,13 is clear and not to be disguised." He offers no solution. B.S. Easton (*The Pastoral Epistles*, p. 64), however, suggests that the statement in 3:13 arises from the Pastor's indignation that "makes him forget his apocalyptic role and predict improvement in place of decay."

89   Commentators have noted the peculiarity of all or part of 3:10–12. J. Moffatt (*An Introduction to the Literature of the New Testament*, revised 3rd ed. [Edinburgh: T. & T. Clark, 1920], p. 403) thinks that the unit sits as an "erratic boulder" in its present context. P.N. Harrison (*The Problem*, p. 124) notes the change in thought and language within this section, and concludes that 3:10–11 is an authentic Pauline note, probably written "on the eve of his martyrdom, or perhaps on the very day."

90   The *hapax legomena* are: ἀγωγή and γόης. The non-Pauline vocabulary includes: παρακολουθέω, εὐσεβῶς, χείρων.

91   H.J. Holtzmann (*Die Pastoralbriefe*, pp. 432f.) notes the oddity of this saying in the present context: "the whole verse is without the necessary context."

in 3:11a/c prompted an editor to tag on the traditional sayings that follow, the first of which involves the idea of persecution (διώκω, 3:12).[92]

3:14–17 Personal admonition (on loyalty to the tradition)

The thought of 3:13 is not developed; the subject returns, rather, to the need for faithfulness to the tradition (cf. 3:10).[93] Included in this unit are two preformed pieces:

> 3:14–15   An admonition on loyalty to the tradition
> 3:16–17   A saying on the role of scripture.

Jewish teaching required that children be taught the sacred writings at an early age.[94] But it is unlikely that the historical Timothy received such training. The fact that his mother Eunice was married to a Greek and had never had her son circumcised (see Acts 16:1–3) raises doubts about her allegiance to Judaism. It is not at all certain, then, that this cluster of materials was originally intended to describe Timothy's training. Perhaps the admonitions were drawn from a homily directed toward catachumens.[95]

It is striking that two different terms, one plural and one singular, are used to refer to the scriptures in 3:15 and 3:16. The phrase τὰ ἱερὰ γράμματα (3:15) appears only here in the NT, although it occurs frequently within the writings of Philo and Josephus to describe the books of the Old Testament.[96] The more usual NT term, γραφή, follows in 3:16; commentators offer various explanations as to why the author chose the peculiar phrase in 3:15 and then reverted to the standard designation in 3:16. E. F. Scott thinks that the two terms are intended to provide a contrast between sacred literature as a whole (including apocryphal and

[92]   The idea that godly living leads to persecution is commonplace within Judaism: see IV Maccabees *passim*, but especially 17:7: "if it were possible for us to paint the history of your piety (εὐσέβεια) as an artist might, would not those who first beheld it have shuddered as they saw the mother of the seven children enduring their varied tortures to death for the sake of religion (εὐσέβεια)?" Compare the connection of διώκω with εὐσεβής in T. Levi 16:2f.

[93]   Again, H. J. Holtzmann (*Die Pastoralbriefe*, p. 433) observes the rough transition: "just as surprising as the way in which the false teachers suddenly appear in the previous verse is the way they are apparently ignored in the following verses."

[94]   See the evidence in Strack–Billerbeck (*Kommentar zum NT*) (Munich: C. H. Beck, 1926), Vol. III, pp. 664ff.

[95]   G. Holtz (*Die Pastoralbriefe*, 2nd ed. [Berlin: Evangelische Verlagsanstalt, 1972], p. 186) thinks that the material may derive from a "baptismal instruction."

[96]   See, for example, Philo, *De vita Mosis* III.39; Josephus, *Antiq.* Proem. 3, X.10.4.

apocalyptic writings, τὰ ἱερὰ γράμματα) and the inspired writings in particular (γραφή). But such precise definitions are scarcely possible.[97]

These attempts to resolve the puzzle all presume the integrity of the text. Perhaps it is better to view this unit (3:14–17) as a cluster of previously independent sayings on loyalty to the traditions that were gathered at some point by an editor. Two references to the scripture, originally unrelated, were thus joined.

4:1–5 Charge and admonition

Another miscellaneous cluster of admonitions is introduced by the expression διαμαρτύρομαι ἐνώπιον τοῦ θεοῦ (cf. I 5:21; II 2:14). The adjuration is elaborated here by fixed liturgical language. The cluster comprises the following elements:

4:1	Introductory charge
4:2	Admonition (to ordinand?)
4:3–4	Polemic against false teachers
4:5	Admonitions (to ordinand?).

Apparent discontinuities within this passage caused P. N. Harrison to break it into various fragments, only parts of which he regarded as genuinely Pauline.[98] R. Falconer also noted the internal disunity of the text, and argued that 4:3–4 must be editorial additions since they "break the connexion between vv. 2 and 5" and contain a distinct vocabulary.[99]

Both writers highlight the problems involved in trying to read this text as if it were the product of one author. But neither seems to recognize that the section has a formal, if not logical, unity. The string of admonitions in 4:2 is linked to the polemic in 4:3–4 by the catch-word διδαχή (4:2; compare διδασκαλία in 4:3). Another string of personal admonitions (4:5), introduced by the formulaic σὺ δέ, has been added at the end of the unit.

---

[97] N. J. D. White (*The Epistles of Timothy and Titus*, p. 174) thinks that "Paul here deliberately uses an ambiguous term in order to express vigorously the notion that Timothy's first lessons were in Holy Scripture." Unfortunately, we have no other evidence to corroborate White's conjecture.

[98] P. N. Harrison (*The Problem*, p. 127) regards 4:1–2a, 4:5b as a last charge that Paul laid upon Timothy to complete his task.

[99] R. Falconer, *The Pastoral Epistles*, p. 95. Falconer notes the presence of five non-Pauline words: ὑγιαίνω, ἐπισωρεύω, κνήθω, μῦθος, ἐκτρέπω.

4:6–8 Autobiographical material

This unit consists of a personal confession and farewell that draw upon a Jewish understanding of the sacrificial value of a martyr's death.[100] It is a well-ordered and coherent statement.

But the unit is oddly situated in the present context; as a final testimony and a confident farewell the passage would seem a fitting close to a letter; but in its present setting the confession only introduces an anti-climactic and rather puzzling mixture of personalia and reminiscence (4:9–22). Both the tone and the mood of the following unit differ considerably from that of 4:6–8. The concern over Paul's imminent death is abruptly left off, and the subject turns oddly to other less urgent affairs.[101]

4:9–21 Personalia

There is no compelling reason to deny the authenticity of this material; although the tone of the passage seems odd in its present context,[102] the unit as a whole carries all the marks of genuine composition, and is probably best read as a separate Pauline letter that at some point in transmission was fused onto the other materials that make up II Timothy.[103]

4:22 Concluding benediction

A more elaborate benediction than that of I Timothy or Titus concludes the letter. Two benedictions appear to have been joined together here, the first oddly enough in the singular (μετὰ τοῦ πνεύματός σου, 4:22a) and the second in the plural (ἡ χάρις μεθ' ὑμῶν, 4:22b). The form of the first benediction is similar but not

---

100 See, for example, the words of the martyr Eleazar in IV Macc. 6:28: "Be merciful to your people and let our punishment suffice for them. Make my blood their purification, and take my life in exchange for theirs." Cf. 17:21f. The concept may derive from such texts as Num. 28:7; see also Phil. 2:17; Ign. Rom. 2:2.

101 J. Calvin (*Commentary on Timothy, Titus*, p. 341) notes the problem: "here someone will ask what Paul meant by asking for a cloak if he thought he was going to die immediately. This difficulty is another reason why I think that he means a chest [filled with books], but there may have been some other use for a cloak at that time, unknown to us today."

102 For example, Paul's confident assertion that "the Lord will deliver me" (4:18) seems to contrast with the attitude of resignation to his fate reflected in 4:6–8.

103 The view presented here is shared in part by W. Lock (*The Pastoral Epistles*, pp. xxxii–xxxiii), who conjectures that two letters have been combined in II Timothy, one pastoral and general (1:1–4:8, 22b), the other personal (4:9–22a).

identical to those found in Galatians (6:18), Philippians (4:23), and Philemon (25). In each of those benedictions (even Philemon!) the recipient of the blessing is denoted by the plural pronoun ("you all"). But none of Paul's recognized letters conclude with a singular benediction. This fact suggests that the benediction of II Tim. 4:22a may be part of an authentic, personal note from Paul to his co-worker.

Most commentators think that the second greeting here is intended for the benefit of the congregation while the more personal (4:22a) is directed toward Timothy. If two originally separate letters are imbedded within II Timothy, however, it would not be surprising to find two benedictions of this sort.

5

TITUS: A COMPOSITIONAL ANALYSIS

1:1–4 Epistolary salutation

The sheer length of this letter's salutation marks it as unusual. Not only are Paul's formal apostolic credentials put forward as in the other Pastorals, but an elaborate creedal statement appears as well (1:1b–3).[1] The grammatical structure of the greeting, consisting of one long and involved sentence, is notoriously complicated and confusing.[2]

The difficulties inherent in this salutation (its overloaded style, confusing grammar, and unusual content) are not easily explained. E. F. Scott argues that the peculiar features are partially due to the writer's "anxiety" over the possibility that in this mainly practical letter the religious basis of the Christian life might be forgotten; consequently, the author "has tried to crowd in a large number of Pauline ideas."[3]

But this is surely to minimize the problems that the salutation presents. The sentence, with its compact phrases and rough transitions, does not read well as a whole.

The closest parallel both in form and content to this greeting

---

[1] Commentators who defend the authenticity of this letter suggest that the formal salutation is due to the "semi-official" character of the letter. See, for example, John Calvin, *Commentary on the Epistles to Timothy and Titus*, ed. D. Torrance and T. Torrance (Edinburgh: Oliver & Boyd, 1964), p. 351. The inclusion, however, of the slur against all Cretans (1:12) makes this unlikely, and leads D. Guthrie (*The Pastoral Epistles* [Leicester: Inter-Varsity Press, 1957], p. 188) to conclude that the letter must have been intended as a private correspondence. But in that case, why the formal salutation?

[2] Note, for example, the perplexing collection of prepositional phrases in 1:1–2. J. Jeremias (*Die Briefe an Timotheus und Titus* [Göttingen: Vandenhoeck & Ruprecht, 1953], p. 59) remarks on the "very compact language" of the salutation, while E. F. Scott (*The Pastoral Epistles*, The Moffatt New Testament Commentary Series [London: Hodder & Stoughton, 1936], p. 149) observes that it is "so complicated in structure that the thought is difficult to follow."

[3] Scott, *The Pastoral Epistles*, p. 149.

appears in the salutation to the Romans (1:1–7). It is widely acknowledged that Paul has included a preformed creedal fragment in this his longest greeting.[4] But, as J. C. O'Neill has observed, two factors count against the view that Paul was responsible for the inclusion of the fragment: first, it seems odd that Paul makes no further use of the terms of the creed in his subsequent argument, and secondly, the inclusion of this creed makes the salutation "a grammatical monstrosity, which no one writer would have perpetrated."[5]

O'Neill suggests that the fragment looks more like an editorial insertion than a Pauline citation. And he finds striking support for his conjecture in the omission of the entire section (Rom. 1:2–5) from codex G (Boernerianus), the greeting of which simply reads:

> Paul, servant of Jesus Christ, called an apostle among all the gentiles on his behalf.

The fact that this late (thirteenth-century) MS is the only one that preserves this reading of the text may argue against O'Neill's conjecture. But it is a scrap of evidence that must be considered. O'Neill remarks that "it is hard to imagine a scribe omitting such a long and important section, even by accident," and concludes that the creedal fragment must be a marginal comment or interpolation that found its way into the text of Romans at an early stage of transmission.[6]

These observations touch upon many of the difficulties that appear within Titus 1:1–4. Like the Romans passage, the greeting to Titus also seems to be overloaded by a creedal fragment that has no real place in the larger context. It is not unlikely that the peculiarities of the salutation to Titus are due (as in Rom. 1:1–7) to editorial expansion.

If Paul's apostolic credentials (unnecessary in a personal letter) and the preformed creedal material are removed, a warm and intimate greeting from Paul to his colleague Titus remains.

The recognition of this material as a later editorial addition has

---

4 See, for example, C. H. Dodd, *The Epistle of Paul to the Romans* (London: Hodder & Stoughton, 1932), pp. 4–5.
5 J. C. O'Neill, *Paul's Letter to the Romans* (Harmondsworth: Penguin, 1975), p. 26.
6 Ibid.

the added advantage of absolving the author from what A. T. Hanson calls a "rather muddled soteriology" (referring to the double reference to God and Jesus as σωτήρ, 1:3, 4).[7]

1:5 Epistolary motive

The salutation leads immediately into the body of the letter; as in I Timothy, the lack of any epistolary thanksgiving is a striking omission and weighs against the view that this letter is a careful imitation of the Pauline epistolary style (see pp. 1–2; 8–10; 59 above).

Titus 1:5 provides the earliest evidence that Paul was involved in a missionary campaign on the island of Crete.[8] The historicity of such a mission cannot be ruled out, and the general information presented here may well have been part of an authentic letter from Paul to Titus.

The sentence, whether genuine or not, serves the formal purpose of linking the salutation with the clearly traditional materials that follow; a similar sentence does the same thing in I Tim. 1:3.

1:6–9 Qualities required of a good leader

Although a thematic unity (on the qualities of a good leader) serves to tie this material together, there are clear signs that originally it was not the composition of one author; the tradition, for example, from the plural πρεσβυτέρους (1:5–6) to the singular ἐπίσκοπον (1:7–9) is abrupt and unexpected;[9] the qualities required of elders in 1:6 (beginning with ἀνέγκλητος) are followed by the sudden appearance of a new list of qualities required of the overseer (also beginning with ἀνέγκλητος); and the form of the regulation presented in 1:6 (εἴ τίς ἐστιν) differs significantly from that of 1:7 (δεῖ plus the infinitive). Such features have led some to conclude that

---

7   A. T. Hanson, *The Pastoral Epistles*, The New Century Bible Commentary (Grand Rapids, MI: Eerdmans, 1982), p. 171.

8   The reference to Crete in Acts 27:7f. does not allow opportunity for active church planting by the apostle; consequently, if Paul evangelized Crete, he must have done so after the events recorded in Acts 28.

9   If the titles were precisely synonymous, one would expect the plural of "overseer" to match the plural of "elders." F. J. A. Hort (*The Christian Ecclesia* [London: Macmillan, 1900], p. 191) argues that πρεσβύτερος describes the official, while ἐπίσκοπος describes the function. See, however, the article on πρεσβύτερος by G. Bornkamm, in *Theological Dictionary of the New Testament*, ed. G. Kittel and G. Friedrich, ET and ed. G. Bromiley (9 vols., Grand Rapids: Eerdmans, 1964–1974) (henceforth *TDNT*), Vol. VI, pp. 667ff.

1:7–9 must be a later interpolation.[10] The excision of this passage restores, they maintain, the original conjunction of ἀνυπότακτα in 1:6 with ἀνυπότακτοι in 1:10. But although this conjecture takes seriously the problems of the text's discontinuity, it seems very unlikely that an author writing continuous prose would end one sentence with ἀνυπότακτα and begin the next with ἀνυπότακτοι.

It seems better to attribute breaks in form and content between these materials to the composite character of this document. It is probable that at least two previously independent pieces have been brought together here:

> 1:5–6   The qualities required of elders
> 1:7–9   The qualities required of an overseer.[11]

Word association again appears to be responsible for the linking together of these two units (cf. ἀνέγκλητος, 1:6, 7).

Not only do the variations in form suggest that all of these pieces have probably been taken over from different sources, but the original unity of 1:7–9 must also be doubted on the basis of its form. This block of materials seems to be composed of at least two originally independent pieces. The seam becomes clear when the material is set out according to its form:

> (1:7a)   δεῖ γὰρ τὸν ἐπίσκοπον ἀνέγκλητον εἶναι ὡς
>   θεοῦ οἰκονόμον...

> (1:7b)   μὴ αὐθάδη
>   μὴ ὀργίλον
>   μὴ πάροινον
>   μὴ πλήκτην
>   μὴ αἰσχροκερδῆ

> (1:8)   ἀλλὰ
>   φιλόξενον
>   φιλάγαθον

[10] For example, A. von Harnack (*Geschichte der altchristlichen Literatur bis Eusebius* [4 vols., Leipzig: Zentralantiquariat, 1958 (1893–1904)], Vol. II [*Chronologie*], part 1, p. 482) recognized that Titus 1:7–9 was independent of its context, and considered it (along with I 3:1–13, and parts of I Tim. 5) to be interpolations taken from a church order around AD 130. Similarly, R. Falconer (*The Pastoral Epistles* [Oxford: Clarendon Press, 1937], p. 104); O. Ritschl, *ThLZ* 10 (1885), 609.

[11] G. Bornkamm (πρεσβύς, in *TDNT*, Vol. VI, p. 667) remarks that the role of bishop is "a surprising point in the Pastorals" and concludes that "the passages about the bishop reflect a different constitutional principle from those about presbyters."

σώφρονα
δίκαιον
ὅσιον
ἐγκρατῆ

(1:9)   ... ἀντεχόμενον τοῦ κατὰ τὴν διδαχὴν πιστοῦ
λόγου, ἵνα δυνατὸς ᾖ καὶ παρακαλεῖν ἐν τῇ
διδασκαλίᾳ τῇ ὑγιαινούσῃ καὶ τοὺς ἀντιλέγοντας
ἐλέγχειν.

It seems likely that in this case a brief regulation concerning the
overseer (1:7a, 9) was later expanded by the addition of a general
vice/virtue list (1:7b, 8).[12]

The scribal tendency to add traditional materials to an existing
text is aptly illustrated by the lengthy addition (following 1:9) that
appears in minuscule 460, a thirteenth-century Venetian MS. This
cluster of regulations (see below) was loaded onto the received text
with no indication that the original text had been modified:

> Do not ordain those who have been twice married or make
> them deacons; do not have wives from a second marriage,
> let (such people) not approach the altar for divine service.
> Rebuke as a servant of God the rulers who are unjust and
> swindlers and liars and merciless.[13]

1:10–16 Polemical warnings

The instructions regarding church order (cf. 1:6–9, 2:1ff.) are
interrupted by a group of polemical statements directed against
unspecified opponents (1:10–16); they may have been intentionally
placed here by a compiler who wished to underscore the need for
care to be exercised in the selection of church leaders. The unit
comprises diverse elements, including:

12 The virtues and vices seem to draw upon a traditional schema. See A. Vögtle,
Tugend- und Lasterkataloge im Neuen Testament (Münster: Aschendorff, 1936),
pp. 52, 239–242. Vögtle argues that the unspecified character of these qualities
shows their secondary employment.

13 It is significant that in addition to the textual evidence (which in this case
confirms the secondary character of this material), the change in literary form
between 1:7–9 and this addition also indicates that they did not originally belong
together: note, for example, the opening imperative infinite μὴ χειροτονεῖν
διγάμους (see A. T. Robertson, *A Grammar of the Greek New Testament in the
Light of Historical Research* [2nd ed., New York: George H. Doran, 1914],
pp. 1092–1093). Compare the discussion at I 1:3b. The variant appears in full in
the Nestle–Aland (26th ed.) text of the NT.

1:10–11   Polemic against the opponents
1:12–13a A pagan citation
1:13b–14 Saying on how to deal with the opponents
1:15–16   Polemic against the opponents.

Although this block of material is unified by its polemical concerns, there is no real movement of thought between the various elements that comprise it; in fact the logical connections within the unit are often strained and obscure (see below).

The term ἀνυπότακτοι probably serves as the link-word connecting this material to that which precedes (see 1:6). But it seems strange that the "insubordinate" people in 1:6 are children of potential elders, while in 1:11 the "insubordinates" refer to the seditious opponents. It is hard to imagine an author using, in such close proximity, the same word to label two very different groups.

The charges of the first polemical saying (1:10–11) are for the most part purely conventional, the opponents remaining nameless and faceless (πολλοί, 1:10; οἵτινες, 1:11); however, at 1:10b there is a very specific reference to "those of the circumcision" (οἱ ἐκ τῆς περιτομῆς). This specific allusion to the Jews (or Jewish practices) seems out of place in this otherwise vague and nondescript passage;[14] it is especially strange since the Pastorals as a whole do not emphasize the Jewish background of the opponents.[15] The mention of "Jewish" myths in 1:14 is the only place in the Pastorals where the myths are so specified.[16]

The reference to Jews (or Jewish converts) in 1:10 is made more

14 The phrase can refer to Jews (see Rom. 4:12); M. Dibelius and H. Conzelmann (henceforth D–C) (*The Pastoral Epistles* [Philadelphia: Fortress Press, 1972], p. 135) and B.S. Easton (*The Pastoral Epistles* [London: SCM, 1948], p. 88) think that the reference is to Jews. But the phrase can also describe Jewish Christians (cf. Acts 10:45; 11:2; Gal. 2:12; Col. 4:11); E.E. Ellis ("Those of the Circumcision," in *Texte und Untersuchungen* 102, Studia Evangelica IV [Berlin: Akademie-Verlag, 1968], pp. 390–399) argues that it refers here to Jewish converts. J. Moffatt translates the phrase, "those who have come over from Judaism."

15 J.B. Lightfoot ("The Date of the Pastoral Epistles," in *Biblical Essays* [London: Macmillan, 1893], p. 411) thinks that I 1:7–8 and Titus 3:9 also signal the Jewish origin of the heretics, but he interprets the meaning of both of these passages in light of Titus 1:10, 14.

16 Compare I 1:4; 4:7; II 4:4. See also II Pet. 1:16. Scholars who assume the literary unity of the Pastorals allow this text to color their understanding of other polemical passages within the Pastorals. F. Büchsel (γενεά, γενεαλογία, in *TDNT*, Vol. I, pp. 662–665), for example, argues in this way: "From I Tim. 1:4 we learn that γενεαλογία cannot be separated from μῦθοι. Tit. 1:14 mentions μῦθοι Ἰουδαϊκοί. It thus follows that the γενεαλογίαι, too, are Jewish in content."

problematic by the quotation of the hexameter by Epimenides that follows (1:12); the phrase introducing the citation ("one of their own prophets") must in the present context refer back to someone within "the circumcision" (1:10), but such a reading causes obvious difficulties since Epimenides was obviously not a Jew.[17]

All of these difficulties vanish if the Jewish references within this unit (1:10, 14) are regarded as anti-Jewish glosses, and removed from the text; it is easy to imagine how a copyist, desiring to underscore Christianity's departure from all things Jewish, could be responsible for just such a gloss. When these references to the Jews are removed, the remaining polemical materials correspond to the kind of conventional language that we find elsewhere in the Pastorals.

Minuscule 460 adds another community rule following 1:11:

> Silence the children who mistreat and beat their own parents; reprove and admonish them as a father to children.

This regulation hardly fits the surrounding context, but it is not logic that led a scribe to insert this text here. The admonition to silence (ἐπιστομίζειν) the insubordinate in 1:11 has clearly prompted a scribe to add another community admonition, this one emphasizing the need to silence (ἐπιστόμιζε) the children.

2:1–10 Domestic rules: qualities of good community members

The traditional character of this block of materials is clear from the parallels that exist within pagan, Jewish, and early Christian literature.[18] It is introduced here by the formulaic σὺ δέ (cf. I 6:11; II 3:10, 14), is marked by a distinct vocabulary,[19] and is tied only

---

[17] C.K. Barrett (*The Pastoral Epistles* [Oxford: Clarendon Press, 1963], p. 131) notes the problem: "the introduction of the 'Cretans' is not easy to understand after the reference in v. 10 to Jewish converts." But Barrett's solution is less than satisfactory: "Either the author has not fully thought through his material ... or the Jews are to be thought of as in great measure assimilated to Cretan life."

[18] See the excursus following Col. 4:1 in M. Dibelius and H. Greeven, *Kolosser, Epheser, Philemon* (Tübingen: J.C.B. Mohr [Paul Siebeck], 1953). See also J. Crouch's *The Origin and Intention of the Colossian Haustafel* (Göttingen: Vandenhoeck & Ruprecht, 1972) for a detailed survey of the source materials.

[19] Ten *hapax legomena* appear within these ten verses: πρεσβῦτις, κατάστημα, ἱεροπρεπής, καλοδιδάσκαλος, σωφρονίζω, φίλανδρος, φιλότεκνος, οἰκουργός, ἀφθορία, ἀκατάγνωστος.

loosely to the surrounding context, all of which suggest that it is a preformed independent unit. The qualities required of the various groups have little specifically Christian emphasis, a feature that may indicate the pre-Christian origin of the material.[20]

The cluster of instructions include five (or six) different groups of people:

2:2	Old men
2:3	Old women
2:4–5	Young women
2:7a	Young men
(2:7b	Leaders[21])
9–10	Slaves.

The form of the code here differs considerably from those which appear elsewhere in the NT;[22] in this schema the community of the Pastorals is divided by age and sex (2:1–7), not by family relationships (wives, husbands, children, fathers, masters, slaves). It does not follow the pattern of "reciprocal" exhortations that appear in the Ephesian and Colossian *Haustafeln*.

J. Crouch suggests that the *Haustafel* schema (as viewed, for example, in Col. 3:18–4:1) has been modified in the Pastorals by "the ecclesiastical concerns of these works," but the assertion is very difficult to demonstrate;[23] the form of Titus 2:1–10 cannot be explained in terms of specific ecclesiastical concerns. Like other parenetic units of material the domestic code here has a "casual" quality about it; no conclusions about the life of the church or of the community of the Pastorals can be drawn from its arrangement; the variations in the NT codes alone suggest that various schemata of domestic rules existed; there is no reason to think that the catalogue in Titus 2 has been adapted to fit the unique circumstances of the church (or the readership) of the Pastorals.

It seems far more likely that the materials in Titus came

---

20 K. Weidinger (*Die Haustafeln: Ein Stück urchristlicher Paränese* [Leipzig: Hinrichs, 1928], p. 53) notes that the specifically Christian content of the house rules in Titus (2:1–10) is less than in other NT domestic codes. It is especially interesting that the code here is grounded upon the teaching of "our savior God" (2:10) but lacks any reference to Jesus.

21 H. von Campenhausen ("Polykarp von Smyrna und die Pastoralbriefe," in *Aus der Frühzeit des Christentums* [Tübingen: J. C. B. Mohr (Paul Siebeck), 1963], p. 231, n. 132) thinks that 2:7b refers to community leaders, but if so, it is a very subtle reference.

22 Compare, for example, Eph. 5:22–6:9; Col. 3:18–4:1; I Pet. 2:18–3:7.

23 Crouch, *The Origin and Intention*, p. 12.

preformed into the hands of a compiler who inserted them unmodified into the text. The independent nature of this material helps explain why the terms used here for older men and women (πρεσβύτης, πρεσβῦτις, 2:2, 3) contrast with those that appear in I Timothy (πρεσβύτερος, πρεσβύτερας, 5:1, 2). The differences in terminology stem from the differences in source materials that were incorporated into the Pastorals.

The double appearance of ὡσαύτως (2:3, 6) reflects the traditional character of these materials (see I 3:8, 3:11).

2:11-14 Creedal fragment

The prosaic catalogue of rules for the community is followed by an elaborate confessional piece. Most commentators point to the connective γάρ in 2:11 and argue that 2:11–14 provides the theological foundation upon which the domestic rules are grounded. But such a logical progression is by no means clear; no explicit references are made within 2:11–14 to the preceding list of rules or to the concerns that may have prompted them. Nor does the reference to slaves in 2:10 lead one to expect the saying on "the epiphany of grace" (2:11) that follows. The liturgical material in 2:11–14, in fact, interrupts the catalogue of rules that continues in 3:1–2 (cf. ὑποτάσσεσθαι, 2:9; 3:1). In the form that we have it, the transition is not smooth and the logical links are not readily apparent.

The discontinuity leads C. K. Barrett to regard the passage as "a digression" and to suggest that "the reference to God as Savior proves to be the point of departure."[24] This latter remark is significant, for it suggests that word association (rather than logic) is responsible for the change of subject matter here; Barrett, of course, thinks that the digression is the work of an author; but the marked change in literary style, the distinct vocabulary, and the liturgical character of this material suggest that the two units (2:1–10, 2:11–14) are not the products of a single hand.[25]

The fixed nature of the language lends credence to the theory that this material was not written ad hoc but, on the contrary, came preformed as a traditional piece into the hands of a compiler, who

---

[24] Barrett, *The Pastoral Epistles*, p. 136.
[25] The style shifts suddenly at 2:11 from catalogues of virtues to prose. The vocabulary includes three *hapax legomena* (σωτήριος, σωφρόνως, περιούσιος) and five other non-Pauline words (ἐπιφαίνω, ἀρνέομαι, κοσμικός, εὐσεβῶς, λυτρόω). Illustrative of the liturgical character is the phrase: "awaiting the blessed hope and the appearance of the glory of the great God."

incorporated it into Titus.[26] Parallels to Titus 2:11–14, both in thought and language, appear in I Pet. 1:13b–19,[27] a text that has long been suspected of incorporating various preformed liturgical elements.[28] Such parallels may reflect the use of common liturgical materials.

The mention of "God our savior (σωτῆρος)" in 2:10 may be the link word that prompted the compiler to include 2:11–15 (cf. σωτήριος, 2:11); in any case, the passage reads like a confessional piece and should probably be regarded as a fragment from a hymn or a creed.[29]

2:15 Literary marker

The admonition to "speak these things" (2:15) seems odd in the present context since the material that immediately precedes is liturgical rather than parenetic. But the stereotyped nature of this admonition is clear from its use elsewhere (see the discussion at I 4:6); it seems likely that the phrase ταῦτα λάλει is functioning here as a literary marker, signaling the inclusion of the preceding traditional materials, including, perhaps, the entire section 2:1–14 (note the introductory σὺ δὲ λάλει, 2:1).

3:1–2 Domestic rule: submission to authorities

The subject reverts to the concern for proper conduct within the

---

26 Compare, for example, Titus 2:14 and Ps. 130 [129]: 8: ἵνα λυτρώσηται ἡμᾶς ἀπὸ πάσης ἀνομίας (Titus 2:14); καὶ αὐτὸς λυτρώσεται τὸν Ἰσραηλ ἐκ πασῶν τῶν ἀνομιῶν αὐτοῦ (Ps. 129:8 LXX).

27 Compare: Titus 2:11 ("the epiphany of grace"), I Pet. 1:13b ("the grace that is coming to you"); Titus 2:12 ("training us to renounce ... worldly passions [ἐπιθυμίας]"), I Pet. 1:14 ("do not be conformed to the passions [ἐπιθυμίαις]); Titus 2:14 ("He gave himself ... to ransom [ἵνα λυτρώσηται] us"), I Pet. 1:18 ("knowing that [εἰδότες ὅτι] you were ransomed [ἐλυτρώθητε])."

28 See the detailed discussion in F. L. Cross, *I Peter, a Paschal Liturgy* (London: A. R. Mowbray, 1954); a number of fixed materials, both liturgical and parenetic, appear in I Peter; see, for example, the apparent citations in 1:18–21; 2:21–25; the domestic code (2:13–3:6); the catalogue of vices; (4:3–5), and virtues (4:7–11). On the liturgical character of Titus 2:11–14, see A. T. Hanson, "Elements of a Baptismal Liturgy in Titus," in *Studies in the Pastoral Epistles* (London: SPCK, 1968), pp. 78–96.

29 E. E. Ellis ("Traditions in the Pastoral Epistles," in *Early Jewish and Christian Exegesis: Studies in Memory of William Hugh Brownlee*, ed. Craig Evans and W. Stinespring [Atlanta: Scholars Press, 1987], pp. 243–244) suggests that the unit has "all the earmarks of traditioned material," and regards it as a "confessional hymn."

community (cf. 2:1–10).³⁰ The commonplace character of the
admonition (on submission to authorities) is presupposed by the
introductory phrase, "remind them."³¹ In the present context,
however, it is not clear to whom the pronoun "them" is referring;
the obscurity of the antecedent is puzzling, and may signal that this
material has been lifted from a preexisting source.

A close parallel to the regulation presented here occurs at the
beginning of the domestic code in I Peter (2:13f.).³² The emphasis
on submission to authorities, the need to supplement this by good
works (ἔργον ἀγαθόν, Titus 3:1; ἀγαθοποιοῦντος, I Pet. 2:15), and
the admonition to show kindness (or honor) to all men (Titus 3:2; I
Pet. 2:17) appear in both regulations.

At the beginning of I Clement (1:3) a summary of a domestic
code appears, many of the concerns of which can also be detected
in Titus 2:1–10 and 3:1–2:

> For you did all things without respect of persons, and
> walked in the laws of God,
>
>> obedient to your *rulers*, and
>> paying all fitting honor to the *older*
>>> among you.
>> On the *young*, too, you enjoined temperate
>>> and seemly thoughts,
>> And to the *women* you gave instruction that
>>> they should do all things with a
>>> blameless and seemly and pure conscience,
>>> yielding a dutiful affection to their *husbands*.
>
> And you taught them to remain in the rule of obedience
> and to manage their households with seemliness, in all
> circumspection (my italic).

---

³⁰ A. R. C. Leaney (*The Epistles to Timothy, Titus and Philemon* [London: SCM Press, 1960], p. 125) notes the discontinuity: "With [2:15] the author appeared to close, but now seems to resume his task after reflection."

³¹ The verb ὑπομιμνῄσκω is often associated with cited or traditional materials. In II Tim. 2:14, for example, ὑπομιμνῄσκω immediately follows the "faithful word" of II 2:11–13. In IV Macc. 18:14, the same verb introduces a citation from Isa. 43:2. In I Clem. 7:1 the phrase "we remind ourselves" is followed by a reference to "the glorious and venerable rule of our tradition" (τὸν ... τῆς παραδόσεως ἡμῶν κανόνα, 7:2).

³² Compare also I Tim. 2:1–2; Rom. 13:1–7. Philo (*Spec. Leg.* 226) suggests that "for those who take account of virtue," rulers are above subjects (that is, they deserve honor).

There does not appear to be any logical connection between 3:1–2 and the preceding liturgical material (2:11–14). The references, however, to "good works" (καλῶν ἔργων, 2:14) and "every good work" (πρὸς πᾶν ἔργον ἀγαθόν, 3:1) may provide the catch-word that ties these two units of traditional materials together.[33]

3:3–8 Creedal fragment

The traditional character of this section is marked by the faithful word formula that appears in 3:8a. Virtually all commentators think that the formula refers to this material rather than that which follows.[34] But there is less agreement over how much of 3:3–8 is part of the citation.[35]

There is no doubt that a striking change in literary style occurs between 3:3 (a seven-member vice list) and 3:4–7 (a rhythmic, liturgical confession). This may signal that two previously separate preformed pieces have been joined here. But the two units cannot easily be detached from one another, for they combine to present a unified picture: 3:3 presenting a graphic account of the preconversion lifestyle, and 3:4–7 declaring the saving effects of God's epiphany of love and kindness. The appearance of the particle ποτέ in 3:3 also seems to require the contrast provided by 3:4–7.

The traditional nature of this material is also evident from the many parallels to this schema that exist. The train of thought and language is especially close to that which appears in Eph. 2:2f.[36] A. T. Hanson argues that the similarities between Titus 3:3–8, Eph. 2:1–10, and I Pet. 1:3–5 suggest that the respective authors drew

---

[33] It is remarkable how often allusions to "good works" appear in Titus: 1:16; 2:7, 14; 3:1, 8; 3:14. Elsewhere in the Pastorals, see: I 2:10; 3:1; 5:10 (twice), 25; 6:18; II 1:9; 2:21; 3:17; 4:18.

[34] E. F. Scott (*The Pastoral Epistles*, p. 178), however, thinks that the "faithful word" formula refers to the sentence that follows ("those who have faith in God make a point of practising honorable occupations"), but his decision is clearly governed by the presupposition that the formula "invariably applies to some concise statement." Scott's line of argument here seems to beg the question.

[35] The majority of scholars regard 2:4–7 as the citation (for example, Barrett, Simpson, Ellicott, Jeremias, Brox, Guthrie, White, Moffatt); a few commentators think that the creedal fragment comprises 3:5–7 or portions thereof (see Spicq, Easton, Lock, Kelly); D–C, and perhaps Leaney, argue for the entire section 2:3–7.

[36] The common features shared by Titus 3:3–8 and Eph. 2:1–10 are noteworthy; both passages contrast present with past behavior; both allude to past "disobedience" and evil "passions"; both emphasize that salvation is by grace and not works; and both refer to regeneration and new life.

upon the same preformed baptismal prayer or act of praise "which they adapted to their own use independently of each other."[37]

But Hanson's theory is weakened by the fact that Titus 3:3–8 shows no signs of being adapted to its present context. The first-person plural pronouns (and verbs) abruptly appear at 3:3 and are left off at 3:8b.[38] No explicit link is made between this material and that which precedes (3:1–2: submission to authorities) or follows (3:8c–11: miscellaneous admonitions). The transitions are not tightly drawn as we would expect them to be if an author were at work. Rather, the entire piece (3:3–8) protrudes distinctly from the surrounding context in a way that suggests it was placed there as a preformed piece, without modification or adaptation. The faithful word formula (3:8a) seems to confirm that this fragment is a citation (rather than a loose adaptation) from a traditional and well-known community liturgy.

The reference to "good works" (καλῶν ἔργων) in 3:8b may again be the link-word responsible for the placement of this material here (cf. 3:1: πᾶν ἔργον ἀγαθόν).[39] The saying in 3:8c ("these are good and profitable to men") seems rather pointless. R. Falconer calls it "an editorial platitude," while A. T. Hanson remarks that "nowhere does the author descend lower in mere banality than here."[40] Not only does the sentence appear unnecessary, but its precise meaning is obscure as well. To what, for example, does the demonstrative pronoun ταῦτα refer? Does it refer to the "good works" mentioned in 3:8b, or the preceding blocks of traditional materials (3:1–7), or to the admonitions within the letter as a whole?[41] It is likely that this saying is functioning here as a formal literary marker, signaling the end of another cluster of traditional materials.

---

[37] See the detailed discussion by A. T. Hanson, "Elements of a Baptismal Liturgy in Titus," in *Studies in the Pastoral Epistles*, p. 86.

[38] Note the use of the second-person imperative (ὑπομίμνῃσκε) at 3:1, and first-person indicative (βούλομαι) at 3:8b.

[39] E. E. Ellis ("Traditions in the Pastoral Epistles," p. 245) regards ταῦτα as a marker of the traditional nature of 3:3–8, but it is not clear to which ταῦτα (3:8b or 3:8c) he is referring.

[40] Falconer, *The Pastoral Epistles*, p. 117; Hanson, *The Pastoral Epistles*, p. 194.

[41] Some commentators think that it refers to the entire message of the letter (so, for example, Kelly, Guthrie); others to the immediately preceding injunctions (Bernard).

3:9–11 Polemical admonitions: on dealing with opponents

The appearance of this unit in its present context is sudden and unexpected;[42] the catch-word association ὠφέλιμα and ἀνωφελεῖς may be the editorial link that brought these two units together.

The material may be genuine, charging Titus to beware of the sources of potential dissension within his community. If so, it has striking similarities to the charge given to Timothy in I Tim. 1:1–7. Both passages treat the subject of how to deal with the opponents, and employ similar terms:

μωρὰς ζητήσεις	(cf. I Tim. 1:4)
γενεαλογίας	(cf. I Tim. 1:4)
μάταιοι	(cf. I Tim. 1:6)

3:12–15 Personalia and greetings

Apart from the salutation, this unit provides the only personal remarks that appear within the whole of Titus. There is no compelling reason to doubt the authenticity of this material. The passage reads well as a unit and may represent an authentic Pauline "core" around which the rest of the materials within Titus were gathered (see chapter 6 below).

3:15c Benediction

The benediction that concludes the letter parallels closely those of I and II Timothy. It may have been added when the letters began to be used within the larger Christian community.

[42] J. N. D. Kelly (*A Commentary on the Pastoral Epistles* [London: Adam & Charles Black, 1963], p. 255) regards this passage as a digression.

6

SUMMARY AND CONCLUSIONS

The problem of the Pastorals

If the foregoing analysis of the Pastorals is anywhere near correct, then the problems that confront the interpreter of these letters are even more complex than most scholars have allowed. The letters do not reflect the sort of literary construction that one expects from the hand of an author writing narrative prose; the reader is seldom carried along by the development of thought, much less the force of argument; the letters have no driving concern, no consistent focus of interest; instead, they read like an anthology of traditions, many arranged mechanically together by topic, some simply juxtaposed.

It is precisely in the literary discontinuities, the flashes of different material, the lack of sustained argument, that the compositional integrity of the Pastorals is most seriously called into question. The diversity of literary forms within these letters, the variations in content, the traditional character of much of the material, all converge to suggest that these documents are composite works, consisting of gathered collections of community traditions.

Theories of composition

But if the Pastorals are made up of various preformed elements, how did they come to take the shape they now have? What is to account for the puzzling mixture of materials within these documents? Among those who recognize that the Pastorals contain previously independent materials, a number of theories have been put forward to account for the literary peculiarity of these letters.

Collections of an imitator

M. Dibelius remains the most influential proponent of the view that the traditional materials within the Pastorals were collected and passed off as Pauline by a pseudonymous author. According to this theory, the epistolary framework of these documents is a carefully employed literary device designed to confer apostolic authority upon the traditional materials; the fictional "occasion" of the letters (that is, Paul writing to two men in charge of whole provinces) was intended to ensure the widest possible reading of these materials.[1]

This approach allows for a full appreciation of the diversity of the traditional materials that have been incorporated within the Pastorals. The preformed character of the domestic rules, church order regulations, liturgical pieces, and the like is properly recognized and given its rightful place in the interpretation of the letters.

But in spite of its considerable strengths, Dibelius's approach (and the many variations that derive from it) founders on the assumption that these letters are the product of a skilled imitator, writing in Paul's name, and mimicking his epistolary style;[2] in too many respects these letters lack the Pauline stamp. It is hard to attribute, for example, the abrupt ending of I Timothy, and its lack of any closing greetings, to a Pauline imitator; and why would a pseudonymous author omit the customary thanksgivings in I Timothy and Titus? Paul's letters usually have a distinct parenetic section, but the Pastorals are permeated by parenetical advice and instructions.[3] In matters of literary style, language, and form, the Pastorals deviate too widely from the Pauline corpus to be regarded as carefully crafted imitations.

The internal ordering of the materials within the Pastorals also militates against the view that these documents are the product of one author. Organization and development of thought are expected from an author, but the Pastorals are characterized by a remarkable

---

[1] So M. Dibelius and H. Conzelmann (henceforth DC), *The Pastoral Epistles* (Philadelphia: Fortress Press, 1972), pp. 5–8.

[2] Dibelius does not claim any special craftiness on the part of the pseudonymous writer; nevertheless, his descriptions of the author's use of literary devices and pseudepigraphical techniques (see *The Pastoral Epistles*, p. 127) imply a considerable expertise and sophistication.

[3] W. Doty (*Letters in Primitive Christianity* [Philadelphia: Fortress Press, 1973], p. 69) observes this oddity of the Pastorals: "I find it characteristic of [the Pastorals] that the Pauline paraenetic section is now lost to view formally."

lack of both. Topics are abruptly left off only to reappear later; even obviously related church-order materials are detached from one another, their arrangement showing no clear logical sequence.[4]

Equally problematic is the question: why three Pastorals? Or, more specifically, what would motivate a pseudonymous author to write both I Timothy and Titus, documents so similar in outlook, content, and concerns as to seem tautologous? Dibelius's hypothesis suggests that I Timothy is intended for the leader of the congregation, while Titus is directed primarily toward the missionary.[5] But this is surely to place a greater burden upon Titus 1:5 than it can bear, since there is no other evidence to support such a distinction.[6]

Collections of Paul

Another view that takes seriously the presence of preformed traditions argues that Paul himself collected and employed traditional materials in his writings.[7] G. E. Cannon argues this case in his published dissertation *Traditional Materials in Colossians*.[8] Cannon begins by noting that the major problems in ascribing Colossians to Paul revolve around theological, lexical, and stylistic matters; he then attempts to show that most of the controversial issues within these letters are directly related to the sections where traditional forms are present.

E. E. Ellis, as we observed earlier, argues a similar position in relation to the Pastorals.[9] Following Harnack and Lightfoot, Ellis

---

[4] See, for example, the material on deacons (I 3:8–10, 12–13); church leaders (I 3:1–7; 5:17ff.).

[5] DC, *The Pastoral Epistles*, p. 154.

[6] H. Binder, ("Die historische Situation der Pastoralbriefe," in *Geschichtswirklichkeit und Glaubensbewährung: Festschrift für F. Müller* [Stuttgart: Evangelisches Verlagswerk, 1967], p. 72) recognizes the difficulty: "We can better explain the fact that three editorial letters with approximately the same message are handed down when we presume genuine Pauline letters to Timothy and Titus that later underwent an ecclesiastical addition, than if we think of a subsequent historical basis of general utterances concerning contemporary issues in the church, since in the latter case only one letter would have been necessary."

[7] E. Norden (*Agnostos Theos* [Berlin/Leipzig: Teubner, 1913], pp. 250–254) was an early exponent of this view, arguing that Col. 1:15–20 was a liturgical piece. A. M. Hunter (*Paul and his Predecessors* [Philadelphia: Westminster Press, 1940]) argued that Paul's letters are punctuated by various preformed traditional materials (see especially pp. 136–146).

[8] G. E. Cannon, *Traditional Materials in Colossians* (Macon, GA: Mercer University Press, 1983).

[9] Ellis, "Traditions in the Pastoral Epistles," pp. 237–253.

accepts a post-Acts 28 ministry of Paul,[10] and suggests that during this period Paul

> apparently found traditions, some with a soteriological and church order idiom and emphasis reminiscent of the Jerusalem church, which he incorporated into his letters to Timothy and Titus.[11]

Ellis concludes by noting the genre-affinities of the Pastorals with the Qumran Manual of Discipline, and suggests that Paul's last three letters functioned as "virtual manuals of traditions and commentary" for the various congregations to whom they were circulated (via Timothy and Titus).[12]

This theory provides a credible motive and *Sitz im Leben* for the Pastorals, and also makes sense of the many Pauline features present within these letters. But, nonetheless, the appeal to Pauline authorship is met with a host of serious difficulties. As we observed above, the Pastorals do not easily lend themselves to any theory of authorship; they do not read like the writings of a single author. But even assuming that Paul wrote these documents as we now have them, it is hard to understand what could have motivated such a remarkable change in his epistolary habits; by Ellis's own count, traditional materials occur within the Pastorals "in much greater abundance" than within the other Pauline letters, comprising 41 per cent of I Timothy, 16 per cent of II Timothy, and 46 per cent of Titus.[13] To what can we attribute this marked increase in the inclusion of traditional materials?

And if Paul is responsible for the collection of these materials, why did he incorporate elements that seem at cross-purposes with some of his most deeply held theological convictions? The references to the law, for example, in I Tim. 1:8–11 are hardly in keeping with Paul's statements on the subject elsewhere in his letters; it is hard to imagine Paul affirming the idea that "the law is not laid down for the just, but for the lawless" (1:9).[14] Ellis correctly

---

[10] A. von Harnack, *Geschichte der altchristlichen Literatur bis Eusebius* (Leipzig: Zentralantiquariat, 1958 [1893–1904], Vol. II [*Chronologie*], part 1, p. 240n.; J. B. Lightfoot, *The Apostolic Fathers* (2 vols., London: Macmillan, 1890), Vol. I, part 2, pp. 30ff.

[11] Ellis, "Traditions in the Pastoral Epistles," p. 252.

[12] Ibid., pp. 252–253.

[13] Ibid., pp. 250, 247. By comparison, Ellis thinks that traditional materials make up about 15 percent of I Corinthians. See his article "Traditions in I Corinthians," *NTS* 32 (1986), 481–502.

[14] C. K. Barrett (*The Pastoral Epistles* [Oxford: Clarendon Press, 1963], pp. 42–43)

identifies I Tim. 1:9–11 as a pre-Pauline unit, but if Paul himself were the collector of these traditions, why would he include this piece?

Collections of a Pauline school

The Pastorals may be the product, not of an individual (be it Paul or a pseudo-Paul), but of a "school" – that is, a group of editors charged with the preservation and circulation of Pauline teaching and traditions. The existence of such schools is suggested by analogy from the known organized teaching practices within contemporary pagan circles and those of the Hellenistic synagogue.[15] Allusions to the presence of prophetic schools are also contained within the OT itself.[16] The view that organized schools existed within early Christian communities has been frequently advanced, notably by K. Stendahl on the Matthean school and O. Cullmann on the Johannine "circle."[17]

The idea that Paul had disciples who functioned during his lifetime and after his death as collectors and editors of his teaching has much to commend it. The distinctive features of the Deutero-Pauline literature are well attributed to the work of a school.[18] And

---

finds this text in tension with the Pauline understanding of the law as presented in Rom. 3:19: "Now we know that whatever the law says it speaks to those who are under the law, so that every mouth may be stopped."

[15] For example, the Pythagoreans, Epicureans, Stoics, and Essenes probably all had some kind of "school" community during the first century. For a thorough canvassing of both pagan and Jewish "schools," see the dissertation by R. A. Culpepper, *The Johannine Schools: An Evaluation of the Johannine-School Hypothesis based on an Investigation of the Nature of Ancient Schools*, SBL Dissertation Series 26 (Missoula, MT: Scholars Press, 1974). Culpepper's definition of a school consists of nine characteristics, one of which includes an emphasis on "teaching, learning, studying, and writing" (p. 259).

[16] See II Kgs. 6:1; I Sam. 10:10. Compare the remarks on this subject by G. von Rad, *Wisdom in Israel* (London: SCM, 1972), p. 17.

[17] K. Stendahl (*The School of St. Matthew and its Use of the Old Testament* [Uppsala: Gleerup, 1954], p.35) understands the Matthean school as a school for teachers and church leaders, and argues that the gospel is a product of the school, designed as a manual for teaching and administration within the church. O. Cullmann (*The Johannine Circle* [London: SCM, 1976], p. 5) thinks that the "author" of John's gospel had disciples who functioned as redactors in its production and revision.

[18] H. Conzelmann (*Studies in Luke–Acts*, ed. L. Keck and J. Martyn [Nashville: Abingdon Press, 1966], p. 307) thinks that "we can understand the existence of the deutero-Pauline literature only if we assume that Paul founded an actual school." See also his article, "Paulus und die Weisheit," *NTS* 12 (1965), 231–244. G. Bornkamm (*Paul* [London: Hodder & Stoughton, 1971 (1969)], p. 86) suggests

the peculiar characteristics of the Pastorals, in particular, seem to lend themselves to such an explanation; the diversity of forms and the sudden changes in subject matter suggest that collectors were at work.

But this theory is also confronted by a massive problem: if the Pastorals are the products of a Pauline school, why do they deviate so considerably from the teachings of the master? Major Pauline concerns find little or no place in these letters: the work of the Spirit is rarely discussed (I 4:1; II 1:14; Titus 3:5); Paul's rich use of the formula "in Christ" is almost completely lost to view;[19] the Pauline use of "faith" as the justifying principle never appears;[20] and perhaps most surprisingly of all, no explicit mention is made of the cross, or of Jesus' resurrection except in II 2:8.

The theological orientation of the Pastorals is likewise in tension with Pauline teaching at a number of points. We have already noted the non-Pauline treatment of the law in I Tim. 1:8–11. But other tensions exist; the increased identification of faith ("the faith") with the contents of the gospel seems to reflect a strange transformation of the customary Pauline understanding of the term;[21] the tendency to link πίστις with other virtues (see, for example, the virtue lists at I 2:15; 4:12, 6:11, II 2:22, II 3:10; Titus 2:2) also marks a movement away from the Pauline usage.[22]

More significantly, non-Pauline elements appear in the Chris-

that the Pastorals, as well as Colossians and Ephesians, are the product of a Pauline school.

[19] The expression "in Christ" occurs nine times in the Pastorals (I 1:14; 3:13; II 1:1, 9, 13; 2:1, 10; 3:13, 15). J. A. Allan ("The 'In-Christ' Formula in the Pastoral Epistles," *NTS* 10 [1963], 115–121) notes that "as compared with Paul, the Pastorals show a very great improvement of expression. The formula survives only in a single stereotyped form" (p. 118).

[20] See the remarks by B. S. Easton, *The Pastoral Epistles* (London: SCM, 1948), p. 203. I. H. Marshall ("Faith and Works in the Pastoral Letters," *SNTU* A, 9 [1984], 207) takes issue with Easton, arguing that Paul does not always link the concepts of faith and justification (cf. Rom. 3:20; 9:11f.); Marshall's point is well taken, but it does not diminish the striking fact that no explicit reference to faith as the means of salvation appears in the Pastorals.

[21] The objective meaning of πίστις occurs only four times in the earlier Pauline letters (I Cor. 16:13; II Cor. 13:5; Gal. 1:23; Phil. 1:27; [Col. 1:23; 2:7]); in the Pastorals the word has this meaning seventeen times (I 1:2, 19; 3:9, 13; 4:1, 6; 5:8; 6:10, 12, 21; II 2:18; 3:8; 4:7; Titus 1:1, 4, 13; 2:2. See the discussion by O. von Merk, "Glaube und Tat in den Pastoralbriefen," *ZNW* 66 (1975), 91–112.

[22] The combination of faith with other Christian virtues appears also in Paul (for example, Gal. 5:22), but the frequency of the lists within the Pastorals is striking. I. H. Marshall ("Faith and Works") regards such linking as "the most character-istic feature of the Pastorals"; he notes fourteen instances (p. 214).

tology (Christologies?)[23] of the Pastorals; H. Windisch is probably right in seeing some pre-Pauline Christological ideas within certain passages of these letters (especially I 2:5–6); but other passages seem to reflect an equally un-Pauline "epiphany" Christology (I 3:16; II 1:10; Titus 2:11, 3:4).

The Pastorals may be the product of a school, but the lack of emphasis of key Pauline ideas, and the tensions caused by the appearance of non-Pauline theological positions, make it unlikely that the letters are the product of a specifically *Pauline* school.

Distinctive features of the Pastorals

None of the above hypotheses seems adequate to explain the literary peculiarities of the Pastorals. Before I offer my own theory of the origin of these letters, it may be helpful to reexamine the various features that make the interpretation of these documents so difficult:

1   the letters claim to be by Paul, and contain what appears to be genuine Pauline material;
2   the letters do not closely "mimic" the Pauline letters in form or style;
3   all three letters are made up of a miscellany of preformed materials;
4   some of the material appears to be non-Pauline;
5   the materials are not arranged in any logical order;
6   the traditional character of the materials is very pronounced.

The origin of the Pastorals

The peculiar features of the Pastorals suggest that, in their present form at least, they cannot be attributed to the work of any one man, writing at a specific time and place, in response to a particular situation or request. But if this assessment be correct, then what kind of documents are they? How did they come together, and what can we say about their origin?

---

[23] According to H. Windisch ("Zur Christologie der Pastoralbriefe," *ZNW* 34 [1935], 213–238) the Pastorals show no unified Christology, "but rather, Christian teachings about Christ in the form of 'sayings,' 'formulas,' and 'hymns' that came from various circles and levels of learning."

The documents read like composite works, and appear to possess complicated compositional histories.

In light of our review of the complex compositional histories underlying other Jewish and early Christian texts (see ch. 2), such conclusions come as no surprise. The composite character of the Pastorals simply reflects the widespread practices of the literary environment out of which they emerged.[24]

Genuine Pauline notes?

There is good reason to believe that the present text of the Pastorals incorporates genuine Pauline notes that were written to Timothy and Titus at some time during Paul's missionary activity. The presence of authentic material within the Pastorals has been advocated since 1836, but the greatest proponent of the theory remains P. N. Harrison. On literary, historical, and doctrinal grounds, Harrison advocates the presence of three genuine notes in the Pastorals: (1) Titus 3:12–15; (2) II Tim. 4:9–15, 20–21a, 22b; and (3) II Tim. 1:16–18; 3:10f; 4:1, 2a, 5b–8, 16–19, 21b, 22a.[25] His unique dissection and recombination of these notes is open to debate, but his argument for accepting the presence of some genuine material within the Pastorals seems compelling.

C. K. Barrett affirms the basic thrust of Harrison's position, and suggests that by the acceptance of this theory "both the Pauline characteristics of certain verses, and the non-Pauline characteristics of the Epistles as a whole, receive their due."[26]

But the major drawback of the "fragments" hypothesis, as Harrison and Barrett propound it, is that it provides no convincing explanation as to how or why splintered bits from various Pauline letters were preserved prior to their being collected and placed in the artificial framework of the Pastorals. This is the problem that led A. T. Hanson to abandon the "fragments" theory and treat the Pastorals as wholly pseudonymous.[27]

---

[24] Some textual evidence still survives that indicates how easily the Pastorals lent themselves to additions and expansion; in codex 460, two lengthy "regulations" have been added to the text at Titus 1:9 and 1:11; in II Tim. 3:11, the sufferings that Paul underwent in Antioch, Iconium, and Lystra (II 3:11) are attributed to Thecla (from the Acts of Paul and Thecla) in codex 181; the same MS adds the names of three persons to the greetings in II 4:19 (also taken from the Acts of Paul and Thecla).

[25] P. N. Harrison, *Paulines and Pastorals* (London: Villiers, 1964), pp. 106–128.

[26] Barrett, *The Pastoral Epistles*, p. 10.

[27] Hanson defends the "fragments" hypothesis in his commentary on the Pastorals

Hanson's reservations are justified; the likelihood of such nondescript fragments surviving seems remote. But the difficulties are greatly lessened if the fragments are regarded not as miscellaneous scraps of worn-out Pauline letters, but as the original Pastoral letters themselves; that is, each of our three Pastorals originated as an authentic note written by the apostle to Timothy and Titus. These three notes were read by the recipients, who then handed them over to the scribes responsible for preserving the community's sacred writings. Over the course of transmission, the notes were expanded by the addition of other sacred community traditions; the expansion was not intended to make the letters "look" Pauline; rather, it was motivated by the community's desire to preserve the traditions and to be instructed by them.

This theory, of course, involves considerable speculation, but it is not without significant supporting evidence; the book of Jeremiah, for example, in its present form, cannot be attributed to any one man; it is clearly made up of a variety of traditional materials. But there is little doubt that the book originated as a collection of genuine prophetic oracles from the great Jeremiah himself. Other materials were added later during the process of transmission. Similar literary histories are shared by most of the prophetic books.

If the Pastorals originated in this way, the question, "why three Pastorals?" no longer presents difficulties; we possess three letters because three Pauline notes were written and preserved. If these original notes were expanded by editorial activity, it becomes easier to understand why the Pastorals in their present form are characterized by abrupt and sudden shifts in subject matter and literary form. The lack of organization and development of thought is likewise clarified, and the letters can be read for what they are, not as the carefully honed products of an author, but as anthologies of traditional materials brought together by editors.

But if an original Pauline note is embedded within each of the Pastorals, can it still be identified? The early proponents of this theory often responded affirmatively to this question and sought to extricate each of the three notes from its respective matrix.[28] But

in the Cambridge Bible Commentary series published in 1966. His change of opinion is discussed in his later commentary, *The Pastoral Epistles*, p. 11.

[28] J. Moffatt canvasses the nineteenth-century attempts to identify the original Pauline letters within the Pastorals in the appendix of *The Historical New Testament* (Edinburgh: T. & T. Clark, 1901), pp. 700–704. See also the attempts by A. von Harnack (*Geschichte*, Vol. II [*Chronologie*], part 1, pp. 480ff.) and H. Binder, "Die historische Situation," pp. 70–83.

the sheer variety of their conclusions cautions one against such an attempt. It is probably no longer possible to determine the shape or the limit of the original Pauline letters with exact precision. Barrett rightly regards Harrison's neat distinctions with skepticism.[29]

Identification of authentic "core"

It seems better to present what appears to be the "core" of the original notes, without making any attempt to delimit them further. Additional study may show that other passages, regarded here as later traditions on Paul's life and ministry, should, in fact, be added to this authentic "core" (for example, I Tim. 1:12–17; 4:12–14; II Tim. 1:12b–14; 2:8–10, 17b–18).

> I Timothy
> 1:1–7   Salutation and occasion
> 1:18–20⎫
> 3:14–15⎭   Charges to Timothy (and current news)
> 6:20–21   Concluding charge and benediction

When these four passages are read consecutively, a plausible Pauline note emerges that instructs Timothy to remain in Ephesus because of serious disturbances that have arisen in that region of the Pauline mission. If traditions contained in Paul's farewell speech to the Ephesian elders are reliable (Acts 20:17–35), there is reason to believe that difficulties similar to those addressed in I Timothy were, in fact, encountered in Ephesus:[30]

> I know that after my departure fierce wolves will come in among you, not sparing the flock; and from among your own selves will arise men speaking perverse things, to draw away the disciples after them.   (Acts 20:29–30)

The dating and occasion of the note cannot be established; very little can be determined about Paul's situation. It is plain that he had recently been in Ephesus, leaving Timothy behind as he traveled on to Macedonia (I Tim. 1:3); at the time the letter was

---

[29] Barrett, *The Pastoral Epistles*, p. 11.
[30] The historical reliability of this passage is still a matter of debate. F.F. Bruce (*The Acts of the Apostles* [London: Tyndale Press, 1956], p. 377) finds much authentic material within the speech. *Pace* M. Dibelius, *Studies in the Acts of the Apostles*, ET by Mary Ling (London: SCM, 1956), pp. 155–158.

written Paul was clearly at liberty and was hoping to return soon to Ephesus (I Tim. 1:3; 3:14).

The situation described in the note could fit within the framework of the Ephesian ministry as described in Acts. As K. and S. Lake have noted:

> Modern scholars are increasingly aware that a comparison of I Corinthians with Acts shows that Luke left out much which one would have thought he must have known concerning Paul's life, and his account of what happened to Paul in Ephesus is probably quite as sketchy as his picture of the Corinthian church.[31]

C. K. Barrett also thinks it possible to fit I Timothy into Acts, although in his view "the evidence is too slight to warrant any decisive judgment."[32]

Since we do not know the outcome of Paul's trial in Rome (see Acts 28), it is possible that I Timothy was written by Paul sometime after the events described by Luke. That Paul was released from his Roman imprisonment and conducted other missionary campaigns (including Crete?) is very probable, as J. B. Lightfoot's summary of the evidence has shown.[33]

The purposes behind the note (as we have identified it) appear to have included the following:

1 to confirm previous instructions;
2 to provide Timothy with written apostolic authorization in support of his work;
3 to highlight the problem of false teachers in Ephesus;
4 to provide current news (1:19–20; 3:14);
5 to encourage Timothy in his charge.

Like the authentic letter imbedded within I Timothy, an original Pauline "core" can also be detected within Titus; it, too, has been splintered by the inclusion of various traditional materials:

---

[31] K. Lake and S. Lake, *An Introduction to the New Testament* (London: Christophers, 1938), p. 156.

[32] Barrett, *The Pastoral Epistles*, p. 8.

[33] J. B. Lightfoot, *Biblical Essays* (London: Macmillan, 1893), pp. 421–437 (esp. pp. 423ff.). N. Brox (*Die Pastoralbriefe*, Regensburger Neues Testament VII.2 [Regensburg: F. Pustet, 1969], p. 29), who argues for the pseudonymity of the Pastorals, nonetheless concludes that "according to [the friendly attitude of the authorities] it is very unlikely that this captivity and the trial [described in Acts 28] brought about the end for Paul."

Titus 1:1–5   Salutation and occasion
      3:9–11   Charge to Titus
      3:12–15   Current news and greetings
      3:15c   Benediction

The precise dating and occasion of this note are equally obscure. It is unlikely, however, that the writer of Acts would omit a major missionary campaign of the kind alluded to here; this may tilt the evidence in favor of a post-Acts 28 dating.

The note has a structure very much like that of I Timothy, a fact that suggests that its purposes may also have been similar. Again, the following concerns are discernible:

1   to confirm previous instructions;
2   to provide Timothy with written apostolic authorization for his reforms;
3   to highlight the problem of church order and dissension in Crete (1:5; 3:99ff.);
4   to provide current news (3:12);
5   to encourage Titus in his charge.

At least one, and possibly two (see below), Pauline notes (hereafter called II Tim. "A," II Tim. "B") appear imbedded within II Timothy:

II Timothy "A"

II Tim. 1:1–2   Salutation and occasion
      (1:3–5   Thanksgiving?)
      1:15–18 Personalia and current news
      4:6–8   Paul's situation
      4:22a   Closing benediction

Unlike the Pauline notes to Timothy (I Timothy) and Titus (above), II Timothy "A" was not intended to provide an apostolic authorization for Timothy's work. It is, rather, a brief farewell exhortation from Paul to Timothy, and contains a moving account of Paul's circumstances and expected fate (4:6–8) as a prisoner (1:8) in Rome (1:17). From Paul's remarks in 4:6–8, it seems likely that the note was written shortly before his execution.

There is no compelling reason to deny the authenticity (or the unity) of II Tim. 4:9–21, although a number of difficulties make it unlikely that this passage was originally a part of the letter outlined above. The "routine" remarks and casual greetings that appear in

4:9ff. hardly seem appropriate following Paul's moving description of his "finished course" in 4:6–8; the abrupt break in thought and tone between II Tim. 4:8 and 4:9 could scarcely be more pronounced. Paul's clear resignation to his fate in 4:6–8 is difficult to square with his confident assertion that "the Lord will deliver me" in 4:18. In light of such incongruities, it seems best to regard II Tim. 4:9–21, 22b as another genuine Pauline note (II Tim. "B") that at some point was editorially fused onto the letter outlined above;[34] that independent documents of considerable length could be appended onto existing texts in this way (without any editorial acknowledgment of the fact) is clear from the evidence examined in chapter 2 of this study. The original salutation of this note was most likely omitted when the note was appended to the end of II Timothy "A." The note addresses the following concerns:

II Timothy "B"

II Tim. 4:9	Occasion
4:10–18	Current news and requests
4:19–21	Greetings
4:22b	Closing benediction

Each of these four Pauline notes is plausible as a complete and independent letter. The fact that the notes are very brief, relatively innocuous, and directed to individuals rather than communities might raise doubts about the church's interest in preserving them. But there are good reasons for thinking that these notes would have been treasured by at least some early Christian communities.

The notes imbedded within the letters of I Timothy and Titus were probably used by Timothy and Titus as seals of apostolic "authorization," providing written certification of the tasks which they had been called upon to fulfil. Later, the churches may have preserved the notes, using to good effect the apostle's general warning of the threat of false teachers.

The personal note to Timothy (II Timothy "A") was probably immediately cherished by early Christians in Pauline circles, both for its record of Paul's final days and its moving farewell testimonial.

---

[34] A similar solution to the literary difficulties of II Tim. 4:9–22 has been offered by W. Lock, *The Pastoral Epistles* (Edinburgh: T. & T. Clark, 1924), p. xxxiii: "It is therefore most probable that an earlier note, or perhaps more than one earlier note, from Paul to Timothy, has been, whether intentionally or unintentionally, added to the main letter at the end, as apparently Rom. 16 was added to 1–15."

Although the reasons for preserving II Timothy "B" are not as obvious as those for the other three letters, at least two possible motives present themselves: (1) the note provides significant information on the whereabouts of other co-workers within the Pauline circle; this could explain Timothy's initial desire to retain the note; (2) but more significantly, the note identifies Alexander the coppersmith (4:14) as an enemy to Paul and his circle; the identification of a Pauline opponent by the great apostle himself would have been of great importance to early Christian communities seeking to defend themselves against such opponents and their teachings. The polemical weight that such a note could carry is obvious. It is no surprise that a note like that would be preserved.

In each of the above letters (except II Timothy "B") the original Pauline notes have been splintered; blocks of non-Pauline materials have been editorially sandwiched between genuine Pauline elements with no indication that redactional activity has taken place. Such editorial license, as we observed in chapter 2, was commonplace within the literary circles out of which the Pastorals emerged.

The process of splintering genuine letters by the inclusion of other materials is roughly paralleled in the long recension of the Ignatius corpus. Admittedly, the Ignatian additions were inserted much later (AD 400?) into non-apostolic letters and, consequently, do not precisely parallel the redactional situation that we encounter in the Pastorals. But the fact that genuine letters *could* be enlarged and splintered by editorial additions is surely confirmed by the Ignatian evidence.

A community of scribes

But if the Pastoral letters originated in the way we have conjectured, what kind of community must we envisage that could effectively collect, transcribe, and circulate these sacred materials? Several fundamental requirements immediately present themselves; such a community would need to possess:

1 a zeal to preserve the sacred traditions;
2 some sort of communal "library" or archives where the sacred traditions could be preserved;
3 a facility where the copying and collecting could take place;
4 a group of trained scribes;

5   an organizational scheme whereby the basic needs of the scribes would be provided.

The existence of such facilities within Christian communities is a matter of speculation; considerable evidence, however, suggests that organized and highly trained religious groups did exist, dedicated to preserving and passing on sacred traditions. Perhaps the most notable example is that of the Qumran community. As J. van der Ploeg has noted:

> At Qumran, men busied themselves with writing, reading and studying. The first we know, apart from other proofs, from the ink-wells which have been found in the remains of the building and those of the secondary buildings at Ain Feshkha, the second from the many manuscripts in the neighboring caves, the third from the prescriptions of the Rules.[35]

If, as seems likely, the Jewish sect known as the Essenes and the Qumran community were one and the same,[36] then we have additional testimony from Josephus of the "extraordinary interest" that the members displayed in "the writings of the ancients," each novitiate being required to swear "carefully to preserve the books of the sect."[37]

Qumran: the scriptorium

Archaeological evidence also suggests that a "scriptorium" existed at Qumran in which the compiling and copying of sacred MSS took place.[38] Concerning the tables and ink-wells found in the long room at Khirbet Qumran, R. de Vaux remarks:

[35] J. van der Ploeg, *The Excavations at Qumran: A Survey of the Judean Brotherhood and its Ideals*, ET by K. Smyth (London: Longmans, Green, 1958), p. 150. On the prescriptions, see IQS 6.7–8: "And the congregation shall watch in community for a third of every night of the year, to read the Book and to study Law and to pray together" (Vermes's translation).

[36] This is the verdict rendered by the majority of scholars; see the evidence offered by A. Dupont-Sommer, *The Essene Writings from Qumran*, ET by G. Vermes (Oxford: Basil Blackwell, 1961), pp. 39–67. See also G. Vermes, *The Dead Sea Scrolls: Qumran in Perspective* (London: SCM, 1982), pp. 116–136.

[37] Josephus, *The Jewish War* 136, 142 (LCL). See also Philo's accounts of the Essenes in *Every Good Man is Free* (75–91) and *Hypothetica* (11.1–18).

[38] That such a facility existed at Qumran has been widely accepted. See, for example, F. M. Cross, *The Ancient Library of Qumran and Modern Biblical Studies* (New York: Scribners, 1958), p. 67; J. T. Milik, *Ten Years of Discovery in*

Is it not reasonable to regard these tables and inkwells as the furniture of a room where writing was carried on, a *scriptorium* in the sense in which this term later came to be applied to similar rooms in monasteries in the Middle Ages?[39]

A zeal to preserve sacred traditions would naturally lead to the development of such a facility. The seriousness with which the Qumran community regarded its task to transmit the community's traditions is reflected not only in the enormous collection of MSS that was discovered in the nearby caves, but also in the apparent emphasis that was placed upon the training of scribes. The quality of the Qumran MSS leads Dupont-Sommer to conclude that

> the Qumran scribes could not have acquired such mastery of the art of writing as seen in the discovered manuscripts without a long apprenticeship.[40]

Other evidence uncovered at Qumran also suggests that scribal apprentices were trained there. A potsherd, for example, found among the ruins, appears to have served as an exercise tablet for a trainee scribe. The letters of the Hebrew alphabet are inscribed upon the piece, and these letters correspond exactly to those of some of the scrolls found in the caves; some of the letters on the potsherd have been corrected, suggesting that it was the work of an apprentice.

If this reading of the evidence be correct, we have in Qumran a clear first-century illustration of the kind of religious community that could produce documents like the Pastorals – a monastic community zealous to preserve the sacred traditions, furnished with trained scribes, and equipped with adequate facilities for the transcription of such documents. This is not, of course, to say that the Pastorals were written at Qumran! The discoveries at Qumran, however, are of prime importance for our study, for they provide

the Wilderness of Judea, ET by J. Strugnell (London, SCM, 1958), p. 22; B. M. Metzger, "The Furniture in the Scriptorium at Qumran," *Revue de Qumran* 1 (1958–1959), 509–515. But see also the objections of G. R. Driver, who maintains that the room thought to be the scriptorium at Qumran was actually a refectory ("Myths of Qumran," *Annual of Leeds Oriental Society* 6 [1966–1968], 23–27).

[39] R. de Vaux, *Archaeology of the Dead Sea Scrolls* (London: Oxford University Press, 1973); pp. 29–30; de Vaux argues that MSS were both copied and composed at Qumran (cf. p. 104).

[40] Dupont-Sommer, *The Essene Writings*, p. 63.

convincing evidence that the sort of community we have imagined necessary for the production of the Pastorals did, in fact, exist.

The Therapeutae

But how widespread were such communities? Is there any reason to think that there were Qumran-like organizations elsewhere? We know from a number of sources that various Essene communities existed, though the members' lifestyle in the "camps" seems to have varied considerably from that of the monastic setting of Qumran.[41] But there is also evidence that non-Essene communities dedicated to the sanctified life and the preservation of sacred traditions were thriving too. Philo tells us of the Therapeutae, another Jewish group which zealously guarded the sacred traditions:

> They read the Holy Scriptures ... They also have writings of men of old, the founders of their way of thinking.[42]

Philo describes the Therapeutae in terms that carry some of the marks of later monasticism, an institution which is nowhere else described within the literature of the period.[43] The members of this community lived in simple huts clustered closely enough together to provide opportunities for fellowship as well as to protect against robbers (*CL* 24). In each of the huts was a consecrated room called a μοναστήριον in which the Therapeutae would meditate upon the sacred texts and the mysteries of the sanctified life:

> They take nothing into it, either drink or food or any other of the things necessary for the needs of the body, but laws and oracles delivered through the mouth of prophets, and psalms and anything else which fosters and perfects knowledge and piety.   (*CL* 25)

It is clear from Philo's account that members of this community

---

[41] The existence of various "camps" is attested in the Damascus Document (XII.19, 23). In spite of his tendency to eulogize the Essenes, there is no compelling reason to deny Philo's report that "they live in many cities of Judea and in many villages and grouped in great societies of many members" (*Hypothetica* 11.1).

[42] Philo, *The Contemplative Life* (hereafter *CL*) 28–29 (LCL).

[43] In his introduction to the LCL translation of *CL* (Vol. IX, p. 105), F. H. Colson remarks on the historical importance of Philo's description of the monastic Therapeutae community (or communities?).

were also involved, like the Essenes, in the composition of sacred texts:

> And so they do not confine themselves to contemplation but also compose hymns and psalms to God in all sorts of metres and melodies which they write down.   (*CL 29*)

It is not clear what meaning is to be derived from Philo's cryptic remark that "this kind [of community] exists in many places in the inhabited world."[44] His mention of the widespread diffusion of these groups may be referring, not to the Therapeutae specifically, but to diverse and independent groups of religious enthusiasts who banded together in communities for the purpose of achieving a common goal. Such a reading would suggest that other religious communities similar in some respects to those of the Therapeutae and the Essenes were in existence at the time the Pastorals were produced.

The community of the Pastorals

Given the existence of such religious communities, it must be regarded as possible, if not likely, that some early Christian groups banded together in a similar fashion in order to preserve and circulate their own sacred writings.

But even if this be granted, major questions still remain regarding the production of a corpus like the Pastorals by such a community. How did such an editorial process occur? What kind of community would preserve such brief Pauline notes, enlarge them by the incorporation of a variety of traditional materials, and eventually circulate them to the churches? What purposes would motivate such extensive editorial activity? And what could account for the inclusion within the documents of sometimes very tiny fragments of traditional materials?

Becuse of the lack of evidence we find ourselves in a quandary of conjecture. Few questions regarding the compositional history of ancient texts can be easily or confidently answered. Scholars are equally bereft of information that might explain precisely how, for example, the composite book of Jeremiah was produced, and by what kind of scribal community. Even the redaction- and form-critics do not help us here; little work has been done (can be done?)

---

[44] *CL* 21. In his introduction to this work, F. H. Colson (Vol. IX, pp. 105–106) doubts that the Therapeutae were anything by a "small and ephemeral" group.

on the actual scribal practices that brought into existence the sacred
Jewish and Christian literature. To go forward at this point, we
must rely heavily upon historical imagination and plausible conjecture.

In this spirit, a few tentative proposals can be put forward that
may throw some light on how the compositional process, as we
have envisioned it for the Pastorals, may have actually occurred.

The community that produced the Pastorals clearly revered Paul
and his teachings. His letters were cherished as part of the larger
sacred tradition which the community felt under obligation both to
preserve and to circulate. The community must have had a
scriptorium-like setting in which the work of transcription and
compilation took place. They must also have had access to an
extensive archive room in which the collections of sacred texts were
preserved.[45]

It is not unlikely that such a community would be patterned after
the prophetic schools within Judaism. J. Lindblom describes such
schools in these words:

> Every prophet had a circle of disciples who transmitted the
> utterances of their master, various communications made
> by him, and, in addition, what they themselves remem-
> bered of the lives of the prophets. Generally speaking the
> task of the collectors was to bring this material together in
> larger or smaller collections which then became the
> groundwork of the prophetic books.[46]

A similar kind of collecting process seems to have been behind the
production of the Pastorals as we now possess them. But the
community out of which the Pastorals emerged was not only
devoted to Paul and his teachings. It saw itself as a guardian of all
the church's sacred traditions and, consequently, felt free to mix

---

[45] The existence of such "libraries" is well known. See the study by E.C.
Richardson, *Biblical Libraries: A Sketch of Library History from 3400 B.C. to
A.D. 150* (Princeton: University Press, 1914), p.183: "during the period say
between the birth of Jesus and the death of the last of those who figure in the
New Testament, one may distinguish at least six kinds or classes of libraries
known to have existed in Palestine; the temple libraries, a public central archive
in Jerusalem, local public archives in many and various places outside Jerusalem,
a probable public Greek library, the monastic libraries of the Essenes in
considerable numbers, hundreds and probably thousands of synagogue and other
school libraries, and a great number of private libraries."
[46] J. Lindblom, *Prophecy in Ancient Literature* (Oxford: Basil Blackwell, 1973),
pp. 239ff.

and blend sources together according to their particular needs and aims. This helps explain why the Pastorals seem to deviate from time to time from Paul's teaching as we know it elsewhere in his letters (cf. I Tim. 1:8).

Apart from the general desire to preserve sacred traditions, did the community have a particular aim in mind in compiling the materials that currently appear within the Pastorals? It seems very likely. The letters, in their own miscellaneous and rambling way, address concerns that would have been of great practical interest and benefit to Pastors and other leaders within the early church. They are a treasure-house of information on how to deal with various situations that arise in the church.

A school for Pastors

It is possible, then, that the school from which the Pastorals emerged was especially interested in the training and care of church leaders. The authentic Pauline letters to the two "Pastors," Timothy and Titus, which the community possessed, were perfectly suited as the framework upon which other materials appropriate to Pastors might be added.

The process of compiling such manuals for church leaders can be readily imagined. Traditional materials offering general instruction and guidance on, say, "leadership" would be collected from the archives. These would be sewn together and added to the Pauline notes. Other more specific matters of concern to church leaders would be similarly treated; for example, collections of instructions would be gathered on such issues as: the care and maintenance of widows, proper conduct in worship, and discipline of elders, the importance of prayer, the dangers of false teachings, the preservation of the traditions, guidelines for upright living, proper conduct toward outsiders, etc.

The compilation of such materials may also help explain the appearance of very short isolated sayings within the Pastorals. We know from the work of the form-critics that independent units of material, some of them very short, were circulating among, and being collected by, the early churches. The Gospel of Thomas may well represent such a collection of previously independent sayings by Jesus.

A scribal community dedicated to the preservation of sacred traditions, and equipped with archives, might have possessed many such collections of previously independent sayings. In the compilation of these "letters for Pastors," however, only the sayings that were considered relevant would be added in. This would account for the appearance within the Pastorals of very small isolated units that do not fit easily within their present context.

It must not be thought that the compilation of these materials, or the production of the Pastorals, was accomplished at any one specific time. It was most probably a lengthy process that went on for a considerable period; the documents may have gone through many stages of development, with additional materials being added as they came into the community's possession. Similar developmental processes are visible throughout the literature within, for example, the documents produced by the prophetic schools and wisdom schools, and even within such documents as the Didache and the Epistle of Barnabas.[47]

The origin of the Pastorals remains shrouded in mystery. In this study we have only begun to explore, as with eyes blinded, the literary environment out of which these letters emerged. The more scholarship can learn about ancient scribal communities and their organization, and about the methods used to preserve and circulate the sacred traditions, the more confident and less speculative will be our answers to these most tantalizing questions.

---

[47] See the remarks on the growth of prophetic literature, ibid., p. 279: "There are countless examples of additions, enlargements and comments, which show that the text was not regarded as in any way sacrosanct, but was subjected to alterations in accordance with the taste and the needs of later times." Compare the similar observations on wisdom literature in G. Fuhrer, *Introduction to the OT* (New York: Abingdon, 1968), pp. 316ff.

APPENDIX A

THE PASTORALS: COMPOSITIONS OR COLLECTIONS?

Are the pastorals, in their present form, the product of an author or the collections of a compiler? This, of course, is to put the question too simply, since ancient authors often functioned as compilers, drawing from and incorporating preexisting sources into their own work. The features, consequently, that distinguish an "author" from a "compiler" are admittedly blurred.

But granting the inherent difficulties in making such judgments, the question of composition versus collection remains central to a proper interpretation of any document. How one understands the book of Isaiah, for example, is largely determined by whether one reads it as the product of one author, or as a collection of various prophetic voices. The interpretation of the Pastorals is equally affected by such questions. The importance of correctly understanding the compositional method by which these letters were produced can scarcely be overstated.

If the Pastorals are the product of an author, one could presumably expect them to show some evidence of structure, a certain unity of thought, and a basic progression of argument.

Most commentators on the Pastorals do not address the question of literary structure within these letters. The documents are usually regarded (by scholars on both sides of the authenticity question) as loosely structured according to the form of ancient letters. Beyond that very little is said as to any authorial intent behind the structuring of these documents. It appears to be generally assumed that the epistolary genre in general, and the Pauline letter form in particular, was responsible for the structural forms that are revealed within these letters.

To some extent this judgment is accurate; the Pastorals do generally follow an epistolary format. But the structure that the letters take often deviates from that of the other Paulines – a difficulty for those who claim Paul or a Pauline imitator as the author. Why would an author intentionally change the internal structure of the "Pauline" letters? Why deviate, for example, from Paul's customary habit of placing the parenetic section at the end of the document? Why break the parenesis up and distribute it throughout the letters? It is possible that Paul dramatically changed his writing style, but it does not seem likely.

A. T. Hanson suggests that a pesudonymous author carefully structured the diverse blocks of material within these letters so that the writings would not look "too much like a manual of church order, or an exposition of Paul, or a book of worship, and [the pseudonymous author] wanted to give the impression he was writing letters."[1] But by arguing this, Hanson attributes the very features that make the Pastorals read so oddly as Pauline letters to a pseudonymous author wishing to imitate Paul!

Other larger questions of the Pastorals' literary structure, such as "why three Pastorals?" are also rarely discussed by the commentators. L. Houlden tries to make sense of the external structure of the letters by suggesting that the Pastorals were designed as a triptych, I Timothy and Titus written specifically to admonish and instruct, while II Timothy, the middle section, was intended to appeal to the reader's loyalty and sympathy.[2] Houlden is right in recognizing that the Pastorals seem to be treating similar matters, but it is not clear from this whether the similarity is the result of authorial intention or the collection of related materials by a compiler.

Both the internal and the external structure of the Pastorals, then, do not seem to yield any firm results regarding clear authorial intent in their design.

Whether the Pastorals show a clear unity of thought continues to be debated. C. K. Barrett includes in his commentary a brief, but detailed, section entitled "Theology and Practice" in which he presents the thinking of the Pastorals on such questions as "Man and Sin," "Salvation: Eschatology," etc. Barrett's method, like that of many other commentators, is to collect isolated passages on related subjects and view them as a whole. By so doing he makes a reasonable case for the basic harmony of thought within the Pastorals, although he finds the collection of passages on "Ethics" more difficult to hold together:

[1]   A. T. Hanson, *The Pastoral Letters*, The Cambridge Bible Commentary (Cambridge: University Press, 1966), p. 46.
[2]   L. Houlden, *The Pastoral Epistles* (Harmondsworth: Penguin, 1976), pp. 18ff.

Paul himself was deeply concerned about the moral beha-
viour of his churches, but he always makes clear the
theological and Christocentric basis of the moral demands
that he makes. It cannot be said that the Pastorals always
do this. Lists of moral duties are laid down, and sometimes
at least appear to exist in their own right, and as ends in
themselves.[3]

Other scholars have read the evidence differently from Barrett.
H. Windisch, for example, finds conflicting Christologies within the
Pastorals, as does A. T. Hanson, who occasionally tends (as here)
to make the author of the Pastorals a rather passive compiler:

[The author] does not have any doctrine of his own, but
makes use of whatever comes to him in the sources he uses
... The consequence is that we find several different ways
of expressing the significance of Christ in the Pastorals, not
all consistent with each other.[4]

We must conclude that the evidence for unity of thought in the
Pastorals is ambiguous.

The question of logical progression within the Pastorals remains.
B. S. Easton echoes a widely accepted view on these letters when he
observes that they show "no sustained thought beyond the limits of
the separate paragraphs; from paragraph to paragraph – and sometimes even within paragraphs – the topic changes without prepara-
tion and sometimes apparently without motive."[5]

Easton, of course, is not arguing here that the Pastorals should
be read as the collections of a compiler. Rather, he suggests that the
logical discontinuity of the materials within the letters is due to the
fact that the author was an unsystematic thinker who took little
interest in organizing the sources he employed.[6] It is this authorial
idiosyncrasy that accounts for the lack of clear logical progression
between the various literary elements within the letters.

---

[3]   C. K. Barrett, *The Pastoral Epistles* (Oxford: Clarendon Press, 1963), pp. 25–26.
[4]   H. Windisch, "Zur Christologie der Pastoralbriefe," *ZNW* 34 (1935), pp. 213f.
      A. T. Hanson, *The Pastoral Epistles*, The New Century Bible Commentary
      (Grand Rapids, MI: Eerdmans, 1982), pp. 38–39.
[5]   B. S. Easton, *The Pastoral Epistles* (London: SCM, 1948), p. 14. For similar
      views see M. Dibelius and H. Conzelmann, *The Pastoral Epistles* (Philadelphia:
      Fortress, 1972), pp. 8–10, N. Brox, *Die Pastoralbriefe*, Regensburger Neues
      Testament VII.2 (Regensburg: F. Pustet, 1969), pp. 49–55, and Hanson, *The
      Pastoral Epistles*, pp. 42–48.
[6]   See, for example, Brox, *Die Pastoralbriefe*, pp. 49–55.

Recently, however, this reading of the Pastorals has been vigorously disputed; a number of studies have been published that seek
to refute the view that these letters lack continuity of thought and
logical progression. The author of the Pastorals, it is argued, far
from being uninterested in organization and continuous argument,
has taken considerable care in the organization and presentation of
his materials. Since this line of argument runs directly counter to
that maintained in this book, an account of these studies must be
considered here in some detail.

Robert Karris's commentary *The Pastoral Epistles* briefly addresses the question of how the materials within the Pastorals are
ordered.[7] The brevity of this commentary restricted the extent to
which Karris could pursue the issue, but it is clear throughout the
work that he believes the Pastorals are carefully constructed letters
written by one pseudonymous author.

In commenting on II Tim. 2:14–26, for example, Karris begins a
section entitled "How the Author Thinks" with the sentence: "The
author of the Pastorals thinks quite differently from most of us."[8]
Karris goes on to argue that the apparent oddities are due to the
fact that II Timothy is an "exhortatory" letter and, as such, follows
the customs and norms of such letters.[9]

In treating the difficult passage I Tim. 1:3–20, Karris provides a
note entitled "How the Author Argues in this Section."[10] Here he
not only emphasizes the exhortatory nature of the letter, but adds
the suggestion that the author of the Pastorals "argues by means of
link words."

Karris's commentary is noteworthy since it attempts to demonstrate, albeit briefly, that logic and continuity of thought are not
alien to the Pastorals. His suggestion that the "Pastor" argues by
means of "contrasts" and "link words" is worthy of further
consideration.

Another study that argues for cogency and development of
thought within the Pastorals is D. Verner's *The Household of God:
The Social World of the Pastoral Epistles.*[11] Verner offers a "socio-
logical" reading of the Pastorals that seeks to show "the way in
which the author has used the traditional *Haustafel* schema and

[7] R. Karris, *The Pastoral Epistles* (Wilmington, DE: Michael Glazier, 1979).
[8] Ibid., p. 25.
[9] Ibid. See Karris's brief remarks on exhortatory letters on pp. 7–10.
[10] Ibid., pp. 53f.
[11] D. Verner, *The Household of God: The Social World of the Pastorals*, SBL
Dissertation Series 71 (Chico, CA: Scholars Press, 1983).

traditional materials to express his concept of the household of God.''[12]

Verner investigates the general nature of parenesis and concludes (*pace* Dibelius) that parenetic discourse can take the form of developed moral argumentation.[13] He defends this view by citing at some length the results of H. Cancik's study on the structure of parenetic discourse in Seneca's *Epistulae morales*. In her study, Cancik seeks to demonstrate that the diatribe style of argumentation in the epistles of Seneca is logically coherent. Verner finds Cancik's arguments convincing and suggests that her insights may be helpful in clarifying the kind of argumentation that is found within the Pastorals.

B. Fiore's monograph, *The Function of Personal Example in the Socratic and Pastoral Epistles*, is another significant contribution to the debate over method (or methods) of argumentation within the Pastorals.[14] Fiore's study is of limited value, however, in understanding the reasoning of the Pastorals as a whole, since he is primarily concerned with the function of personal example within the letters. Consequently, many puzzling passages within the Pastorals are not addressed in his work.

Nonetheless, Fiore makes a strong case that these letters should be read as the product of one author who carefully structured and organized his material. Fiore does this by examining the hortatory role of personal example in Greco-Roman literature, giving pride of place to the Socratic letters, which he thinks present the best literary parallels to the Pastorals:

> The editor of the [Socratic] corpus, who is also the pseudonymous author of a good part of it, has moulded and arranged his disparate sources into a collection of harmonious, if not uniform, letters.[15]

Although Fiore thinks that personal example is the principal hortatory device within the Pastorals, he allows that the author has

---

[12] Ibid., p. 25. This concern is addressed most directly in the Excursus on Paraenetic Discourse (pp. 112–125).

[13] Verner, like L. Donelson (see below), relies heavily upon the results of H. Cancik's research into the parenesis of Seneca's *Epistulae morales*.

[14] B. Fiore, *The Function of Personal Example in the Socratic and Pastoral Epistles* (Rome: Biblical Institute Press, 1986). See the positive reviews of Fiore's work by H. D. Betz in *JBL* 107 (1988), 335–337, and by R. Karris in *CBQ* 50 (1988), 134–135.

[15] Fiore, *The Function*, p. 107. In ch. 6 (pp. 101–163) Fiore presents a detailed examination of "personal example" in the Socratic letters.

utilized other rhetorical devices as well. He suggests, for example, that the argumentation of the Pastorals may occasionally reflect the influence of the developed "chria."[16] Elsewhere he remarks that "the tension of opposites provides what loose, overall structure there is in the [Pastoral] letters."[17]

Fiore's monograph is complemented in many respects by L. Donelson's study entitled *Pseudepigraphy and Ethical Argument in the Pastoral Letters*, published in the same year (1986).[18] Donelson's monograph provides the most comprehensive analysis yet available of the rhetorical methods of argumentation within the Pastorals. In a recent review of the work, R. Karris suggests that it may provide "major clues to solving the mystery of the Pastoral Epistles."[19]

In the second chapter (pp. 67–113), entitled "Forms of Argument," Donelson begins by suggesting that the Pastorals must be read as documents that "present carefully structured arguments which follow the parenetic canons of their day."[20] He seeks to demonstrate that the style of argumentation within the Pastorals follows closely that which appears within ancient rhetorical handbooks, especially as presented in Aristotle's *Art of Rhetoric*. When the Pastorals are evaluated according to the canons of ancient rhetoric it becomes clear, according to Donelson, that the author argues rhetorically by employing a method of deduction called enthymeme and a method of induction called paradigm.[21]

Considerable space (pp. 81–90) is given over to a comprehensive examination of the enthymemes that appear within the Pastorals. Donelson begins, for example, with I Tim. 1:15, in which he finds the syllogistic argument:

    A   Major premise: Jesus saves sinners.

    B   Minor premise: I am a sinner.

    C   Conclusion: Thus Jesus saved me.

---

[16] Ibid. See, especially, pp. 95–100.

[17] Ibid., p. 21.

[18] L. Donelson, *Pseudepigraphy and Ethical Argument in the Pastoral Epistles* (Tübingen: J. C. B. Mohr [P. Siebeck], 1986).

[19] R. Karris, review of *Pseudepigraphy*, *JBL* 107 (1988), 558–560. See, however, the much more critical review of Donelson's book by L. Johnson in *CBQ* 50 (1988), 131–133.

[20] Donelson, *Pseudepigraphy*, p. 69.

[21] Donelson's introduction to Aristotle's use of these terms is clearly presented on pp. 70–81. On the meaning of enthymeme and paradigm, he cites Aristotle: "I call an enthymeme a rhetorical syllogism, and a paradigm a rhetorical induction" (p. 75).

The author of the Pastorals does not actually state the conclusion (C), but, according to Donelson, this is intentional, for it allows readers (following the principles of enthymematic rhetoric) to draw it themselves.

Donelson then examines inductive and illustrative paradigms (pp. 90–108).[22] He argues that Paul is the source of the inductive paradigms in the Pastorals in a way analogous to the use of Socrates as a paradigm in the Socratic epistles, Seneca, and Epictetus. By Donelson's count the Pastorals contain six of these paradigms (all consisting of Pauline biographical material), four of which appear in I Timothy and two in II Timothy.[23]

Similarly, Donelson finds numerous illustrative paradigms in the Pastorals.[24] Most of these, he notes, offer a negative "portrait" of certain people and are usually followed in the Pastorals by a positive description of some sort. Donelson maintains that this method of argument is "reminiscent of the use of positive and negative paradigms in Seneca and Epictetus."[25]

In ch. 3 (pp. 115–198), entitled "The Cosmological and Ethical System," Donelson attempts to show that "the author of the Pastorals has put forward a cogent and consistent ethical system." In order to give this system warrant and authority, "the author uses the pseudepigraphical letter to rewrite the history of the church, so that his own faction and vision can enjoy apostolic support."[26]

Donelson's work is well researched, and his conclusions require close attention, for they clearly present a major challenge to those (including me) who argue that the Pastorals lack both continuity of thought and sustained argument. His work deserves much closer scrutiny than can be given in this short excursus. But some brief comments will not be out of place.

---

[22] Donelson's conclusions about the use of paradigms in Aristotle, Epictetus, Seneca, and the Cynic epistles are given on p. 100. Regarding the terms themselves, he writes: "In Aristotle, inductive paradigms are self-sufficient proofs used independently of enthymematic argument, and illustrative paradigms are witnesses or epilogues used to prove what has been deduced through enthymemes."

[23] Cf. I 1:12–17, 1:19–20; II 1:11–12; 2:9–10; 3:10–13; 4:6–22. Donelson finds no inductive paradigms in Titus.

[24] Donelson, *Pseudepigraphy*, pp. 106ff. Donelson groups the illustrative paradigms into two groups: those in which the person or persons are named (I 1:19–20; II 1:15–17; II 2:17–18; II 4:9–15) and those in which no names appear (I 1:3–4, 6–7; 6:3–5; II 3:1–9; II 4:3–4; Titus 1:10–16).

[25] Ibid., p. 108.

[26] Ibid., p. 198.

A critical response

In one sense the above works complement and supplement each other; they all find, for instance, that the Pastorals are best understood within the matrix of Greco-Roman pseudepigraphical literature, and are all in agreement that the Pastorals have been carefully designed by one pseudonymous author.

Each of the works, however, presents a different case for the unity and cohesion that they claim to find in the Pastorals. The flow of argument that Verner finds, for example, in the material on widows in I Tim. 5:3–16 is quite different from the enthymematic schema that Donelson detects.[27] Karris argues that the author of II Tim. 2:14–16 is arguing by means of contrasts, but Donelson suggests that the continuity lies in another enthymeme.[28] These differences in detecting the order within this material does not invalidate any one of the above approaches. Each must be examined on its own merits. The disparity does, however, considerably lessen the cumulative impact that these studies might otherwise have had on the question of coherent argumentation within the Pastorals. The reader is left wondering why, if there is such order within these letters, the experts cannot seem to agree among themselves as to what it is.

Another disturbing element within each of the above works is the almost complete neglect of Jewish sources. Donelson's reasons for omitting these writings derive from his belief that Christian *pseudepigraphical* letters most likely originated within a Greco-Roman and not a Jewish milieu.[29] This may or may not be true (A. Meyer among others strongly argues the contrary),[30] but in either case it has significance for us only if the Pastorals *are* pseudepigraphical, and it is precisely here that Donelson's work seems to beg the question. His study builds, and in many respects depends, upon the presupposition that the Pastorals are pseudonymous documents.[31] The possibility that authentic Pauline letters might lie imbedded

---

[27] See Verner, *The Household of God*, pp. 161–166; Donelson, *Pseudepigraphy*, pp. 86–90.

[28] Karris, *The Pastoral Epistles*, p. 25; Donelson, *Pseudepigraphy*, p. 87.

[29] Donelson draws heavily upon M. Smith; see his remarks in *Pseudepigraphy*, pp. 13–15.

[30] See A. Meyer, "Religiöse Pseudepigraphie als ethisch-psychologisches Problem," in *Pseudepigraphie in der heidnischen und jüdisch-christlichen Antike*, ed. N. Brox (Darmstadt: Wissenschaftliche Buchgesellschaft, 1977).

[31] Donelson, *Pseudepigraphy*, p. 8.

within the Pastorals is never considered.[32] Fiore's study also ignores Jewish literature, but at least he recognizes the relevance of such literature to a proper understanding of the Pastorals.[33]

In summary, it may be said that the arguments presented here for the presence of coherent and logical thinking within the Pastorals must be judged to be far from conclusive. This is not to say that the writings reviewed here do not have much to contribute to the study of the Pastorals. Donelson's approach, in fact, gives some force to the notion that the more atomistic reading of certain portions of the Pastorals (as proposed in this book) may have to be revised so as to permit more readily the occurrence of small groups of sentences which belong structurally together.

---

[32] Even if one were to grant the pseudonymity of the Pastorals, Donelson's presumption that Greco-Roman pseudepigraphical letters provide the best matrix within which to understand the Pastorals would have to be challenged. See, especially, D. Meade's monograph *Pseudonymity and Canon*, Wissenschaftliche Untersuchungen zum Neuen Testament 39 (Tübingen: J. C. B. Mohr [Paul Siebeck], 1986).

[33] At the close of chapter 2 (on "personal example") Fiore remarks in a footnote: "A study of example in the literature of the Jewish milieu is important for a complete understanding of the device in the Pastoral Epistles. The scope of this study, however, does not permit such an examination within these pages" (n. 67).

APPENDIX B

A FORMAL ANALYSIS OF THE PASTORAL LETTERS

If the Pastorals are made up of diverse and preformed elements, one would expect to find variations of style and form within these letters. The strophic divisions within our modern editions of the NT suggest that such is, indeed, the case; the Nestle–Aland edition,[1] for example, sets apart (by various forms of indentation) no fewer than eight passages within the Pastorals.[2] In the opinion of the editors these passages show significant differences in form and literary style from the surrounding materials. The paragraph and strophic divisions, consequently, have been created by the editors

> to aid the reader's understanding of the writings by clarifying their structure, e.g., in the Gospels distinguishing the primitive units.[3]

The purpose of the following analysis is to give the reader a kind of visual image of the various literary elements and forms which, in my view, permeate these letters. The advantage of viewing the Pastorals according to their respective formal elements is two-fold:

1   the "clustering" of materials according to topics or by word association stands out in clear relief;
2   the preformed elements (virtue/vice lists; community rules, etc.) protrude within their context by virtue of their distinctive forms.

The form analysis presented below attempts to separate the various formal and preformed elements that have been editorially joined together. It is remarkable how often these materials seem to

[1]   *Novum Testamentum Graece*, ed. E. Nestle, K. Aland, et al., 26th ed. (Stuttgart: Deutsche Bibelstiftung, 1979.
[2]   See, for example, I 2:5–6; 3:16; 6:7–8, 11–12, 15b–16; II 1:9–10; 2:11–13; Titus 3:4–7.
[3]   *Novum Testamentum Graece*, p. 44 (introduction).

fall neatly into independent "clusters" of related materials or forms. I have tried to highlight the various independent elements within the letters by setting the first words of the new "cluster" to the left of the rest of the material. So, for example, distinctive blocks of material begin, I think, at I Tim. 1:1, 3c, 8, 9. My analysis also seeks to highlight the presence of formal literary "signals" or "markers" that often appear at the beginning or at the end of preformed traditions within the Pastorals. See, for example, οἴδαμεν δὲ ὅτι (I 1:8); εἰδὼς τοῦτο, ὅτι (I 1:9).

I Timothy

1:1 Παῦλος

ἀπόστολος Χριστοῦ Ἰησοῦ
κατ᾽ ἐπιταγὴν θεοῦ σωτῆρος ἡμῶν
καὶ Χριστοῦ Ἰησοῦ τῆς ἐλπίδος ἡμῶν

1:2 Τιμοθέῳ γνησίῳ τέκνῳ ἐν πίστει · χάρις, ἔλεος, εἰρήνη
ἀπὸ θεοῦ πατρὸς καὶ Χριστοῦ Ἰησοῦ τοῦ κυρίου ἡμῶν.

1:3 Καθὼς παρεκάλεσά σε προσμεῖναι ἐν Ἐφέσῳ
πορευόμενος εἰς Μακεδονίαν, ἵνα παραγγείλῃς τισὶν

1:3c μὴ ἑτεροδιδασκαλεῖν μηδὲ προσέχειν μύθοις καὶ
γενεαλογίαις ἀπεράντοις, αἵτινες ἐκζητήσεις
παρέχουσιν μᾶλλον ἢ οἰκονομίαν θεοῦ τὴν ἐν πίστει.
τὸ δὲ τέλος τῆς παραγγελίας ἐστὶν ἀγάπη ἐκ καθαρᾶς
καρδίας καὶ συνειδήσεως ἀγαθῆς, καὶ πίστεως
ἀνυποκρίτου ὧν τινες ἀστοχήσαντες ἐξετράπησαν εἰς
ματαιολογίαν, θέλοντες εἶναι νομοδιδάσκαλοι, μὴ
νοοῦντες μήτε ἃ λέγουσιν μήτε περὶ τίνων
διαβεβαιοῦνται.

1:8 Οἴδαμεν δὲ ὅτι
καλὸς ὁ νόμος ἐάν τις αὐτῷ νομίμως χρῆται,

1:9 εἰδὼς τοῦτο, ὅτι
δικαίῳ νόμος οὐ κεῖται,
ἀνόμοις δὲ καὶ ἀνυποτάκτοις,
ἀσεβέσι καὶ ἁμαρτωλοῖς,
ἀνοσίοις καὶ βεβήλοις,
πατρολῴαις καὶ μητρολῴαις,
ἀνδροφόνοις,

πόρνοις,
ἀρσενοκοίταις,
ἀνδραποδισταῖς,
ψεύσταις,
ἐπιόρκοις,

καὶ εἴ τι ἕτερον τῇ ὑγιαινούσῃ
διδασκαλίᾳ ἀντίκειται,

1:11   κατὰ τὸ εὐαγγέλιον τῆς δόξης
τοῦ μακαρίου θεοῦ, ὃ ἐπιστεύθην ἐγώ.

1:12   Χάριν ἔχω τῷ ἐνδυναμώσαντί με Χριστῷ Ἰησοῦ
τῷ κυρίῳ ἡμῶν, ὅτι πιστόν με ἡγήσατο θέμενος εἰς
διακονίαν. τὸ πρότερον ὄντα βλάσφημον καὶ διώκτην
καὶ ὑβριστήν ·

ἀλλὰ ἠλεήθην, ὅτι ἀγνοῶν ἐποίησα ἐν
ἀπιστίᾳ, ὑπερεπλεόνασεν δὲ ἡ χάρις τοῦ κυρίου ἡμῶν
μετὰ πίστεως καὶ ἀγάπης τῆς ἐν Χριστῷ Ἰησοῦ.

1:15   πιστὸς ὁ λόγος καὶ πάσης ἀποδοχῆς ἄξιος, ὅτι

Χριστὸς Ἰησοῦς ἦλθεν εἰς τὸν κόσμον
ἁμαρτωλοὺς σῶσαι · ὧν πρῶτός εἰμι ἐγώ,

1:16   ἀλλὰ διὰ τοῦτο ἠλεήθην, ἵνα ἐν ἐμοὶ πρώτῳ
ἐνδείξηται Χριστὸς Ἰησοῦς τὴν ἅπασαν
μακροθυμίαν, πρὸς ὑποτύπωσιν τῶν μελλόντων
πιστεύειν ἐπ' αὐτῷ εἰς ζωὴν αἰώνιον.

1:17   τῷ δὲ βασιλεῖ τῶν αἰώνων,
ἀφθάρτῳ,
ἀοράτῳ,
μόνῳ θεῷ,
τιμὴ καὶ δόξα εἰς τοὺς αἰῶνας τῶν αἰώνων · ἀμήν.

1:18   Ταύτην τὴν παραγγελίαν παρατίθεμαί σοι, τέκνον
Τιμόθεε, κατὰ τὰς προαγούσας ἐπὶ σὲ προφητείας, ἵνα
στρατεύῃ ἐν αὐταῖς τὴν καλὴν στρατείαν, ἔχων πίστιν
καὶ ἀγαθὴν συνείδησιν, ἥν τινες ἀπωσάμενοι περὶ τὴν
πίστιν ἐναυάγησαν, ὧν ἐστιν Ὑμέναιος καὶ
Ἀλέξανδρος, οὓς παρέδωκα τῷ Σατανᾷ
ἵνα παιδευθῶσιν μὴ βλασφημεῖν.

2:1   Παρακαλῶ οὖν πρῶτον πάντων ποιεῖσθαι

δεήσεις,
προσευχάς,
ἐντεύξεις,
εὐχαριστίας,
ὑπὲρ πάντων ἀνθρώπων,
ὑπὲρ βασιλέων καὶ πάντων τῶν ἐν ὑπεροχῇ ὄντων,
ἵνα ἤρεμον καὶ ἡσύχιον βίον διάγωμεν ἐν πάσῃ
εὐσεβείᾳ καὶ σεμνότητι.

2:3   τοῦτο καλὸν καὶ ἀπόδεκτον ἐνώπιον τοῦ
      σωτῆρος ἡμῶν θεοῦ,

2:4   ὃς πάντας ἀνθρώπους θέλει σωθῆναι
      καὶ εἰς ἐπίγνωσιν ἀληθείας ἐλθεῖν.

2:5   εἷς γὰρ θεός,
      εἷς καὶ μεσίτης θεοῦ καὶ ἀνθρώπων,
      ἄνθρωπος Χριστὸς Ἰησοῦς,
      ὁ δοὺς ἑαυτὸν ἀντίλυτρον ὑπὲρ πάντων,
      τὸ μαρτύριον καιροῖς ἰδίοις.

2:7   εἰς ὃ ἐτέθην ἐγὼ
      κῆρυξ καὶ ἀπόστολος – ἀλήθειαν λέγω, οὐ ψεύδομαι –
      διδάσκαλος ἐθνῶν ἐν πίστει καὶ ἀληθείᾳ.

2:8   Βούλομαι οὖν

      προσεύχεσθαι τοὺς ἄνδρας ἐν παντὶ τόπῳ,
        ἐπαίροντας ὁσίους χεῖρας
        χωρὶς ὀργῆς καὶ διαλογισμοῦ ·

2:9   ὡσαύτως καὶ γυναῖκας
        ἐν καταστολῇ κοσμίῳ μετὰ αἰδοῦς καὶ σωφροσύνης
          κοσμεῖν ἑαυτάς,
        μὴ ἐν πλέγμασιν καὶ χρυσίῳ ἢ μαργαρίταις
          ἢ ἱματισμῷ πολυτελεῖ,
        ἀλλ' ὃ πρέπει γυναιξὶν ἐπαγγελλομέναις
          θεοσέβειαν, δι' ἔργων ἀγαθῶν.

2:11 γυνὴ ἐν ἡσυχίᾳ μανθανέτω ἐν πάσῃ ὑποταγῇ ·

2:12 διδάσκειν δὲ γυναικὶ οὐκ ἐπιτρέπω, οὐδὲ αὐθεντεῖν
      ἀνδρός, ἀλλ' εἶναι ἐν ἡσυχίᾳ.

2:13 Ἀδὰμ γὰρ πρῶτος ἐπλάσθη, εἶτα Εὕα ·
        καὶ Ἀδὰμ οὐκ ἠπατήθη, ἡ δὲ γυνὴ ἐξαπατηθεῖσα

ἐν παραβάσει γέγονεν. σωθήσεται δὲ διὰ τῆς
τεκνογονίας, ἐὰν μείνωσιν ἐν πίστει καὶ ἀγάπῃ καὶ
ἁγιασμῷ μετὰ σωφροσύνης.

3:1a   Πιστὸς ὁ λόγος.

3:1b   εἴ τις ἐπισκοπῆς ὀρέγεται, καλοῦ ἔργου ἐπιθυμεῖ.

3:2   δεῖ οὖν τὸν ἐπίσκοπον ἀνεπίλημπτον εἶναι,
       μιᾶς γυναικὸς ἄνδρα,
       νηφάλιον,
       σώφρονα,
       κόσμιον,
       φιλόξενον,
       διδακτικόν,

3:3   μὴ πάροινον,
       μὴ πλήκτην,
       ἀλλὰ ἐπιεικῆ,
       ἄμαχον,
       ἀφιλάργυρον,

3:4   τοῦ ἰδίου οἴκου καλῶς προϊστάμενον,
       τέκνα ἔχοντα ἐν ὑποταγῇ
          μετὰ πάσης σεμνότητος ·

3:5   εἰ δέ τις τοῦ ἰδίου οἴκου προστῆναι οὐκ οἶδεν,
       πῶς ἐκκλησίας θεοῦ ἐπιμελήσεται;

3:6   μὴ νεόφυτον,
          ἵνα μὴ τυφωθεὶς εἰς κρίμα ἐμπέσῃ τοῦ διαβόλου.

3:7   δεῖ δὲ καὶ μαρτυρίαν καλὴν ἔχειν ἀπὸ τῶν ἔξωθεν,
          ἵνα μὴ εἰς ὀνειδισμὸν ἐμπέσῃ καὶ παγίδα τοῦ
          διαβόλου.

3:8   Διακόνους ὡσαύτως
          σεμνούς,
          μὴ διλόγους,
          μὴ οἴνῳ πολλῷ προσέχοντας,
          μὴ αἰσχροκερδεῖς,
             ἔχοντας τὸ μυστήριον τῆς πίστεως ἐν καθαρᾷ
             συνειδήσει.
          καὶ οὗτοι δὲ δοκιμαζέσθωσαν πρῶτον, εἶτα
          διακονείτωσαν ἀνέγκλητοι ὄντες.

3:11   γυναῖκας ὡσαύτως
          σεμνάς,
          μὴ διαβόλους,
          νηφαλίους,
          πιστὰς ἐν πᾶσιν.

3:12   διάκονοι ἔστωσαν
          μιᾶς γυναικὸς ἄνδρες,
          τέκνων καλῶς προϊστάμενοι καὶ τῶν ἰδίων οἴκων ·
          οἱ γὰρ καλῶς διακονήσαντες βαθμὸν
          ἑαυτοῖς καλὸν περιποιοῦνται καὶ πολλὴν
          παρρησίαν ἐν πίστει τῇ ἐν Χριστῷ Ἰησοῦ.

3:14   Ταῦτά σοι γράφω, ἐλπίζων ἐλθεῖν πρὸς σὲ τάχιον ·
          ἐὰν δὲ βραδύνω, ἵνα εἰδῇς πῶς δεῖ ἐν οἴκῳ θεοῦ
          ἀναστρέφεσθαι, ἥτις ἐστὶν ἐκκλησία θεοῦ ζῶντος,
          στῦλος καὶ ἑδραίωμα τῆς ἀληθείας.

3:16   καὶ ὁμολογουμένως μέγα ἐστὶν
          τὸ τῆς εὐσεβείας μυστήριον ·

              ὃς ἐφανερώθη ἐν σαρκί,
              ἐδικαιώθη ἐν πνεύματι,
              ὤφθη ἀγγέλοις,
              ἐκηρύχθη ἐν ἔθνεσιν,
              ἐπιστεύθη ἐν κόσμῳ,
              ἀνελήμφθη ἐν δόξῃ.

 4:1   Τὸ δὲ πνεῦμα ῥητῶς λέγει ὅτι

          ἐν ὑστέροις καιροῖς ἀποστήσονταί τινες τῆς πίστεως
          προσέχοντες πνεύμασιν πλάνοις
              καὶ διδασκαλίαις δαιμονίων,
          ἐν ὑποκρίσει ψευδολόγων, κεκαυστηριασμένων τὴν
              ἰδίαν συνείδησιν,
          κωλυόντων γαμεῖν,
          ἀπέχεσθαι βρωμάτων ἃ ὁ θεὸς ἔκτισεν εἰς
              μετάλημψιν μετὰ εὐχαριστίας τοῖς πιστοῖς καὶ
              ἐπεγνωκόσι τὴν ἀλήθειαν.
          ὅτι πᾶν κτίσμα θεοῦ καλόν,
              καὶ οὐδὲν ἀπόβλητον μετὰ εὐχαριστίας
                  λαμβανόμενον, ἁγιάζεται γὰρ διὰ λόγου θεοῦ
                  καὶ ἐντεύξεως.

4:6   Ταῦτα ὑποτιθέμενος τοῖς ἀδελφοῖς καλὸς ἔσῃ διά-
       κονος Χριστοῦ ᾽Ιησοῦ, ἐντρεφόμενος τοῖς λόγοις τῆς
       πίστεως καὶ τῆς καλῆς διδασκαλίας ᾗ
       παρηκολούθηκας·

4:7a   τοὺς δὲ βεβήλους καὶ γραώδεις μύθους παραιτοῦ.

4:7b   γύμναζε δὲ σεαυτὸν πρὸς εὐσέβειαν·

4:8   ἡ γὰρ σωματικὴ γυμνασία πρὸς ὀλίγον ἐστὶν ὠφέλιμος,
       ἡ δὲ εὐσέβεια πρὸς πάντα ὠφέλιμός ἐστιν, ἐπαγγελίαν
       ἔχουσα ζωῆς τῆς νῦν καὶ τῆς μελλούσης.

4:9   πιστὸς ὁ λόγος καὶ πάσης ἀποδοχῆς ἄξιος·

       εἰς τοῦτο γὰρ κοπιῶμεν καὶ ἀγωνιζόμεθα,
       ὅτι ἠλπίκαμεν ἐπὶ θεῷ ζῶντι,
       ὅς ἐστιν σωτὴρ πάντων ἀνθρώπων, μάλιστα πιστῶν.

4:11   παράγγελλε ταῦτα καὶ δίδασκε.

4:12   μηδείς σου τῆς νεότητος καταφρονείτω,
       ἀλλὰ τύπος γίνου τῶν πιστῶν
       ἐν λόγῳ,
       ἐν ἀναστροφῇ,
       ἐν ἀγάπῃ,
       ἐν πίστει,
       ἐν ἁγνείᾳ.

4:13   ἕως ἔρχομαι πρόσεχε τῇ ἀναγνώσει,
       τῇ παρακλήσει,
       τῇ διδασκαλίᾳ.

4:14   μὴ ἀμέλει τοῦ ἐν σοὶ χαρίσματος.
       ὃ ἐδόθη σοι διὰ προφητείας μετὰ ἐπιθέσεως
       τῶν χειρῶν τοῦ πρεσβυτερίου.

4:15   ταῦτα μελέτα, ἐν τούτοις ἴσθι,
       ἵνα σου ἡ προκοπὴ φανερὰ ᾖ πᾶσιν.

4:16a ἔπεχε σεαυτῷ καὶ τῇ διδασκαλίᾳ·
       ἐπίμενε αὐτοῖς·

4:16b τοῦτο γὰρ ποιῶν καὶ σεαυτὸν σώσεις
       καὶ τοὺς ἀκούοντάς σου.

5:1–2 Πρεσβυτέρῳ μὴ ἐπιπλήξῃς, ἀλλὰ παρακάλει
            ὡς πατέρα,
        νεωτέρους   ὡς ἀδελφούς,
        πρεσβυτέρας ὡς μητέρας,
        νεωτέρας   ὡς ἀδελφὰς
            ἐν πάσῃ ἁγνείᾳ.

5:3   Χήρας τίμα τὰς ὄντως χήρας.

5:4   εἰ δέ τις χήρα τέκνα ἢ ἔκγονα ἔχει,
        μανθανέτωσαν πρῶτον τὸν ἴδιον
        οἶκον εὐσεβεῖν καὶ ἀμοιβὰς ἀποδιδόναι
            τοῖς προγόνοις,

5:4c τοῦτο γάρ ἐστιν ἀπόδεκτον ἐνώπιον τοῦ θεοῦ.

5:5   ἡ δὲ ὄντως χήρα καὶ μεμονωμένη ἤλπικεν ἐπὶ θεὸν καὶ
        προσμένει ταῖς δεήσεσιν καὶ ταῖς προσευχαῖς νυκτὸς
        καὶ ἡμέρας·

5:6   ἡ δὲ σπαταλῶσα ζῶσα τέθνηκεν.

5:7   καὶ ταῦτα παράγγελλε, ἵνα ἀνεπίλημπτοι ὦσιν.

5:8   εἰ δέ τις τῶν ἰδίων καὶ μάλιστα οἰκείων
        οὐ προνοεῖται, τὴν πίστιν
        ἤρνηται καὶ ἔστιν ἀπίστου χείρων.

5:9   χήρα καταλεγέσθω
        μὴ ἔλαττον ἐτῶν ἑξήκοντα γεγονυῖα,
        ἑνὸς ἀνδρὸς γυνή,
        ἐν ἔργοις καλοῖς μαρτυρουμένη,
            εἰ ἐτεκνοτρόφησεν,
            εἰ ἐξενοδόχησεν,
            εἰ ἁγίων πόδας ἔνιψεν,
            εἰ θλιβομένοις, ἐπήρκεσεν,
            εἰ παντὶ ἔργῳ ἀγαθῷ ἐπηκολούθησεν.

5:11 νεωτέρας δὲ χήρας παραιτοῦ·
        ὅταν γὰρ καταστρηνιάσωσιν τοῦ Χριστοῦ,
            γαμεῖν θέλουσιν,
        ἔχουσαι κρίμα ὅτι τὴν πρώτην πίστιν ἠθέτησαν·
        ἅμα δὲ καὶ ἀργαὶ μανθάνουσιν,

περιερχόμεναι τὰς οἰκίας, οὐ μόνον δὲ
ἀργαὶ ἀλλὰ
καὶ φλύαροι
καὶ περίεργοι,
λαλοῦσαι τὰ μὴ δέοντα.

5:14   βούλομαι οὖν
νεωτέρας γαμεῖν,
τεκνογονεῖν,
οἰκοδεσποτεῖν,
μηδεμίαν ἀφορμὴν διδόναι τῷ ἀντικειμένῳ
λοιδορίας χάριν·
ἤδη γάρ τινες ἐξετράπησαν ὀπίσω
τοῦ Σατανᾶ.

5:16   εἴ τις πιστὴ ἔχει χήρας,
ἐπαρκείτω αὐταῖς,
καὶ μὴ βαρείσθω ἡ ἐκκλησία,
ἵνα ταῖς ὄντως χήραις ἐπαρκέσῃ.

5:17   Οἱ καλῶς προεστῶτες πρεσβύτεροι διπλῆς τιμῆς
ἀξιούσθωσαν, μάλιστα οἱ κοπιῶντες ἐν λόγῳ καὶ
διδασκαλίᾳ·

5:18a   λέγει γὰρ ἡ γραφή,
Βοῦν ἀλοῶντα οὐ φιμώσεις·
καί,

5:18b   Ἄξιος ὁ ἐργάτης τοῦ μισθοῦ αὐτοῦ.

5:19a   κατὰ πρεσβυτέρου κατηγορίαν μὴ παραδέχου,
ἐκτὸς εἰ μὴ ἐπὶ δύο ἢ πριῶν μαρτύρων.

5:20   τοὺς ἁμαρτάνοντας ἐνώπιον πάντων ἔλεγχε,
ἵνα καὶ οἱ λοιποὶ φόβον ἔχωσιν.

5:21   διαμαρτύρομαι ἐνώπιον τοῦ θεοῦ
καὶ Χριστοῦ Ἰησοῦ
καὶ τῶν ἐκλεκτῶν ἀγγέλων,
ἵνα ταῦτα φυλάξῃς χωρὶς προκρίματος,
μηδὲν ποιῶν κατὰ πρόσκλισιν.

5:22a   χεῖρας ταχέως μηδενὶ ἐπιτίθει,
μηδὲ κοινώνει ἁμαρτίαις ἀλλοτρίαις·

5:22b   σεαυτὸν ἁγνὸν τήρει.

5:23   μηκέτι ὑδροπότει, ἀλλὰ οἴνῳ ὀλίγῳ χρῶ
        διὰ τὸν στόμαχον καὶ τὰς πυκνάς σου
        ἀσθενείας.

5:24   τινῶν ἀνθρώπων αἱ ἁμαρτίαι πρόδηλοί εἰσιν,
        προάγουσαι εἰς κρίσιν,
        τισὶν δὲ καὶ ἐπακολουθοῦσιν ·
        ὡσαύτως
        καὶ τὰ ἔργα τὰ καλὰ πρόδηλα,
        καὶ τὰ ἄλλως ἔχοντα κρυβῆναι οὐ δύνανται.

6:1   Ὅσοι εἰσὶν ὑπὸ ζυγὸν δοῦλοι,
        τοὺς ἰδίους δεσπότας
        πάσης τιμῆς ἀξίους ἡγείσθωσαν,
        ἵνα μὴ τὸ ὄνομα τοῦ θεοῦ καὶ ἡ διδασκαλία
        βλασφημῆται.
        οἱ δὲ πιστοὺς ἔχοντες δεσπότας
        μὴ καταφρονείτωσαν,
            ὅτι ἀδελφοί εἰσιν ·
        ἀλλὰ μᾶλλον δουλευέτωσαν,
            ὅτι πιστοί εἰσιν καὶ ἀγαπητοὶ
            οἱ τῆς εὐεργεσίας ἀντιλαμβανόμενοι.

6:2c   Ταῦτα δίδασκε καὶ παρακάλει.

6:3   εἴ τις ἑτεροδιδασκαλεῖ καὶ μὴ προσέρχεται
        ὑγιαίνουσιν λόγοις, τοῖς τοῦ κυρίου ἡμῶν ᾽Ιησοῦ
            Χριστοῦ,
        καὶ τῇ κατ' εὐσέβειαν διδασκαλίᾳ,
        τετύφωται,
        μηδὲν ἐπιστάμενος,

6:4b   ἀλλὰ νοσῶν περὶ ζητήσεις καὶ λογομαχίας,
        ἐξ ὧν γίνεται
            φθόνος,
            ἔρις,
            βλασφημίαι,
            ὑπόνοιαι πονηραί,
        διαπαρατριβαὶ διεφθαρμένων ἀνθρώπων τὸν νοῦν καὶ
            ἀπεστερημένων τῆς ἀληθείας,
        νομιζόντων πορισμὸν εἶναι τὴν εὐσέβειαν.

6:6   ἔστιν δὲ πορισμὸς μέγας ἡ εὐσέβεια μετὰ αὐταρκείας ·

6:7   οὐδὲν γὰρ εἰσηνέγκαμεν εἰς τὸν κόσμον, ὅτι οὐδὲ
       ἐξενεγκεῖν τι δυνάμεθα ·

6:8   ἔχοντες δὲ διατροφὰς καὶ
       σκεπάσματα, τούτοις ἀρκεσθησόμεθα.

6:9   οἱ δὲ βουλόμενοι πλουτεῖν ἐμπίπτουσιν
       εἰς πειρασμὸν καὶ παγίδα
       καὶ ἐπιθυμίας πολλὰς ἀνοήτους καὶ βλαβεράς,
       αἵτινες βυθίζουσιν τοὺς ἀνθρώπους
       εἰς ὄλεθρον καὶ ἀπώλειαν ·

6:10   ῥίζα γὰρ πάντων τῶν κακῶν ἐστιν ἡ φιλαργυρία,
       ἧς τινες ὀρεγόμενοι ἀπεπλανήθησαν ἀπὸ τῆς
       πίστεως καὶ ἑαυτοὺς περιέπειραν ὀδύναις πολλαῖς.

6:11   Σὺ δέ, ὦ ἄνθρωπε θεοῦ,
           ταῦτα φεῦγε · δίωκε δὲ
           δικαιοσύνην,
           εὐσέβειαν,
           πίστιν,
           ἀγάπην,
           ὑπομονήν,
           πραϋπαθίαν.

6:12   ἀγωνίζου τὸν καλὸν ἀγῶνα τῆς πίστεως,
       ἐπιλαβοῦ τῆς αἰωνίου ζωῆς,
           εἰς ἣν ἐκλήθης καὶ ὡμολόγησας τὴν καλὴν
           ὁμολογίαν ἐνώπιον πολλῶν μαρτύρων.

6:13   παραγγέλλω σοι
           ἐνώπιον τοῦ θεοῦ τοῦ ζῳογονοῦντος τὰ πάντα
           καὶ Χριστοῦ ᾿Ιησοῦ τοῦ μαρτυρήσαντος
           ἐπὶ Ποντίου Πιλάτου τὴν καλὴν ὁμολογίαν,
           τηρῆσαί σε τὴν ἐντολὴν ἄσπιλον ἀνεπίλημπτον

6:14   μέχρι τῆς ἐπιφανείας τοῦ κυρίου ἡμῶν ᾿Ιησοῦ
               Χριστοῦ,
               ἣν καιροῖς ἰδίοις δείξει ὁ μακάριος
               καὶ μόνος δυνάστης,

6:15b   ὁ βασιλεὺς τῶν βασιλευόντων
               καὶ κύριος τῶν κυριευόντων,
               ὁ μόνος ἔχων ἀθανασίαν,
               φῶς οἰκῶν ἀπρόσιτον,

ὃν εἶδεν οὐδεὶς ἀνθρώπων οὐδὲ ἰδεῖν δύναται ·
ᾧ τιμὴ καὶ κράτος αἰώνιον · ἀμήν.

6:17 Τοῖς πλουσίοις ἐν τῷ νῦν αἰῶνι παράγγελλε
μὴ ὑψηλοφρονεῖν
μηδὲ ἠλπικέναι ἐπὶ πλούτου ἀδηλότητι,
ἀλλ᾽ ἐπὶ θεῷ τῷ παρέχοντι ἡμῖν πάντα πλουσίως εἰς
ἀπόλαυσιν,
ἀγαθοεργεῖν,
πλουτεῖν ἐν ἔργοις καλοῖς,
εὐμεταδότους εἶναι,
κοινωνικούς,
ἀποθησαυρίζοντας ἑαυτοῖς θεμέλιον καλὸν εἰς τὸ
μέλλον, ἵνα ἐπιλάβωνται τῆς ὄντως ζωῆς.

6:20 Ὦ Τιμόθεε, τὴν παραθήκην φύλαξον,
ἐκτρεπόμενος τὰς βεβήλους κενοφωνίας καὶ
ἀντιθέσεις τῆς ψευδωνύμου γνώσεως,
ἥν τινες ἐπαγγελλόμενοι περὶ τὴν πίστιν
ἠστόχησαν.

6:21 Ἡ χάρις μεθ᾽ ὑμῶν.

II Timothy

1:1 Παῦλος

ἀπόστολος Χριστοῦ Ἰησοῦ διὰ θελήματος θεοῦ
κατ' ἐπαγγελίαν ζωῆς τῆς ἐν Χριστῷ Ἰησοῦ

Τιμοθέῳ ἀγαπητῷ τέκνῳ · χάρις, ἔλεος, εἰρήνη ἀπὸ
θεοῦ πατρὸς καὶ Χριστοῦ Ἰησοῦ τοῦ κυρίου ἡμῶν.

1:3 Χάριν ἔχω τῷ θεῷ, ᾧ λατρεύω ἀπὸ προγόνων ἐν
καθαρᾷ συνειδήσει, ὡς ἀδιάλειπτον ἔχω τὴν περὶ σοῦ
μνείαν ἐν ταῖς δεήσεσίν μου νυκτὸς καὶ ἡμέρας,
ἐπιποθῶν σε ἰδεῖν, μεμνημένος σου τῶν δακρύων, ἵνα
χαρᾶς πληρωθῶ, ὑπόμνησιν λαβὼν τῆς ἐν σοὶ
ἀνυποκρίτου πίστεως, ἥτις ἐνῴκησεν πρῶτον ἐν τῇ
μάμμῃ σου Λωΐδι καὶ τῇ μητρί σου Εὐνίκῃ, πέπεισμαι
δὲ ὅτι καὶ ἐν σοί.

1:6 δι᾽ ἣν αἰτίαν ἀναμιμνῄσκω σε ἀναζωπυρεῖν

τὸ χάρισμα τοῦ θεοῦ, ὅ ἐστιν ἐν σοὶ διὰ τῆς ἐπιθέσεως
τῶν χειρῶν μου ·

1:7   οὐ γὰρ ἔδωκεν ἡμῖν ὁ θεὸς πνεῦμα δειλίας,
ἀλλὰ δυνάμεως καὶ ἀγάπης καὶ σωφρονισμοῦ.

1:8   μὴ οὖν ἐπαισχυνθῇς τὸ μαρτύριον τοῦ κυρίου ἡμῶν
μηδὲ ἐμὲ τὸν δέσμιον αὐτοῦ,
ἀλλὰ συγκακοπάθησον τῷ εὐαγγελίῳ κατὰ δύναμιν
θεοῦ,

1:9   τοῦ σώσαντος ἡμᾶς
καὶ καλέσαντος κλήσει ἁγίᾳ,
οὐ κατὰ τὰ ἔργα ἡμῶν
ἀλλὰ κατὰ ἰδίαν πρόθεσιν καὶ χάριν,
τὴν δοθεῖσαν ἡμῖν ἐν Χριστῷ ᾿Ιησοῦ
πρὸ χρόνων αἰωνίων,
φανερωθεῖσαν δὲ νῦν διὰ τῆς ἐπιφανείας
τοῦ σωτῆρος ἡμῶν Χριστοῦ ᾿Ιησοῦ,
καταργήσαντος μὲν τὸν θάνατον
φωτίσαντος δὲ ζωὴν καὶ ἀφθαρσίαν διὰ τοῦ
εὐαγγελίου,

1:11   εἰς ὃ ἐτέθην ἐγὼ κῆρυξ καὶ ἀπόστολος καὶ διδάσκαλος.
δι᾿ ἣν αἰτίαν καὶ ταῦτα πάσχω,
ἀλλ᾿ οὐκ ἐπαισχύνομαι,

1:12b   οἶδα γὰρ ᾧ πεπίστευκα, καὶ πέπεισμαι ὅτι
δυνατός ἐστιν τὴν παραθήκην μου φυλάξαι
εἰς ἐκείνην τὴν ἡμέραν.

1:13   ὑποτύπωσιν ἔχε ὑγιαινόντων λόγων
ὧν παρ' ἐμοῦ ἤκουσας
ἐν πίστει καὶ ἀγάπῃ τῇ ἐν Χριστῷ ᾿Ιησοῦ ·

1:14   τὴν καλὴν παραθήκην φύλαξον διὰ πνεύματος ἁγίου τοῦ
ἐνοικοῦντος ἐν ἡμῖν.

1:15   Οἶδας τοῦτο, ὅτι ἀπεστράφησάν με πάντες οἱ ἐν
τῇ ᾿Ασίᾳ, ὧν ἐστιν Φύγελος καὶ ῾Ερμογένης.

δῴη ἔλεος ὁ κύριος τῷ ᾿Ονησιφόρου οἴκῳ, ὅτι
πολλάκις με ἀνέψυξεν καὶ τὴν ἅλυσίν μου οὐκ
ἐπαισχύνθη,
ἀλλὰ γενόμενος ἐν ῾Ρώμῃ σπουδαίως ἐζήτησέν με καὶ

εὗρεν – δῴη αὐτῷ ὁ κύριος εὑρεῖν ἔλεος παρὰ
κυρίου ἐν ἐκείνῃ τῇ ἡμέρᾳ –
καὶ ὅσα ἐν Ἐφέσῳ διηκόνησεν,
βέλτιον σὺ γινώσκεις.

2:1 Σὺ οὖν, τέκνον μου,

ἐνδυναμοῦ ἐν τῇ χάριτι τῇ ἐν
Χριστῷ Ἰησοῦ,

2:2 καὶ ἃ ἤκουσας παρ' ἐμοῦ διὰ πολλῶν μαρτύρων,
ταῦτα παράθου πιστοῖς ἀνθρώποις,
οἵτινες ἱκανοὶ ἔσονται καὶ ἑτέρους διδάξαι.

2:3 συγκακοπάθησον ὡς καλὸς στρατιώτης Χριστοῦ Ἰησοῦ.
οὐδεὶς στρατευόμενος ἐμπλέκεται
ταῖς τοῦ βίου πραγματείαις,
ἵνα τῷ στρατολογήσαντι ἀρέσῃ ·

2:5 ἐὰν δὲ καὶ ἀθλῇ τις,
οὐ στεφανοῦται ἐὰν μὴ νομίμως ἀθλήσῃ.

2:6 τὸν κοπιῶντα γεωργὸν δεῖ πρῶτον τῶν καρπῶν
μεταλαμβάνειν.

2:7 νόει ὃ λέγω ·
δώσει γάρ σοι ὁ κύριος σύνεσιν ἐν πᾶσιν.

2:8 Μνημόνευε Ἰησοῦν Χριστὸν
ἐγηγερμένον ἐκ νεκρῶν,
ἐκ σπέρματος Δαυίδ,

2:8c κατὰ τὸ εὐαγγέλιόν μου ·
ἐν ᾧ κακοπαθῶ μέχρι δεσμῶν ὡς κακοῦργος,
ἀλλὰ ὁ λόγος τοῦ θεοῦ οὐ δέδεται.

διὰ τοῦτο πάντα ὑπομένω διὰ τοὺς ἐκλεκτούς,
ἵνα καὶ αὐτοὶ σωτηρίας τύχωσιν τῆς
ἐν Χριστῷ Ἰησοῦ μετὰ δόξης αἰωνίου.

2:11 πιστὸς ὁ λόγος ·

εἰ γὰρ συναπεθάνομεν, καὶ συζήσομεν ·
εἰ ὑπομένομεν, καὶ συμβασιλεύσομεν ·
εἰ ἀρνησόμεθα, κἀκεῖνος ἀρνήσεται ἡμᾶς ·
εἰ ἀπιστοῦμεν, ἐκεῖνος πιστὸς μένει,
ἀρνήσασθαι γὰρ ἑαυτὸν οὐ δύναται.

2:14a   Ταῦτα ὑπομίμνησκε,
        διαμαρτυρόμενος ἐνώπιον τοῦ θεοῦ

2:14b   μὴ λογομαχεῖν, ἐπ' οὐδὲν χρήσιμον, ἐπὶ καταστροφῇ
        τῶν ἀκουόντων.

2:15   σπούδασον σεαυτὸν δόκιμον παραστῆσαι τῷ θεῷ,
        ἐργάτην ἀνεπαίσχυντον,
        ὀρθοτομοῦντα τὸν λόγον τῆς ἀληθείας.

2:16   τὰς δὲ βεβήλους κενοφωνίας περιΐστασο ·
        ἐπὶ πλεῖον γὰρ προκόψουσιν ἀσεβείας,
        καὶ ὁ λόγος αὐτῶν ὡς γάγγραινα νομὴν ἕξει ·

2:17b   ὧν ἐστιν Ὑμέναιος καὶ Φίλητος,
            οἵτινες περὶ τὴν ἀλήθειαν ἠστόχησαν,
            λέγοντες τὴν ἀνάστασιν ἤδη γεγονέναι,
            καὶ ἀνατρέπουσιν τήν τινων πίστιν.

2:19   ὁ μέντοι στερεὸς θεμέλιος τοῦ θεοῦ ἕστηκεν,
        ἔχων τὴν σφραγῖδα ταύτην ·

        Ἔγνω κύριος τοὺς ὄντας αὐτοῦ,
            καί,
        Ἀποστήτω ἀπὸ ἀδικίας πᾶς ὁ ὀνομάζων
            τὸ ὄνομα κυρίου.

2:10   Ἐν μεγάλῃ δὲ οἰκίᾳ οὐκ ἔστιν μόνον σκεύη
        χρυσᾶ καὶ ἀργυρᾶ
            ἀλλὰ καὶ
        ξύλινα καὶ ὀστράκινα, καὶ
        ἃ μὲν εἰς τιμὴν ἃ δὲ εἰς ἀτιμίαν ·

2:21   ἐὰν οὖν τις ἐκκαθάρῃ ἑαυτὸν ἀπὸ τούτων,
        ἔσται σκεῦος εἰς τιμήν,
        ἡγιασμένον,
        εὔχρηστον τῷ δεσπότῃ,
        εἰς πᾶν ἔργον ἀγαθὸν ἡτοιμασμένον.

2:22   τὰς δὲ νεωτερικὰς ἐπιθυμίας φεῦγε, δίωκε δὲ
            δικαιοσύνην,
            πίστιν,
            ἀγάπην,
            εἰρήνην

μετὰ τῶν ἐπικαλουμένων τὸν κύριον
ἐκ καθαρᾶς καρδίας.

2:23 τὰς δὲ μωρὰς καὶ ἀπαιδεύτους ζητήσεις παραιτοῦ,
εἰδὼς ὅτι
γεννῶσιν μάχας ·

2:24 δοῦλον δὲ κυρίου οὐ δεῖ μάχεσθαι,
ἀλλὰ ἤπιον εἶναι πρὸς πάντας,
διδακτικόν,
ἀνεξίκακον,
ἐν πραΰτητι παιδεύοντα τοὺς ἀντιδιατιθεμένους,
μήποτε δώῃ αὐτοῖς ὁ θεὸς μετάνοιαν
εἰς ἐπίγνωσιν ἀληθείας,
καὶ ἀνανήψωσιν ἐκ τῆς τοῦ διαβόλου παγίδος,
ἐζωγρημένοι ὑπ' αὐτοῦ εἰς τὸ ἐκείνου θέλημα.

3:1 Τοῦτο δὲ γίνωσκε, ὅτι
ἐν ἐσχάταις ἡμέραις ἐνστήσονται καιροὶ χαλεποί ·
ἔσονται γὰρ οἱ ἄνθρωποι
φίλαυτοι,
φιλάργυροι,
ἀλαζόνες,
ὑπερήφανοι,
βλάσφημοι,
γονεῦσιν ἀπειθεῖς,
ἀχάριστοι,
ἀνόσιοι,
ἄστοργοι,
ἄσπονδοι,
διάβολοι,
ἀκρατεῖς,
ἀνήμεροι,
ἀφιλάγαθοι,
προδόται,
προπετεῖς,
τετυφωμένοι,
φιλήδονοι μᾶλλον ἢ φιλόθεοι,
ἔχοντες μόρφωσιν εὐσεβείας τὴν δὲ δύναμιν
αὐτῆς ἠρνημένοι ·

3:5b καὶ τούτους ἀποτρέπου.

3:6   ἐκ τούτων γάρ εἰσιν οἱ ἐνδύνοντες εἰς τὰς οἰκίας
        καὶ αἰχμαλωτίζοντες γυναικάρια
        σεσωρευμένα ἁμαρτίαις,
        ἀγόμενα ἐπιθυμίαις ποικίλαις,
        πάντοτε μανθάνοντα καὶ μηδέποτε
        εἰς ἐπίγνωσιν ἀληθείας ἐλθεῖν δυνάμενα.

3:8   ὃν τρόπον δὲ Ἰάννης καὶ Ἰαμβρῆς ἀντέστησαν
        Μωϋσεῖ,
            οὕτως καὶ οὗτοι ἀνθίστανται τῇ ἀληθείᾳ,
            ἄνθρωποι κατεφθαρμένοι τὸν νοῦν,
            ἀδόκιμοι περὶ τὴν πίστιν·
        ἀλλ' οὐ προκόψουσιν ἐπὶ πλεῖον,
            ἡ γὰρ ἄνοια αὐτῶν ἔκδηλος ἔσται
        πᾶσιν, ὡς καὶ ἡ ἐκείνων ἐγένετο.

3:10   Σὺ δὲ
        παρηκολούθησάς μου τῇ διδασκαλίᾳ,

            τῇ ἀγωγῇ,
            τῇ προθέσει,
            τῇ πίστει,
            τῇ μακροθυμίᾳ,
            τῇ ἀγάπῃ,
            τῇ ὑπομονῇ,

            τοῖς διωγμοῖς,
            τοῖς παθήμασιν,

        οἷά μοι ἐγένετο ἐν Ἀντιοχείᾳ,
            ἐν Ἰκονίῳ,
            ἐν Λύστροις,
        οἵους διωγμοὺς ὑπήνεγκα·
        καὶ ἐκ πάντων με ἐρρύσατο ὁ κύριος.

3:12   καὶ πάντες δὲ οἱ θέλοντες ζῆν εὐσεβῶς ἐν
        Χριστῷ Ἰησοῦ διωχθήσονται·

3:13   πονηροὶ δὲ ἄνθρωποι καὶ γόητες
        προκόψουσιν ἐπὶ τὸ χεῖρον,
        πλανῶντες καὶ πλανώμενοι.

3:14   σὺ δὲ
        μένε ἐν οἷς ἔμαθες καὶ ἐπιστώθης,
        εἰδὼς παρὰ τίνων ἔμαθες,

3:15 καὶ ὅτι ἀπὸ βρέφους τὰ ἱερὰ γράμματα οἶδας,
   τὰ δυνάμενά σε σοφίσαι εἰς σωτηρίαν
   διὰ πίστεως τῆς ἐν Χριστῷ Ἰησοῦ.

3:16 πᾶσα γραφὴ θεόπνευστος καὶ ὠφέλιμος
   πρὸς διδασκαλίαν,
   πρὸς ἐλεγμόν,
   πρὸς ἐπανόρθωσιν,
   πρὸς παιδείαν τὴν ἐν δικαιοσύνῃ,
   ἵνα ἄρτιος ᾖ ὁ τοῦ θεοῦ ἄνθρωπος,
   πρὸς πᾶν ἔργον ἀγαθὸν ἐξηρτισμένος.

4:1 Διαμαρτύρομαι ἐνώπιον τοῦ θεοῦ
   καὶ Χριστοῦ Ἰησοῦ,
   τοῦ μέλλοντος κρίνειν ζῶντας καὶ νεκρούς,
   καὶ τὴν ἐπιφάνειαν αὐτοῦ καὶ τὴν βασιλείαν αὐτοῦ ·

4:2 κήρυξον τὸν λόγον,
   ἐπίστηθι εὐκαίρως ἀκαίρως,
    ἔλεγξον,
    ἐπιτίμησον,
    παρακάλεσον,
   ἐν πάσῃ μακροθυμίᾳ καὶ διδαχῇ.

4:3 ἔσται γὰρ καιρὸς ὅτε τῆς ὑγιαινούσης διδασκαλίας οὐκ
   ἀνέξονται,
   ἀλλὰ κατὰ τὰς ἰδίας ἐπιθυμίας
    ἑαυτοῖς ἐπισωρεύσουσιν διδασκάλους
     κνηθόμενοι τὴν ἀκοήν,
    καὶ ἀπὸ μὲν τῆς ἀληθείας τὴν ἀκοὴν ἀποστρέψουσιν,
     ἐπὶ δὲ τοὺς μύθους ἐκτραπήσονται.

4:5 σὺ δὲ
   νῆφε ἐν πᾶσιν,
   κακοπάθησον,
   ἔργον ποίησον εὐαγγελιστοῦ,
   τὴν διακονίαν σου πληροφόρησον.

4:6 Ἐγὼ γὰρ ἤδη σπένδομαι, καὶ ὁ καιρὸς τῆς ἀναλύσεώς
   μου ἐφέστηκεν.
    τὸν καλὸν ἀγῶνα ἠγώνισμαι,
    τὸν δρόμον τετέλεκα,
    τὴν πίστιν τετήρηκα ·
   λοιπὸν ἀπόκειταί μοι ὁ τῆς δικαιοσύνης στέφανος,

ὃν ἀποδώσει μοι ὁ κύριος ἐν ἐκείνῃ τῇ ἡμέρᾳ,
ὁ δίκαιος κριτής,
οὐ μόνον δὲ ἐμοὶ
ἀλλὰ καὶ πᾶσι τοῖς ἠγαπηκόσι τὴν ἐπιφάνειαν
αὐτοῦ.

4:9   Σπούδασον ἐλθεῖν πρός με ταχέως ·
Δημᾶς γάρ με ἐγκατέλιπεν ἀγαπήσας τὸν νῦν αἰῶνα,
καὶ ἐπορεύθη εἰς Θεσσαλονίκην,
Κρήσκης εἰς Γαλατίαν,
Τίτος εἰς Δαλματίαν ·
Λουκᾶς ἐστιν μόνος μετ' ἐμοῦ.
Μᾶρκον ἀναλαβὼν ἄγε μετὰ σεαυτοῦ, ἔστιν γάρ μοι
εὔχρηστος εἰς διακονίαν.
Τύχικον δὲ ἀπέστειλα εἰς Ἔφεσον.

4:13   τὸν φαιλόνην ὃν ἀπέλιπον ἐν Τρῳάδι παρὰ Κάρπῳ
ἐρχόμενος φέρε,
καὶ τὰ βιβλία, μάλιστα τὰς μεμβράνας.

4:14   Ἀλέξανδρος ὁ χαλκεὺς πολλά μοι κακὰ ἐνεδείξατο ·
ἀποδώσει αὐτῷ ὁ κύριος κατὰ τὰ ἔργα αὐτοῦ ·
ὃν καὶ σὺ φυλάσσου, λίαν γὰρ ἀντέστη τοῖς ἡμετέροις
λόγοις.

4:16   Ἐν τῇ πρώτῃ μου ἀπολογίᾳ οὐδείς μοι παρεγένετο,
ἀλλὰ πάντες με ἐγκατέλιπον ·
μὴ αὐτοῖς λογισθείη ·
ὁ δὲ κύριός μοι παρέστη καὶ ἐνεδυνάμωσέν με,
ἵνα δι' ἐμοῦ τὸ κήρυγμα πληροφορηθῇ
καὶ ἀκούσωσιν πάντα τὰ ἔθνη,
καὶ ἐρρύσθην ἐκ στόματος λέοντος.

4:18   ῥύσεταί με ὁ κύριος
ἀπὸ παντὸς ἔργου πονηροῦ
καὶ σώσει εἰς τὴν βασιλείαν αὐτοῦ τὴν ἐπουράνιον,
ᾧ ἡ δόξα εἰς τοὺς αἰῶνας τῶν αἰώνων · ἀμήν.

4:19   Ἄσπασαι Πρίσκαν καὶ Ἀκύλαν καὶ τὸν Ὀνησιφόρου
οἶκον.
Ἔραστος ἔμεινεν ἐν Κορίνθῳ,
Τρόφιμον δὲ ἀπέλιπον ἐν Μιλήτῳ ἀσθενοῦντα.

4:21   Σπούδασον πρὸ χειμῶνος ἐλθεῖν.

'Ασπάζεταί σε
Εὔβουλος καὶ Πούδης
καὶ Λίνος καὶ Κλαυδία
καὶ οἱ ἀδελφοὶ πάντες.

4:22 ὁ κύριος μετὰ τοῦ πνεύματός σου. ἡ χάρις μεθ' ὑμῶν.

Titus

1:1 Παῦλος

δοῦλος θεοῦ, ἀπόστολος δὲ Ἰησοῦ Χριστοῦ
κατὰ πίστιν ἐκλεκτῶν θεοῦ καὶ ἐπίγνωσιν ἀληθείας τῆς
κατ' εὐσέβειαν ἐπ' ἐλπίδι ζωῆς αἰωνίου, ἥν
ἐπηγγείλατο ὁ ἀψευδὴς θεὸς πρὸ χρόνων αἰωνίων,
ἐφανέρωσεν δὲ καιροῖς ἰδίοις τὸν λόγον αὐτοῦ ἐν
κηρύγματι ὃ ἐπιστεύθην ἐγὼ κατ' ἐπιταγὴν τοῦ
σωτῆρος ἡμῶν θεοῦ,

1:4 Τίτῳ γνησίῳ τέκνῳ κατὰ κοινὴν πίστιν· χάρις καὶ
εἰρήνη ἀπὸ θεοῦ πατρὸς καὶ Χριστοῦ Ἰησοῦ τοῦ
σωτῆρος ἡμῶν. Τούτου χάριν ἀπέλιπόν σε ἐν Κρήτῃ,
ἵνα τὰ λείποντα ἐπιδιορθώσῃ καὶ καταστήσῃς κατὰ
πόλιν πρεσβυτέρους, ὡς ἐγώ σοι διεταξάμην,

1:6 εἴ τίς ἐστιν ἀνέγκλητος,
μιᾶς γυναικὸς ἀνήρ,
τέκνα ἔχων πιστά,
μὴ ἐν κατηγορίᾳ ἀσωτίας ἢ ἀνυπότακτα.

1:7 δεῖ γὰρ τὸν ἐπίσκοπον ἀνέγκλητον εἶναι ὡς θεοῦ
οἰκονόμον,
μὴ αὐθάδη,
μὴ ὀργίλον,
μὴ πάροινον,
μὴ πλήκτην,
μὴ αἰσχροκερδῆ,
ἀλλὰ φιλόξενον,
φιλάγαθον,
σώφρονα,
δίκαιον,
ὅσιον,
ἐγκρατῆ,

ἀντεχόμενον τοῦ κατὰ τὴν διδαχὴν πιστοῦ λόγου,
     ἵνα δυνατὸς ᾖ καὶ παρακαλεῖν ἐν τῇ διδασκαλίᾳ
     τῇ ὑγιαινούσῃ καὶ τοὺς ἀντιλέγοντας
     ἐλέγχειν.

1:10   Εἰσὶν γὰρ πολλοὶ καὶ ἀνυπότακτοι,
     ματαιολόγοι
     καὶ φρεναπάται,
          μάλιστα οἱ ἐκ τῆς περιτομῆς,
     οὓς δεῖ ἐπιστομίζειν,
     οἵτινες ὅλους οἴκους ἀνατρέπουσιν
     διδάσκοντες ἃ μὴ δεῖ αἰσχροῦ κέρδους χάριν.

1:12   εἶπέν τις ἐξ αὐτῶν, ἴδιος αὐτῶν προφήτης,
     Κρῆτες ἀεὶ ψεῦσται, κακὰ θηρία, γαστέρες ἀργαί.
     ἡ μαρτυρία αὕτη ἐστὶν ἀληθής.

1:13b   δι' ἣν αἰτίαν ἔλεγχε αὐτοὺς ἀποτόμως,
     ἵνα ὑγιαίνωσιν ἐν τῇ πίστει,
     μὴ προσέχοντες Ἰουδαϊκοῖς μύθοις καὶ ἐντολαῖς
     ἀνθρώπων ἀποστρεφομένων τὴν ἀλήθειαν.

1:15a   πάντα καθαρὰ τοῖς καθαροῖς·

     τοῖς δὲ μεμιαμμένοις καὶ ἀπίστοις οὐδὲν καθαρόν,
          ἀλλὰ μεμίανται αὐτῶν καὶ ὁ νοῦς καὶ ἡ συνείδησις.

1:16   θεὸν ὁμολογοῦσιν εἰδέναι,
     τοῖς δὲ ἔργοις ἀρνοῦνται,
     βδελυκτοὶ ὄντες καὶ ἀπειθεῖς
     καὶ πρὸς πᾶν ἔργον ἀγαθὸν ἀδόκιμοι.

2:1   Σὺ δὲ
     λάλει ἃ πρέπει τῇ ὑγιαινούσῃ διδασκαλίᾳ.

2:2   πρεσβύτας νηφαλίους εἶναι,
     σεμνούς,
     σώφρονας,
     ὑγιαίνοντας τῇ πίστει,
               τῇ ἀγάπῃ,
               τῇ ὑπομονῇ.

2:3   πρεσβύτιδας ὡσαύτως
     ἐν καταστήματι ἱεροπρεπεῖς,
     μὴ διαβόλους

μηδὲ οἴνῳ πολλῷ δεδουλωμένας,
καλοδιδασκάλους,
ἵνα σωφρονίζωσιν.

2:4   τὰς νέας φιλάνδρους εἶναι,
φιλοτέκνους,
σώφρονας,
ἁγνάς,
οἰκουργούς,
ἀγαθάς,
ὑποτασσομένας τοῖς ἰδίοις ἀνδράσιν,
ἵνα μὴ ὁ λόγος τοῦ θεοῦ βλασφημῆται.

2:6   τοὺς νεωτέρους ὡσαύτως παρακάλει σωφρονεῖν ·
περὶ πάντα σεαυτὸν παρεχόμενος τύπον καλῶν ἔργων,
ἐν τῇ διδασκαλίᾳ ἀφθορίαν,
σεμνότητα,
λόγον ὑγιῆ ἀκατάγνωστον,
ἵνα ὁ ἐξ ἐναντίας ἐντραπῇ
μηδὲν ἔχων λέγειν περὶ ἡμῶν φαῦλον.

2:9   δούλους ἰδίοις δεσπόταις ὑποτάσσεσθαι ἐν πᾶσιν,
εὐαρέστους εἶναι,
μὴ ἀντιλέγοντας,
ἀλλὰ πᾶσαν πίστιν ἐνδεικνυμένους ἀγαθήν,
ἵνα τὴν διδασκαλίαν τὴν τοῦ σωτῆρος ἡμῶν θεοῦ
κοσμῶσιν ἐν πᾶσιν.

2:11   Ἐπεφάνη γὰρ ἡ χάρις τοῦ θεοῦ σωτήριος πᾶσιν
ἀνθρώποις, παιδεύουσα ἡμᾶς
ἵνα ἀρνησάμενοι τὴν ἀσέβειαν καὶ τὰς κοσμικὰς
ἐπιθυμίας
σωφρόνως καὶ
δικαίως καὶ
εὐσεβῶς
ζήσωμεν ἐν τῷ νῦν αἰῶνι,
προσδεχόμενοι τὴν μακαρίαν ἐλπίδα καὶ ἐπιφάνειαν
τῆς δόξης
τοῦ μεγάλου θεοῦ καὶ σωτῆρος ἡμῶν Ἰησοῦ Χριστοῦ,

2:14   ὃς ἔδωκεν ἑαυτὸν ὑπὲρ ἡμῶν
ἵνα
λυτρώσηται ἡμᾶς ἀπὸ πάσης ἀνομίας

καὶ καθαρίσῃ ἑαυτῷ λαὸν περιούσιον,
ζηλωτὴν καλῶν ἔργων.

2:15 Ταῦτα λάλει καὶ παρακάλει
καὶ ἔλεγχε μετὰ πάσης ἐπιταγῆς ·
μηδείς σου περιφρονείτω.

3:1 Ὑπομίμνῃσκε αὐτοὺς
ἀρχαῖς ἐξουσίαις ὑποτάσσεσθαι,
πειθαρχεῖν,
πρὸς πᾶν ἔργον ἀγαθὸν ἑτοίμους εἶναι,
μηδένα βλασφημεῖν,
ἀμάχους εἶναι,
ἐπιεικεῖς,
πᾶσαν ἐνδεικνυμένους πραΰτητα πρὸς πάντας
ἀνθρώπους.

3:3 Ἦμεν γάρ ποτε καὶ ἡμεῖς
ἀνόητοι,
ἀπειθεῖς,
πλανώμενοι,
δουλεύοντες ἐπιθυμίαις καὶ ἡδοναῖς ποικίλαις,
ἐν κακίᾳ καὶ φθόνῳ διάγοντες,
στυγητοί,
μισοῦντες ἀλλήλους.

3:4 ὅτε δὲ ἡ χρηστότης καὶ ἡ φιλανθρωπία ἐπεφάνη
τοῦ σωτῆρος ἡμῶν θεοῦ,
οὐκ ἐξ ἔργων τῶν ἐν δικαιοσύνῃ
ἃ ἐποιήσαμεν ἡμεῖς
ἀλλὰ κατὰ τὸ αὐτοῦ ἔλεος
ἔσωσεν ἡμᾶς διὰ λουτροῦ παλιγγενεσίας
καὶ ἀνακαινώσεως πνεύματος ἁγίου,
οὗ ἐξέχεεν ἐφ' ἡμᾶς πλουσίως
διὰ Ἰησοῦ Χριστοῦ τοῦ σωτῆρος ἡμῶν,
ἵνα δικαιωθέντες τῇ ἐκείνου χάριτι
κληρονόμοι γενηθῶμεν κατ' ἐλπίδα ζωῆς αἰωνίου.

3:8a Πιστὸς ὁ λόγος,
καὶ περὶ τούτων βούλομαί σε διαβεβαιοῦσθαι,
ἵνα φροντίζωσιν καλῶν ἔργων προΐστασθαι
οἱ πεπιστευκότες θεῷ.

3:8c ταῦτά ἐστιν καλὰ καὶ ὠφέλιμα τοῖς ἀνθρώποις ·

3:9   μωρὰς δὲ ζητήσεις
         καὶ γενεαλογίας
         καὶ ἔριν
         καὶ μάχας νομικὰς
         περιΐστασο, εἰσὶν γὰρ ἀνωφελεῖς καὶ μάταιοι.

3:10   αἱρετικὸν ἄνθρωπον
         μετὰ μίαν καὶ δευτέραν νουθεσίαν παραιτοῦ,
         εἰδὼς ὅτι ἐξέστραπται ὁ τοιοῦτος καὶ ἁμαρτάνει,
         ὢν αὐτοκατάκριτος.

3:12   Ὅταν πέμψω ᾿Αρτεμᾶν πρὸς σε ἢ Τύχικον, σπούδασον
         ἐλθεῖν πρός με εἰς Νικόπολιν, ἐκεῖ γὰρ κέκρικα
         παραχειμάσαι.
         Ζηνᾶν τὸν νομικὸν καὶ ᾿Απολλῶν σπουδαίως
         πρόπεμψον, ἵνα μηδὲν αὐτοῖς λείπῃ.

3:14   μανθανέτωσαν δὲ καὶ οἱ ἡμέτεροι καλῶν ἔργων
         προΐστασθαι εἰς τὰς ἀναγκαίας χρείας,
         ἵνα μὴ ὦσιν ἄκαρποι.

3:15a   ᾿Ασπάζονταί σε οἱ μετ᾿ ἐμοῦ πάντες.
         ἄσπασαι τοὺς φιλοῦντας ἡμᾶς ἐν πίστει.

3:15c   ἡ χάρις μετὰ πάντων ὑμῶν.

BIBLIOGRAPHY

Aland, K. "Glosse, Interpolation, Redaktion und Komposition in der Sicht der neutestamentlichen Textkritik," in *Studien zur Überlieferung des Neuen Testaments und seines Textes*, Arbeiten zur neutestamentlichen Textforschung. Berlin: de Gruyter, 1967.

Albertz, M. *Die synoptischen Streitgespräche*. Berlin: Trowitzsch und Sohn, 1919.

Allan, J. A. "The In-Christ Formula in the Pastoral Epistles," *New Testament Studies* 10 (1963), 115–121.

Audet, J. P. *La Didachè: instructions des apôtres*, Etudes bibliques. Paris: Gabalda, 1958.

Aune, David. *The New Testament and its Literary Environment*. Philadelphia: Westminster Press, 1987.

Bahr, Gordon. "Paul and Letter Writing in the First Century," *Catholic Biblical Quarterly* 28 (1966), 465–477.

Baillet, M. *Discoveries in the Judaean Desert*. Oxford: Clarendon Press, 1955, Vol. III.

Baltzer, K. *The Covenant Formulary*. ET by D. Green. Philadelphia: Fortress Press, 1971.

Barnett, A. E. *Paul Becomes a Literary Influence*. Chicago: University Press, 1941.

Barnikol, E. "Römer 13: Der nichtpaulinische Ursprung der absoluten Obrigkeitsbejahung von Römer 13.1–7," in *Studien zum Neuen Testament: Erich Klostermann zum 90. Geburtstag dargebracht*, Texte und Untersuchungen 77. Berlin: Akademie-Verlag, 1961.

Barrett, C. K. *A Commentary on the Epistle to the Romans*. London: Adam & Charles Black, 1962 [1957].

A Commentary on the First Epistle to the Corinthians. 2nd ed. London: Adam & Charles Black, 1976.

The Gospel according to St. John. 2nd ed. Philadelphia: Westminster Press, 1978.

The Pastoral Epistles. Oxford: Clarendon Press, 1963.

Barthélemy, D. *Discoveries in the Judaean Desert*. Oxford: Clarendon Press, 1956, Vol. I.

Bartsch, H.-W. *Die Anfänge urchristlicher Rechtsbildungen*. Hamburg: H. Reich, 1965.

Baur, F. C. *Paulus der Apostel Jesu Christi*. 2 vols. Stuttgart: Becher & Müller, 1845.

Die sogenannten Pastoralbriefe. Tübingen: J. G. Gotta'schen, 1835.

Beasley-Murray, G. R. *Jesus and the Future*. London: Macmillan, 1954.

Bernard, J.H. *The Pastoral Epistles.* Grand Rapids, MI: Baker, 1980 [1899].

Betz, H.D. *Essays on the Sermon on the Mount.* Philadelphia: Fortress Press, 1985.

"2 Cor. 6:14–7:1: An Anti-Pauline Fragment?," *Journal of Biblical Literature* 92 (1973), 88–108.

Bigg, C. *Commentary on the Epistles of St. Peter and St. Jude.* Edinburgh: T. & T. Clark, 1910.

Binder, H. "Die historische Situation der Pastoralbriefe," in *Geschichtswirklichkeit und Glaubensbewährung: Festschrift für F. Müller.* Stuttgart: Evangelisches Verlagswerk, 1967, pp. 70–83.

Black, M. *Romans.* Grand Rapids: Eerdmans, 1973.

Blass, F. and Debrunner, A. *A Greek Grammar of the New Testament.* Trans. and ed. R. Funk. Chicago: University Press, 1961.

Bornkamm, G. *Paul.* London: Hodder & Stoughton, 1971.

"πρέσβυς κτλ.," in *Theological Dictionary of the New Testament.* Ed. G. Kittel and G. Friedrich. ET and ed. G. Bromiley. 9 vols. Grand Rapids: Eerdmans, 1964–1974, Vol. VI, pp. 667ff.

Brox, N. *Die Pastoralbriefe*, Regensburger Neues Testament VII.2. Regensburg: F. Pustet, 1969.

"Zu den persönlichen Notizen der Pastoralbriefe," *Biblische Zeitung* 13 (1969), 76–94.

Bruce, F.F. *I and II Corinthians.* London: Marshall, Morgan and Scott, 1971.

Büchsel, F. "γενεά κτλ.," in *Theological Dictionary of the New Testament.* Ed. G. Kittel and G. Friedrich. ET and ed. G. Bromiley. 9 vols. Grand Rapids: Eerdmans, 1964–1974, Vol. I, pp. 662–665.

Bultmann, R. *The Gospel of John: A Commentary.* ET by G.R. Beasley-Murray. Philadelphia: Westminster Press, 1971.

Der Stil der Paulinischen Predigt und kynisch-stoische Diatribe. Göttingen: Vandenhoeck & Ruprecht, 1910.

Der zweite Brief an die Korinther. Göttingen: Vandenhoeck & Ruprecht, 1976.

Campenhausen, H. von. "Polykarp von Smyrna und die Pastoralbriefe," in *Aus der Frühzeit des Christentums.* Tübingen: J.C.B. Mohr (Paul Siebeck), 1963, pp. 195–252.

Candlish, J.S. "On the Moral Character of Pseudonymous Books," *The Expositor*, Series 4. 4 (1891), 91–107, 262–279.

Cannon, G.E. *Traditional Materials in Colossians.* Macon, GA: Mercer University Press, 1983.

Chadwick, H. (trans.). *Sentences of Sextus.* Cambridge: University Press, 1959.

Charles, R.H. *The Apocalypse of Baruch.* London: Adam & Charles Black, 1896.

Charlesworth, J. "Christian and Jewish Self-Definition in Light of the Christian Additions to the Apocryphal Writings," in *Jewish and Christian Self-Definition*, ed. E.P. Sanders, A.I. Baumgarten, and A. Mendelson. Philadelphia: Fortress Press, 1981, Vol. II, pp. 27–55, 310–315.

Charlesworth, J. (ed.). *The Old Testament Pseudepigrapha*. 2 vols. London: Darton, Longman & Todd, 1983–1985.

Conybeare, W. and Howson, J. *The Life and Epistles of Paul*. London: Longmans, Green, 1852.

Conzelmann, H. "Luke's Place in the Development of Early Christianity," in *Studies in Luke–Acts*. Ed. L. Keck and J. L. Martyn. Nashville: Abingdon Press, 1966, pp. 291–307.

"Paulus und die Weisheit," *New Testament Studies* 12 (1965), 231–234.

Cranfield, C. E. B. *Romans IX–XVI*. Edinburgh: T. & T. Clark, 1979, Vol. II.

Cross, F. L. *I Peter, a Paschal Liturgy*. London: A. R. Mowbray, 1954.

Cross, F. M. *The Ancient Library of Qumran and Modern Biblical Studies*. New York: Scribners, 1958.

Crouch, J. *The Origin and Intention of the Colossian Haustafel*. Göttingen: Vandenhoeck & Ruprecht, 1972.

Cullmann, O. *The Johannine Circle*. London: A. R. Mowbray: SCM, 1976.

Culpepper, R. A. *The Johannine School: An Evaluation of the Johannine-School Hypothesis based on an Investigation of the Nature of Ancient Schools*, Society of Biblical Literature Dissertation Series 26. Missoula, MT: Scholars Press, 1974.

Cunliffe-Jones, H. *Jeremiah*. London: SCM, 1960.

Danby, H. *The Mishnah*. Oxford: University Press, 1933.

Daube, D. "The Laying on of Hands," in *The New Testament and Rabbinic Judaism*. London: Athlone Press, 1956.

Davies, W. D. "Reflexions on Traditions: The Aboth Revisited," in *Christian History and Interpretation: Studies Presented to John Knox*. Ed. W. Farmer, C. F. D. Moule, and R. Niebuhr. Cambridge: University Press, 1967.

Denis, A. M. "Evolution de structures dans la secte de Qumran," in *Aux origines de l'église*, Recherches bibliques VII. Bruges: Desclée de Brouwer, 1964, pp. 23–49.

"Les Thèmes de connaissance dans le Document de Damas," *Studia Hellenistica* 15 (1967), 139–146.

Dibelius, M. *Die Briefe des Apostels Paulus an Timotheus I, II und Titus*. Tübingen: J. C. B. Mohr (Paul Siebeck), 1913.

The Epistle of James. Philadelphia: Fortress Press, 1964.

Die Formgeschichte des Evangeliums. Ed. G. Bornkamm. 5th ed. Tübingen: J. C. B. Mohr, 1966.

A Fresh Approach to the NT and Early Christian Literature. London: Ivor Nicholson & Watson, 1936.

From Tradition to Gospel. New York: Scribner, 1934.

Der Hirt des Hermas. Tübingen: J. C. B. Mohr (Paul Siebeck), 1923.

Dibelius, M. and Conzelmann, H. *The Pastoral Epistles*. Translation and revision of M. Dibelius's *Die Briefe der Apostels Paulus an Timotheus und Titus*. Philadelphia: Fortress Press, 1972.

Dibelius, M. and Greeven, H. *Kolosser, Epheser, Philemon*. Tübingen: J. C. B. Mohr (Paul Siebeck), 1953.

Dodd, C. H. *The Epistle of Paul to the Romans*. London: Hodder & Stoughton, 1932.

Donelson, Lewis. *Pseudepigraphy and Ethical Argument in the Pastoral Epistles*. Tübingen: J. C. B. Mohr (Paul Siebeck), 1986.

Dornier, P. *Les Epîtres Pastorales*. Paris: Gabalda, 1969.

Doty, William G. "The Classification of Epistolary Literature," *Catholic Biblical Quarterly* 31 (1969), 183–199.

Contemporary New Testament Interpretation. Englewood Cliffs, NJ: Prentice-Hall, 1972.

Letters in Primitive Christianity. Philadelphia: Fortress Press, 1973.

Driver, G. R. "Myths of Qumran," *Annual of Leeds University Oriental Society* 6 (1966–1968), 23–27.

Dupont-Sommer, A. *The Essene Writings from Qumran*. ET by G. Vermes. Oxford: Basil Blackwell, 1961.

Easton, B. S. "New Testament Ethical Lists," *Journal of Biblical Literature* 51 (1932), 1–12.

The Pastoral Epistles. London: SCM, 1948.

Eichhorn, J.G. *Einleitung in das Neue Testament*. Leipzig: Weidmannische Buchhandlung, 1812.

Ellicott, C. J. *An Official Critical and Grammatical Commentary on the Pastorals*. London: J. Parker and Son, 1856.

Ellis, E. E. "New Directions in Form Criticism," in *Jesus Christus in Historie und Theologie, Festschrift* in honor of H. Conzelmann. Tübingen: J. C. B. Mohr (Paul Siebeck), 1975.

"Those of the Circumcision," in *Texte und Untersuchungen* 102, Studia Evangelica IV. Berlin: Akademie-Verlag, 1968, pp. 390–399.

"Traditions in I Corinthians," *New Testament Studies* 32 (1986), 481–502.

"Traditions in the Pastoral Epistles," in *Early Jewish and Christian Exegesis: Studies in Memory of William Hugh Brownlee*. Ed. Craig Evans and W. Stinespring. Atlanta: Scholars Press, 1987.

Falconer, R. *The Pastoral Epistles*. Oxford: Clarendon Press, 1937.

Fiore, B. *The Function of Personal Example in the Socratic and Pastoral Epistles*. Rome: Biblical Institute Press, 1986.

Fitzmyer, J. A. "Qumran and the Interpolated Paragraph in 2 Cor. 6:14–7:1," *Catholic Biblical Quarterly* 23 (1961), 271–280.

Fohrer, G. *Introduction to the OT*. New York: Abingdon, 1968.

Funk, R. W. *Language, Hermeneutics, and Word of God*. New York: Harper & Row, 1966.

Furnish, V. P. *Paul's Exhortations in the Context of his Letters and Thought*, Microcard Theological Studies 36. Washington: The Microcard Foundation for the American Theological Library Association, 1960.

Gamble, H. "The Redaction of the Pauline Letters and the Formation of the Pauline Corpus," *Journal of the Biblical Literature* 94 (1975), 403–418.

Gealy, F. *The First and Second Epistles to Timothy and the Epistle to Titus*, The Interpreter's Bible, Vol. XI. New York: Abingdon Press, 1955.

Guthrie, D. "The Development of the Idea of Canonical Pseudepigraph in New Testament Criticism," in *Vox Evangelica*. Ed. R. Martin.

London: Epworth Press, 1962. Reprinted in *SPCK Theological Collections 4: Some Recent Studies by Kurt Aland, Donald Guthrie* [et al.]. London: SPCK.

The Pastoral Epistles. Leicester: Inter-Varsity Press, 1957.

Hanson, A. T. *The Pastoral Epistles*, The New Century Bible Commentary. Grand Rapids, MI: Eerdmans, 1982.

The Pastoral Letters, The Cambridge Bible Commentary. Cambridge: University Press, 1966.

Studies in the Pastoral Epistles. London: SPCK, 1968.

Harnack, A. von. *Die Briefsammlung des Apostels Paulus und die anderen vorkonstantinischen Briefsammlungen.* Leipzig: J. C. Hinrichs, 1926.

Geschichte der altchristlichen Literatur bis Eusebius. 2 parts in 4 vols., Leipzig: Zentralantiquariat, 1958 [1893–1904].

Harris, R. "Pindar and St. Paul," *Expository Times* 33 (1921–1922).

Harrison, P. N. "Important Hypotheses Reconsidered. III. The Authorship of the Pastoral Epistles," *Expository Times* 67 (1955), 77–81.

Paulines and Pastorals. London: Villiers, 1964.

Polycarp's Two Epistles to the Philippians. Cambridge: University Press, 1936.

The Problem of the Pastoral Epistles. London: Oxford University Press, 1921.

Hesse, F. *Die Entstehung der neutestamentlichen Hirtenbriefe.* Halle: C. A. Kaemmerer, 1889.

Hilgenfeld, A. "Die Hirtenbriefe des Paulus neu untersucht," *Zeitschrift für wissenschaftliche Theologie* 40 (1897), 1–86.

Holtz, G. *Die Pastoralbriefe.* 2nd ed. Berlin: Evangelische Verlagsanstalt, 1972.

Holtzmann, H. J. *Die Pastoralbriefe kritisch und exegetisch behandelt.* Leipzig: Wilhelm Engelmann, 1880.

Hornig, G. *Die Anfänge der historisch-kritischen Theologie: Johann Salomo Semlers Schriftverständis und seine Stellung zu Luther.* Göttingen: Vandenhoeck & Ruprecht, 1961.

Horst, P. W. van der *The Sentences of Pseudo-Phocylides.* Leiden: E. J. Brill, 1978.

Hort, F. J. A. *The Christian Ecclesia.* London: Macmillan, 1900.

Judaistic Christianity. Cambridge: Macmillan, 1894.

Houlden, L. *The Pastoral Epistles.* Harmondsworth: Penguin, 1976.

Hunter, A. M. *Paul and his Predecessors.* Philadelphia: Westminster Press, 1940.

Jeremias, J. *Die Briefe an Timotheus und Titus.* Göttingen: Vandenhoeck & Ruprecht, 1953.

Jülicher, A. *An Introduction to the New Testament.* ET by Janet Ward. London: Smith, Elder, 1904.

Kallas, J. "Romans XIII. 1–7: An Interpolation," *New Testament Studies* 11 (1964–1965), 365–374.

Karris, R. "The Background and Significance of the Polemic of the Pastoral Epistles," *Journal of Biblical Literature* 92 (1973), 549–564.

"The Function and Sitz im Leben of the Paraenetic Elements in the Pastoral Letters," Ph.D. thesis, Harvard, 1971.

The Pastoral Epistles. Wilmington, DE: Michael Glazier, 1979.

Käsemann, E. "Das Formular einer neutestamentlichen Ordinationsparänese," in *Neutestamentliche Studien für Rudolph Bultmann*. Berlin: A. Töpelmann, 1954, pp. 261–268.

Kelly, J. N. D. *A Commentary on the Pastoral Epistles*. London: Adam and Charles Black, 1963.

Kenyon, F. G. *The Western Text in the Gospels and Acts*, Proceedings of the British Academy 24. London, 1939.

Klijn, A. F. J. "The Apocryphal Correspondence between Paul and the Corinthians," *Vigiliae Christianae* 17 (1963).

"The Sources and the Redaction of the Syriac Apocalypse of Baruch," *Journal of Jewish Studies* 1 (1970).

Knight, G. W. *The Faithful Sayings in the Pastoral Letters*. Grand Rapids, MI: Baker, 1979.

Koester, H. *Introduction to the New Testament*. 2 vols. Philadelphia: Fortress Press, 1982.

Kohler, K. "Didascalia," in *The Jewish Encyclopedia*. Edited by Isidore Singer. New York: Funk and Wagnalls, 1903, Vol. IV, pp. 588–594.

"James," in *The Jewish Encyclopedia*. Edited by Isidore Singer. New York: Funk and Wagnalls, 1903, Vol. VI.

Kraft, R. A. *The Apostolic Fathers*, ed. R. Grant. 6 vols. New York: Thomas Nelson and Sons, 1965, Vol. III, *Barnabas and the Didache*.

Kümmel, W. *Introduction to the New Testament*. ET by H. C. Kee. Revised ed. London: SCM, 1975.

Kurfess, A. "Das Mahngedicht des sogenannten Phokylides im zweiten Buch der Oracula Sibyllina," *Zeitschrift für die neutestamentliche Wissenschaft und die Kunde der älteren Kirche* 38 (1939), 171–181.

Leaney, A. R. C. *The Epistles to Timothy, Titus and Philemon*. London: SCM, 1960.

Lightfoot, J. B. *The Apostolic Fathers*. 2 vols. London: Macmillan, 1889.

"The Date of the Pastoral Epistles," in *Biblical Essays*. London: Macmillan, 1893, pp. 397–418.

Lindblom, J. *Prophecy in Ancient Literature*. Oxford: Basil Blackwell, 1973.

Lock, W. *The Pastoral Epistles*. Edinburgh: T. & T. Clark, 1924.

Marshall, I. H. "Faith and Works in the Pastoral Letters," *Studien zum Neuen Testament und seiner Umwelt* A, 9 (1984), 203–218.

Review of *Luke and the Pastoral Epistles*, by S. G. Wilson, *Journal for the Study of the New Testament* 10 (1981), 69–74.

Martin, M. *The Scribal Character of the Dead Sea Scrolls*. Louvain: University Publications, 1958, Vol. I.

Massyngberde Ford, J. *Revelation*, Anchor Bible Series. Garden City, NY: Doubleday, 1975.

Meade, David. *Pseudonymity and Canon*, Wissenschaftliche Untersuchungen zum Neuen Testament 39. Tübingen: J. C. B. Mohr (Paul Siebeck), 1986.

Merk, O. von. "Glaube und Tat in den Pastoralbriefen," *Zeitschrift für die neutestamentliche Wissenschaft und die Kunde der älteren Kirche* 66 (1975), 91–112.

Metzger, B. M. "The Furniture in the Scriptorium at Qumran," *Revue de Qumran* 1 (1958–1959), 509–515.

"Literary Forgeries and Canonical Pseudepigrapha," *Journal of Biblical Literature* 91 (1972), 1–24.

The Textual Commentary of the Greek New Testament. New York: United Bible Societies, 1971.

Meyer, A. "Religiöse Pseudepigraphie als ethisch-psychologisches Problem," in *Pseudepigraphie in der heidnischen und jüdisch-christlichen Antike.* Ed. N. Brox. Darmstadt: Wissenschaftliche Buchgesellschaft, 1977.

Michaelis, W. "Teilungshypothesen bei Paulusbriefen," *Theologische Zeitschrift* 14 (1958), 321–326.

Michel, O. "ὁμολογέω," in *Theological Dictionary of the New Testament.* Ed. G. Kittel and G. Friedrich. ET and ed. G. Bromiley. 9 vols. Grand Rapids: Eerdmans, 1964–1974, Vol. V, 1967, pp. 199–220.

Milik, J. T. "Problèmes de la littérature hénochique à la lumière des fragments araméens de Qumran," *Harvard Theological Review* 64 (1971).

Ten Years of Discovery in the Wilderness of Judea. ET by J. Strugnell. London: SCM, 1958.

Milik, J. T. and Black, M. *The Books of Enoch: Aramaic Fragments of Qumran Cave 4.* London: SCM, 1976.

Moffatt, J. *The Historical New Testament.* Edinburgh: T. & T. Clark, 1901.

An Introduction to the Literature of the New Testament. Rev. 3rd ed. Edinburgh: T. & T. Clark, 1920.

Moore, C. A. *Daniel, Esther, and Jeremiah: The Additions.* Garden City, NY: Doubleday, 1977.

Moule, C. F. D. "The Problem of the Pastoral Epistles: A Reappraisal," *Bulletin of John Rylands Library* 3 (1965), 430–452.

Moule, C. G. *The Second Epistle to the Corinthians.* London: Pickering & Inglis, 1962.

Murphy-O'Connor, J. "An Essene Missionary Document? CD II, 14–VI, 1," *Revue Biblique* 77 (1970).

Nauck, W. "Die Herkunft des Verfassers der Pastoralbriefe," Th.D. thesis, Göttingen, 1950.

Norden, E. *Agnostos Theos: Untersuchungen zur Formengeschichte religiöser Rede.* Leipzig and Berlin: Teubner, 1913, repr. 1924.

Die antike Kunstprosa. 2 vols. Stuttgart: Teubner, 1958 [1909].

Noth, M. *A History of Pentateuchal Traditions.* Englewood Cliffs, NJ: Prentice-Hall, 1972.

Oesterley, W. O. E. *The Wisdom of Jesus the Son of Sirach or Ecclesiasticus.* Cambridge: University Press, 1912.

O'Neill, J. C. "Glosses and Interpolations in the Letters of St. Paul," in *Texte und Untersuchungen* 126, Studia Evangelica 7. Berlin: Akademie-Verlag, 1982.

Paul's Letter to the Romans. Harmondsworth: Penguin, 1975.

Orr, W. F. and Walther, J. A. *I Corinthians.* New York: Doubleday, 1976.

Parry, R. *The Pastoral Epistles.* Cambridge: University Press, 1920.

Pfister, F. "ἐπιφάνεια," in *Real-Encyclopädie der classischen Altertums-wissenschaften*. Ed. A. Pauly, G. Wissowa. Supplement IV (1924), pp. 277ff.

Ploeg, J. van der *The Excavations at Qumran: A Survey of the Judean Brotherhood and its Ideals*. ET by K. Smyth. London: Longmans, Green, 1958.

Quinn, J. D. "The Last Volume of Luke," in *Perspectives on Luke–Acts*. Ed. C. H. Talbert. Danville, VA: Association of Baptist Professors of Religion, 1978, pp. 62–65.

Rad, G. von. *Wisdom in Israel*. London: SCM, 1972.

Reicke, Bo. "Chronologie der Pastoralbriefe," *Theologische Literatur-zeitung* 101 (1976), 81–94.

Richardson, E. C. *Biblical Libraries: A Sketch of Library History from 3400 B.C. to A.D. 150*. Princeton: University Press, 1914.

Rist, M. "Pseudepigraphy and the Early Christians," in *Studies in New Testament and Early Christian Literature: Essays in Honor of Allen P. Wikren*. Ed. D. E. Aune. Leiden: E. J. Brill, 1972, pp. 75–91.

Roberts, A. and Donaldson, J. (eds.). *The Writings of the Apostolic Fathers*. Edinburgh: T. & T. Clark, 1867, Vol. I.

Roller, O. *Das Formular der Paulinischen Briefe*, Beiträge zur Wissen-schaft vom Alten und Neuen Testament 4.6. Stuttgart: Kohlhammer, 1933.

Sanday, W. *Inspiration*, Bampton Lectures of 1893. London: Longman, Green, 1894.

Sanders, J. T. *Ethics in the New Testament*. Philadelphia: Fortress Press, 1975.

Sayler, G. B. *Have the Promises Failed? A Literary Analysis of 2 Baruch*. Chico, CA: Scholars Press, 1982.

Schlatter, A. *Die Kirche der Griechen im Urteil des Paulus*. Stuttgart: Calwer Vereinsbuchhandlung, 1936.

Schleiermacher, F. "Ueber den sogenannten ersten Brief des Paulos an den Timotheos [sic]," in *Sämmtliche Werke*. 32 vols. Berlin: G. Reimer, 1836, Vol. I, part 2.

Schubert, P. *Form and Function of the Pauline Thanksgivings*. Berlin: A. Töpelmann, 1939.

Schürer, E. *The History of the Jewish People in the Age of Jesus Christ*. Rev. and ed. G. Vermes, F. Millar, and M. Goodman. 3 vols. Edinburgh: T. & T. Clark, 1973–1987.

Schwarz, Roland. *Bürgerliches Christentum im Neuen Testament?*, Österreichische Biblische Studien 4. Klosterneuburg: Österreichisches Katholisches Bibelwerk, 1983.

Schweizer, E. "Traditional Ethical Patterns in the Pauline and Post-Pauline Letters and their Development (Lists of Vices and Housetables)," in *Text and Interpretation: Studies in the NT presented to Matthew Black*. Ed. E. Best and R. Mcl. Wilson. Cambridge: University Press, 1979, pp. 195–209.

Scott, E. F. *The Pastoral Epistles*. The Moffatt New Testament Commen-tary Series. London: Hodder & Stoughton, 1936.

Seeberg, Alfred, *Der katechismus der Urchristenheit*, Theologische Bücherei 26. Munich: Kaiser, 1966 [1903].

Semler, J. S. *Abhandlung von freier Untersuchung des Canon.* Halle: Hemmerde, 1771.

Simpson, E. K. *The Pastoral Epistles.* London: Tyndale Press, 1954.

Spicq, C. *St. Paul: Les Epîtres Pastorales*, Etudes Bibliques. Paris: Gabalda, 1969.

Spitta, F. "Der Brief der Jacobus," in *Zur Geschichte und Literatur des Urchristentums.* Göttingen: Vandenhoeck & Ruprecht, 1896. Vol. II, pp. 1–239.

Stanton, G. N. "The Origin and Purpose of Matthew's Sermon on the Mount," in *Traditions and Interpretation in the New Testament*, Essays in honor of E. E. Ellis. Ed. G. Hawthorne and O. Betz. Grand Rapids: Eerdmans. 1987.

Stendahl, K. *The School of St. Matthew and its Use of the Old Testament.* Uppsala: Gleerup, 1954.

Stenger, W. "Timotheus und Titus als literarische Gestalten," *Kairos* 16 (1974), 252–267.

Strobel, A. "Schreiben des Lukas? Zum sprachlichen Problem der Pastoralbriefe," *New Testament Studies* 15 (1969), 191–210.

Taylor, V. *The Formation of the Gospel Tradition.* London: Macmillan, 1935.

The Gospel According to St. Mark. London: Macmillan, 1966.

Torm, F. "Die Psychologie der Pseudonymität im Hinblick auf die Literatur des Urchristentums," in *Pseudepigraphie in der heidnischen und jüdisch-christlichen Antike*, Studien der Luther-Akademie 2. Gütersloh: C. Bertelsmann, 1932.

Trummer, P. *Die Paulustradition der Pastoralbriefe.* Frankfurt: P. Lang, 1978.

Vaux, R. de. *Archaeology of the Dead Sea Scrolls.* London: Oxford University Press, 1973.

Vermes, G. *The Dead Sea Scrolls in English.* Rev. 3rd ed. Harmondsworth: Penguin, 1987.

Vögtle, A. *Tugend- und Lasterkataloge im Neuen Testament.* Münster: Aschendorff, 1936.

Weidinger, K. *Die Haustafeln: Ein Stück urchristlicher Paränese.* Leipzig: Hinrichs, 1928.

Weiss, B. *Der Briefe Pauli an Timotheus und Titus.* Göttingen: Vandenhoeck & Ruprecht, 1902.

Weiss, J. *Der erste Korintherbrief.* Göttingen: Vandenhoeck & Ruprecht, 1910.

Wendland, P. *Die urchristlichen Literaturformen.* Tübingen: J. C. B. Mohr (Paul Siebeck), 1912.

Wette, W. M. L. de. *Lehrbuch der historisch-kritischen Einleitung in die kanonischen Bücher des Neuen Testaments.* Berlin: G. Reimer, 1860 [1826].

White, J. L. "The New Testament Epistolary Literature in the Framework of Ancient Epistolography," in *Aufstieg und Niedergang der römischen Welt: Geschichte und Kultur Roms im Spiegel der neueren Forschung.*

Ed. H. Temporini and W. Hasse. Berlin: Walter de Gruyter, 1984, II:25.2: 1730–1756.

White, N. J. D. *The First and Second Epistles to Timothy and the Epistle to Titus*, The Expositor's Greek Testament. London: Hodder & Stoughton, 1910. Reprinted Grand Rapids: Eerdmans, 1961.

Wibbing, S. "Die Tugend- und Lasterkataloge im Neuen Testament," *Zeitschrift für die neutestamentliche Wissenschaft* 25 (1959).

Die Tugend- und Lasterkataloge im Neuen Testament und ihre Traditionsgeschichte unter besonderer Berücksichtigung der Qumran-Texte. Berlin: Topelmann, 1959.

Wilson, S. G. *Luke and the Pastoral Epistles*. London: SPCK, 1979.

Windisch, H. "Zur Christologie der Pastoralbriefe," *Zeitschrift für die neutestamentliche Wissenschaft* 34 (1935), 213–238.

Wolter, M. *Die Pastoralbriefe als Paulustradition*. Göttingen: Vandenhoeck & Ruprecht, 1988.

Zahn, T. *Ignatius von Antiochen*. Gotha: Friedrich Andreas, 1873.

Introduction to the New Testament. ET J. Trout et al. 3 vols. Edinburgh: T. & T. Clark, 1909.

INDEX

Main references are in bold type.